Human Science
and Social Order

Human Science and Social Order

Hugo Münsterberg
and the Origins
of Applied Psychology

Matthew Hale, Jr.

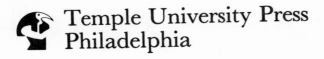 Temple University Press
Philadelphia

Temple University Press, Philadelphia 19122
© 1980 by Temple University. All rights reserved
Published 1980
Printed in the United States of America

Library of Congress Cataloging in Publication Data

Hale, Matthew.
  Human science and social order.

  Includes bibliographical references and index.
  1. Münsterberg, Hugo, 1863–1916. 2. Psychologists
—United States—Biography. 3. Psychology—United
States—History. I. Title.
BF109.M83H34   150.924 [B]   79-20654
ISBN 0-87722-154-5

Frontispiece: Hugo Münsterberg in about 1901.
Courtesy of Harvard University Archives.

To my parents

Contents

Preface   ix

1   Introduction   3

2   The German Years (1863–1892)   11

3   Reductionist Science: Biology, Psychology, and Ethics   26

4   Decision for Harvard (1892–1897)   45

5   Social Idealism and the Social Organism   56

6   Values and Science: A Search for Philosophical Order   70

7   Cultural Diplomacy (1900–1908)   87

8   Psychologies of Measurement   106
     Psychology and Law   111
     Psychology and the Social Organism:
     Vocational Guidance   121

9 Psychologies of Commitment   126
   Individual Therapy   127
   Social Sanity: Propaganda and Art   136

10 Industrial Efficiency   148

11 Science and the State: World War I   164

12 Conclusion   184

   Notes   189

   Index   233

Preface

The German-American Hugo Münsterberg, who taught psychology at Harvard from 1892 to 1916, is remembered today primarily as a German "spy" during World War I. He was, however, a leading figure in the early years of American psychology, and, as much of any of his contemporaries, he laid the groundwork for the new discipline of applied psychology. Although he was known as a psychologist of the old school, he conducted early experiments in industrial psychology, legal psychology, and mental testing; he encouraged students to take up the new studies of comparative psychology and psychometrics; and he campaigned actively in a series of best sellers for a science that could ensure social efficiency. According to some standard sources, this work made him the "founder" of applied psychology.

Whatever his contributions to psychology, Münsterberg was above all a public figure; indeed, he became the best-known psychologist in America at a time when the discipline captured the public's fancy. This notoriety raises a significant question: How and why did attention focus on Münsterberg? How can we explain the fad of psychology and the ambiguous public persona of "Prof. Hugo Monsterwork," as one newspaper called him? The answer is clear: Psychology promised power—over self and others—in years when men and women felt increasingly powerless to control their own lives, and it offered an explanation for the irrational behavior that seemed more and more to dominate public life. I am not addressing the problem of whether an imagined loss of mastery early in the century reflected actual conditions, but only the indisputable fact that millions of Americans sensed a crisis of the will as industrial and urban society emerged. However much professional psychologists of that generation may have asserted their status as scientists, they could not prevent the appropriation of their work by a public seeking short-cut answers. Psychology derived its popular appeal from the same sources as spiritualism, faith healing, hypnotism, astrology, and telepathy. And Münsterberg, who achieved fame partly because he fit the popular image of the scientist so well, was the most aggressive publicist in the discipline.

This public career of Münsterberg and the psyche that impelled him to it offer a seductive topic for the biographer. Here was a man who was motherless from age twelve and orphaned at eighteen, who converted from Judaism to Lutheranism soon after the death of his father, who suffered headaches as a child and nervous disorders as an adult, and who claimed never to have dreamed and never to have experienced anger. His adult behavior could often be described, generously, as immature, and his career was beset by one controversy after another. By the time of his death, he had become an embarrassment to Harvard, and his name was not to be mentioned in polite Cambridge circles. In this study, I have attempted to convey some flavor of Münsterberg's stormy life. On the whole, however, I have tried to set limits both on repeating gossip and psychologizing, and I have chosen not to adopt a psychobiographical approach. To have done so would have run the risk of allowing Münsterberg's eccentricities to obscure his real historical importance.

I have, to be sure, attempted to sketch the interplay of Münsterberg's psyche and his political and philosophical stances, but only with a limited purpose. I hope to demonstrate that his personal failure at self-knowledge mirrored the failure of his theorizing. It is reasonable to suppose that social thought begins with introspection of one sort or another. Münsterberg's unwillingness to face his own motives and interests in a meaningful way severely restricted his perspective on society and allowed him to adopt a behavioristic psychology that eliminated consciousness, while he still professed Idealism in philosphy. I have also argued that many of Münsterberg's actions—for instance, his embracing of applied psychology —satisfied personal needs. But to trace the content of his social thought to his childhood experiences would be to miss the point that this thought was fundamentally political, not psychological, in nature.

I have also generally ignored the development of the profession of psychology, which before World War I was confined almost entirely to the universities. In the first place, by the twentieth century Münsterberg was largely peripheral to this development—indeed, he defied contemporary trends by arguing that psychology had to be grounded in philosophy and by insisting that the psychology program at Harvard remain tied to the Division of Philosophy. In the second place, I believe that the process of "professionalization" has been overemphasized as a historical factor. Histories of professionalization, like histories of bureaucratization, run the risk of assuming that professions grow in a vacuum, fueled by some hidden teleology that guides them through internally constrained stages of growth. Professions, however, do not exist in a vacuum; they are composed of men and women from particular strata of society who have certain personal and social interests and who hold definite views on the just society, which they expect their profession to foster.

My concern in this study of Münsterberg, instead, is to ask, What were his ideas, what was his view of society and human relations, for the transmission of which his psyche and his profession provided a vehicle? And, as a corollary, how were those ideas transformed in the application? What were their political implications and impact? Applied psychology did not appear by accident early in the century. It did not reflect an "inevitable" tendency of the sciences to move from the theoretical to the applied, nor did it develop the way it did simply because psychologists were looking for jobs. In Münsterberg's case, at least, it represented a conscious if belated attempt to bring science to the rescue of traditional principles of authority, self-sacrifice, deferred pleasure, and will. In his first years in America, Münsterberg spoke of family, character-building, and the organic growth of society. By the twentieth century, he had turned to an active, interventionist science of the mind that seemed to deny an autonomous will and resorted to behavioristic manipulation. What held the two views together was a consistent political ideology: Münsterberg subscribed to an ideal of an organic society, lifted from a romanticized preindustrial past and placed in the industrial present, in which everyone knew his or her place and all were eager to perform the functions to which biology, social standing, and their betters had assigned them. In taking this position, Münsterberg was hardly unique: When Americans in the Progressive era enlisted science in the cause of social order, they frequently drew their models of social order from the past.

In writing this study, which began as a dissertation at the University of Maryland, I accumulated many debts. I was supported for three years by a Graduate Fellowship from the University of Maryland, which allowed me to devote full time to research on this project. I received assistance from the staffs of the Manuscript Room of the Library of Congress, Houghton Library, the Harvard University Archives, and especially the Department of Rare Books and Manuscripts of the Boston Public Library, which holds the major collection of Münsterberg papers. Several scholars, including David A. Noble, Donald S. Napoli, and Brigitte

Schroeder-Gudehus, let me see unpublished manuscripts on subjects related to Münsterberg's career, which I have specifically acknowledged in the notes. Dr. Schroeder-Gudehus loaned me microfiche copies of letters from Münsterberg to the Prussian Ministry of Education. Lucy Kressley of the George Washington University German Department transliterated several letters from Wilhelm Wundt to Münsterberg. I especially wish to thank Hugo Munsterberg, Professor of Art at the State University of New York at New Paltz and the nephew of Münsterberg. Dr. Munsterberg made available to me a copy of his grandfather's diary, which gave invaluable information on Hugo's childhood, and shared with me his knowledge of his family's background. Without his help, this study would have been considerably narrower, and the second chapter could not have been written.

Several friends, teachers, and colleagues read all or parts of this study at various stages. I would particularly like to thank Francis C. Haber, Dorothy Ross, and Thomas R. West, who offered extensive and valuable suggestions. Above all, I wish to thank James B. Gilbert, who saw the manuscript through several drafts and encouraged me at all stages of its preparation.

Human Science
and Social Order

Introduction

I want a world of anarchy, Münsterberg one of bureaucracy, and each appeals to "nature" to back him up.
William James in a notebook (1903)

When Hugo Münsterberg, Professor of Psychology at Harvard University, died in December 1916, he was arguably the best-known psychologist in America and the most prominent member of America's largest minority, the German-Americans.[1] Twenty-four years before, in 1892, William James had lured him to Cambridge from Germany's University of Freiburg, where he had been a controversial but promising young experimentalist. For the remainder of his career he taught at Harvard and directed its laboratory, and, with his German credentials, he assumed a senior position in the young profession of psychology. But it was in the public arena, not in the laboratory, that he achieved his fame. He was a publicist, blessed with an uncanny flair for the sensational, and his life can be read as a series of promotions—of himself, his science, and his Fatherland.

At Harvard Münsterberg tired quickly of the experimental studies for which he had been hired, and, like so many of his colleagues, he moved to the more lucrative problems of application. In 1906 he began investigations into the possible contributions of psychology to law. In rapid succession thereafter, he directed his expertise to the fields of psychotherapy, vocational guidance, industrial efficiency, and the film. His work in these various areas fit well with the contemporary Progressive impulse to enlist science in the cause of social order. It also earned him, in the opinion of several respectable textbooks and encyclopedias, the title of "founder" of applied psychology.[2] His German friend William Stern, a rival claimant to that title, offered striking testimony to Münsterberg's work in this field. Stern wrote in 1917:

> During the years when we in Germany had only cautiously and tentatively begun to shape methods for the new problems of application, Münsterberg had penetrated into the fullness of human life, had laid down a general program, and in four books of his own had given a wide outlook into the possibility of making psychology effective in the administration of justice, the healing of the sick, education and industrial life.

Stern conceded that Münsterberg often "showed more boldness and power to imagine future possibilities than he did cautious technical knowledge." But, he argued, Münsterberg's great contribution lay in bringing attention to "this perfectly new method of controlling *Kultur,* and of drawing the great guiding lines for future work."[3]

The most striking feature of Münsterberg's work, and for his fellow professionals the most distressing, was its contentious style. From his early essays on American life, often published collectively under such titles as *American Traits from the Point of View of a German,* he moved increasingly, in the twentieth century, to a form of polemics that he called "social psychology." In articles written for journals from the *Atlantic Monthly* to *Mother's Companion,* he challenged the sacred cows of Progressive thought. His championing of rote memorization angered the educational reformers; his defense of alcohol, the prohibitionists; and his judgment that women were psychologically unfit for jury duty, the feminists. At the same time, he actively took up the application and promotion of his science in a series of spectacular forays into the public sphere. In 1907, for example, he administered a battery of lie detection tests to Harry Orchard, the sole government witness in the murder trial of Big Bill Haywood, the radical labor leader. His public statements during and after the trial became objects of discussion, and in some cases ridicule, on two continents. In 1909 he exposed the celebrated Italian medium Eusapia Palladino, incurring the wrath of both William James, who had been convinced by her performances, and a number of professional psychologists, who criticized his approach as sensationalistic. Moreover, through much of his career rumors circulated that industrial interests had financed one or another of his popular articles or laboratory experiments —rumors that, in the case of his antiprohibition stance at least, had some validity.

Münsterberg's position as an outsider complicated his reception in the

New World, and in a sense he always remained an alien in America. Despite his many years in the United States, he maintained his German citizenship and never abandoned his ambition of securing a full professorship at a major German university. His accent, mannerisms, philosophical idealism, and fascination with problems of theory set him apart from most of his American colleagues, and, by the twentieth century, fostered in him a sense of estrangement from the Harvard community. That estrangement illustrated more than the difficulties of a theoretical-minded German intellectual in the pragmatic New World: It underscored the contradiction within Münsterberg's position as a German academic teaching in an American university.

Münsterberg's call to Harvard affirmed the reality of an international community of scholars that transcended nationality. Yet as a German scholar he had accepted the duty of bearing that nation's particular *Kultur* and owed his fundamental loyalty to the state that had fostered its development. He saw himself as a representative of German *Wissenschaft* in America, a cultural ambassador whose science testified to the vigor of his Fatherland. His organization of the famous International Congress of Arts and Science in St. Louis in 1904, his work in relation to the Harvard-Berlin exchange professorship that began in 1905, and his founding of Berlin's Amerika-Institut in 1910 aimed therefore not only at promoting science but also at furthering German national interests.

The outbreak of World War I in the summer of 1914 brought the conflict between Münsterberg's two roles into the open. Together with virtually every one of his academic colleagues at home, he rallied to the cause of the Reich, and during the war years he wrote a number of widely circulated articles defending the Central Powers. In an America that sympathized with the Allies, Münsterberg's propaganda activities and his ties to figures within the German government encouraged the suspicion (which had cropped up as early as 1901) that he was a "spy" and led to repeated demands from Harvard alumni that the university fire him. In the most sensational case, an Englishman offered a ten-million-dollar bribe for his ouster. Harvard stood firm, but Münsterberg had become a social outcast. The strain apparently proved too much for a man whose health had always been precarious. As he began a lecture at Radcliffe in December 1916, Münsterberg was struck dead, mid-sentence, by a cerebral hemorrhage.

Münsterberg's name fell almost immediately into obscurity. One of his many volumes, *The Photoplay: A Psychological Study,* is currently enjoying a modest revival as a result of the vogue of film criticism, while passages from another, *The Americans,* have been included in a popular collection of essays by foreigners on American life. And several years ago

Business Week honored Münsterberg in a series of articles on "Famous Firsts" in industrial psychology.[4] But the bulk of his work has been forgotten. Standard histories of psychology generally consign to him only a few lines, while accounts of the Progressive Era ignore him entirely. His voluminous writings, often bearing the marks of hasty composition and a foreigner's command of English, did not recommend themselves to posterity, and his "Sunday supplement" style of "yellow psychology" made it easy, then as well as now, to dismiss him as less than a serious figure.

Among his fellow psychologists Münsterberg was controversial. His former student and colleague Knight Dunlap, who became chairman of the department at Johns Hopkins, reminisced in 1930: "I think the modern trends in American psychology, and especially its experimental interests, are easily traceable to Münsterberg as their father." "There was at least one giant in these days," he asserted, "although his publications do not show it." On the other hand, Münsterberg's experimental work was widely criticized for its naiveté, and his theoretical constructions generally did not find a sympathetic audience in America. The alleged judgment of his Cornell rival Edward Bradford Titchener—that Münsterberg had "debased" psychology at Harvard—was harsh, but it expressed the feelings of many of his contemporaries. Like it or not, however, they could not deny that for many in both America and Europe Münsterberg represented psychology. "When American experimental psychology is mentioned in England," the English-born Titchener wrote him in 1912, "the available apperception-mass brings up the name of Münsterberg."[5]

The purpose of this study is not to rehabilitate Münsterberg or to justify for him a place in the pantheon of psychology's founding fathers. Rather, it is to raise a series of issues that were central to his thought and to the historical period in which he lived. Münsterberg's entire career, whether reflected in his metaphysical system-building, his commitment to applied psychology, his promotion of international cultural relations, or even his propaganda work for Germany, can be seen as an attempt to rationalize the world, to organize it as a system in which every part drew its meaning from its function in the whole. The key principles were balance, order, and efficiency. Münsterberg's thought in this sense celebrated the growth of bureaucracy in the modern world—a bureaucracy that, incorporating even the operations of the human mind within its scope, overthrew the traditional nineteenth-century American values of individual autonomy and self-reliance.

A philosophical exchange in 1906 between Münsterberg and William James, that champion of pluralism, vividly illustrated the direction of Münsterberg's thought. "I am satisfied with a free wild Nature," James wrote his colleague. "You seem to me to cherish and pursue an Italian

Garden, where all things are kept in separate compartments, and one must follow straight-ruled walks." In his reply, Münsterberg clarified his position. The world of immediate experience comprised for him also "a wild nature without ways and flowerbeds and plenty of weeds." But, unlike James, he was not satisfied with such a state. "Our life's duty," he continued,

> makes us gardeners, makes us to unweed the weeds of sin and error and ugliness and when we finally come to think over what flowers were left as valuable, and we bring together those which are similar—then we have finally indeed such an Italian garden as the world which we are seeking, as the world which has to be acknowledged as ultimate.[6]

Münsterberg had aptly sketched his intellectual, and indeed temperamental, distance from James, and he caught the spirit of the "life's duty" that informed his adult life. While James spoke of life as a "delicious mess of insanities and realities"[7] and desperately sought a principle of freedom and spontaneity in what he thought was a deterministic world order, Münsterberg, like so many German Idealists before him, worked to expunge all irrationality and unpredictability from the world system. The phenomenal world provided raw material that the mind shaped into a total order. Throughout his American career Münsterberg threw himself energetically into ridding the world of its weeds and domesticating the free, wild nature that he found around him.

It was Münsterberg, not James, whose vision proved the more prophetic in twentieth-century America. To most of their contemporaries the old order was breaking down before the forces of the modern world, and in America the disintegration had reached its most advanced stage. The chaotic exploitation of diminishing natural resources, the homogenization of society into an undifferentiated democratic mass, a pervasive crisis of the individual and national will that left its victims incapable of sustained effort, and the "Europeanization" of American politics and especially of industrial relations—all testified to the weakening of traditional social bonds. They also spawned what Robert Wiebe has aptly described as a "search for order": Efficiency became a code word for progressives of all stripes.[8]

The ambition for social efficiency, or, as Stern put it, the attempt to control *Kultur,* was of course nothing new. But it was widely noted at the time, and has become a commonplace since, that in the early twentieth century centralized planning increasingly replaced "organic" or *ad hoc* forms of social organization. One need only cite such uniquely modern arrangements as the holding company, the College Board examination, and the Dewey Decimal System to prove the point: All were in one sense or another bureaucratic structures consciously designed to meet the new problems of scale in the modern world.

Many intellectuals, particularly in Europe, where their social status and education tied them to the old order, lamented this rationalization of social arrangements. In the late nineteenth century, for example, the German sociologist Friedrich Tönnies made his classic observation that civilization was passing from *Gemeinschaft* to *Gesellschaft,* from a "community" organically evolved and tied together by status, ritual, and personal contact to an impersonalized "society" of interchangeable and contractual relationships; somewhat later Georg Simmel spoke of a new metropolitan culture characterized by "a regimentation of the mind" and emotional deadness. In the wake of World War I, Max Weber grieved over the "disenchantment of the world."[9]

What was striking about Münsterberg's response was the ease with which he combined—sometimes inconsistently—the values of the old, organic society, which in theory had simply grown through "natural" forces, and the new world of bureaucracy; in his synthesis the principles of efficiency and scientific management did not destroy the natural order but allowed its fruition, and a psychology of motivation restored Weber's lost enchantment. Münsterberg's formula may have been less poetic, but it was more consistent with New World optimism.

American progressives tended to assume an affinity between science, democracy, and progress. Efficient production of goods meant a satisfactory life for all; scientific principles of education trained an independent citizenry; systematic vocational guidance expanded the individual's freedom of choice. Yet behind the rhetoric the story was often very different: From another perspective, industrial organization stripped workers of their craft; urban education erased the ethnic traditions of immigrants; vocational guidance preached resignation to one's fate. Science, after all, lent itself as easily to the eugenics of a Charles Davenport, who argued for a selective breeding of men and women, as it did to the anthropology of a Franz Boas, who vigorously defended the equality of mankind. Münsterberg typified the sort of social reformer who turned scientific expertise to traditional purposes and found in it support for established sources of authority.

Like most of his contemporaries, Münsterberg argued that his science was politically neutral. The "efficiencies" that he recommended—in labor management, in propaganda, in social organization—therefore, assumed the aura of technical solutions to problems of administration. The psychologist could tell the employer how to select the best workers, the salesman how to exploit the laws of suggestion, and the judge how to measure the suggestibility of witnesses. As he saw it, these were all technical problems whose solutions fell properly to experts. In taking this position, Münsterberg illustrated the observation of the German sociologist Karl Mannheim that "the fundamental tendency of all bureaucratic thought is to turn all problems of politics into problems of administration";[10] and his practical work, especially in legal and industrial psychology, aimed at extending the sphere of administration at the expense of "politics," in the broadest sense of the word. Münsterberg's career made obvious an important point about this development: The historical form taken by particular efficiencies was thoroughly political, and the principle of "neutrality" often masked political motives.

In Münsterberg's case, I will suggest three ways in which his social assumptions were inextricably linked with his science. His psychology, like that of most of his contemporaries from the psychoanalyst Sigmund Freud to the behaviorist John Watson, undermined the notion that the individual accurately perceived the world around him or indeed was master of his own house—an observation that Münsterberg used to rebut the politically weighted principles of common sense and self-reliance. Also, consistent with his philosophical Idealism (but not entirely with his scientific positivism), he stressed the role of mind in defining the nature of experience, and on that basis he explicitly defined industrial alienation and other social ills as mental illusions, susceptible to psychotherapeutic cures. In doing so, he transformed basic historical conflicts into surface problems of adjustment. Finally, he argued that function in the social order followed form and that the psychologist could measure an individual's "form"—that is, his innate capacities and talents—far more accurately than the individual himself. Münsterberg's view of society, as James's metaphor of the Italian garden made clear, was an organic one in which every unit expressed its true "individuality"—its form—when it performed its appropriate role. The psychologist could assist the individual in fulfilling his role by determining his potential and by molding that potential into its proper shape, just as the gardener brought out the "natural" beauty of one or another shrub.

One final point should be made on the political implications of Münsterberg's concern for social efficiency: Like an earlier generation of social Darwinists, he assumed a continuum between natural and social evolution. "Natural laws" guided the one as well as the other toward increasing organization and differentiation. Münsterberg used this assumption to justify the fundamentally conservative position that what is, is right. The "second nature" of men and women, historically conditioned traits petrified into eternal verities, became prescriptive rules for the just society, and the psychologist, as the expert who understood the laws of mind, became an arbiter of questions that were traditionally personal or political in nature: Should women serve on juries? Should alcohol be prohibited? Who should occupy a particular vocational slot? Furthermore, Münsterberg used this assumption to affirm the nation-state as the highest form of social organization and the indivisible unit of social evolution, for it reconciled within it all social roles. The individual's duty as a citizen coincided with his duty as a family member, a worker, and a moral human being. In Münsterberg's language, therefore, social efficiency only had meaning when it served the nation. His friend Theodore Roosevelt, who did so much to popularize efficiency as the quintessence of Progressivism, would have agreed: Organization, science, and expertise were all measures of national virility.

2

The German Years (1863–1892)

Münsterberg was born in 1863 in the Prussian city of Danzig, a modest-sized Baltic port that enjoyed an ancient and illustrious heritage. German knights had founded the city in a sheltered harbor near the mouth of the Vistula River six hundred years earlier. The woods, lakes, and moors of the Pomeranian plateau lay to its west; to the east and south were the marshes of the Vistula Delta, a nearly impenetrable quagmire that damming eventually transformed into navigable waterways and fertile land. "It is astonishing," wrote one Danzig historian, "what an array of natural difficulties came together at the very place where Danzig grew up." But centuries of improvement, continuing well into Münsterberg's childhood, tamed the environment and changed it into an area that observers could compare to the lowlands of Holland.[1]

In the nineteenth century Danzig preserved a precarious and provincial "Germanness" that was to brand itself indelibly in the mind of the young Münsterberg. From its founding, only native German-speakers could gain citizenship in the city. Consequently, Danzig emerged as an overwhelmingly German city surrounded by a mixed population of Germans, Poles, and Slavs, each with a strong sense of ethnic identity. By the beginning of the fifteenth century it had become not only one of the largest German cities but also an important European trading center. Later in the century, when the city fell under Polish control and the axis of world trade shifted westward, it entered a decline that continued until the second half of the nineteenth century.[2]

Danzig became German once again when Prussia annexed it in 1814, and its commercial fortunes reversed around mid-century as demand for grain and lumber in industrializing England and western Germany stimulated a modest economic revival. But Danzig never regained the glories of its past. Throughout the century it continued to fall behind its more favorably located rivals, and it retained the air of provincialism that it had assumed during years of relative isolation. The city, in fact, bore a distinctive stamp. The major centers of trade and tourism to the south and west, a Danziger observed in 1903, had lost their vigorously local characters to a modern homogeneity. Danzig, however, preserved its German and medieval character, to which its narrow streets and archaic buildings bore witness.[3]

Münsterberg himself was only marginally a Danziger, for he descended from a family of prosperous Breslau Jews, members of one of the largest and most progressive Jewish communities in Germany. His father, Moritz, had emigrated to Danzig in the middle of the nineteenth century and entered the lumber business. He arrived at a critical period in Danzig's economic history, when the city was entering the modern world. Steamships first appeared during the 1840s in the newly improved harbor; railroads arrived in the early 1850s. In 1863, the year of Hugo's birth, Leopold von Winter became mayor, and during his tenure, which lasted until 1890, Danzig emerged as "a great modern city"—its inner walls were knocked down and its trenches filled, water lines and canals built, and further railroads connecting Danzig to Warsaw and elsewhere constructed.[4]

While the old Danzig suggested the values of tradition, history, and individuality, the new testified to the sometimes contradictory need for efficiency and centralization. Merchants like Moritz Münsterberg dealt daily with the political difficulties of international trade in the eastern Baltic and the irrationality, economic and otherwise, that accompanied German disunity. Otto Münsterberg, Hugo's older brother, offered a graphic account of one of these irrationalities in his description of his apprenticeship for a Danzig wholesale grocer. The most difficult and time-consuming part of his job, he wrote, was sorting out the various German currencies and banknotes received by the firm. In 1873 twenty-one states were issuing treasury bills and thirty-three banks were giving out notes in Germany. Many of these, by the time they reached Otto's hands, were torn and illegible. Business in these paper currencies almost always involved a loss for the wholesaler.[5] Businessmen could easily recognize that their future lay with an increasingly rationalized Prussian, and finally German, state. And they could look with envy at the power of the lands to the west. "The feeling of national unity that is expressed everywhere among the English," Moritz wrote in London in 1855, "makes a pleasant if at the same time discouraging impression on a Prussian."[6]

The Münsterberg family in Danzig was typical of thousands of wealthy and cultured Jewish families who were being assimilated into German society through education, language, and local citizenship. The historian Jacob Katz has described the ideological rapprochement between educated Protestants and Jews in the post-Enlightenment years, as each abandoned the orthodoxies of the past for more rationalistic and less explicit faiths. Although Jews were barred in practice from teaching positions and by law from other posts within the Prussian state bureaucracy, they nonetheless came to play an increasingly important role in German economic and political life. The city of Danzig was relatively hospitable to them, perhaps because their number there was so small, and the Danzig Jews, at least the wealthy, were on the whole modernist.[7] Moritz Münsterberg, as a result, found it possible to operate in gentile economic and cultural circles without renouncing his Jewish ties.

By the time of Hugo's birth, the Münsterberg family was well established in Danzig. Moritz was the head (*Vorsteher*) of the Weinberg Synagogue, one of the five synagogues in Danzig's splintered Jewish community of the 1860s,[8] and his lumber business provided him and his family with a comfortable income. He fathered four sons, borne by two different wives. His first wife, Rosalie, gave birth to Otto in 1854 and to Emil a year later. After Rosalie's death in 1857, Moritz brought in her niece, Anna Bernhardi, to take care of the young sons. Five years later, Moritz and Anna married, to the annoyance of their families, and she bore two further sons, Hugo in 1863 and Oscar in 1865.[9]

As a merchant, Moritz generally spent one month of the year abroad on business. During these travels he kept a *Reise-Tagebuch,* a journal of personal impressions, that provides insight into the family in which Hugo grew up. The journal has a strongly pious tone, though it completely lacks any reference to Jewish custom or dogma. God appears frequently in a personal but abstracted form—he was to be thanked for good fortune and success in life, but not, apparently, to be worshipped. Moritz's journal reveals a strong sense of duty and self-sacrifice. He considered his business a chore and regretted that his trips took him away from the life he preferred to live, but they were necessary if he was to provide for the future of his family and to leave his sons comfortably independent. That work itself might be a source of joy he never considered, but, like his son Hugo, he regarded it as duty and service to a higher ideal.[10]

The Münsterberg family expressed a patriotic and nationalist outlook, tempered by a political liberalism that was typical of its middle-class background. Perhaps, too, because they were Jewish and therefore of marginal status, the Münsterbergs identified strongly with the emerging German nation. The family regularly celebrated the Kaiser's birthday with a dinner, and Hugo's earliest memory, he later recalled, was of troops passing beneath his window in 1870 on the way to battle with the French. "He also remembered," his daughter wrote, "how his mother with other ladies had eagerly made bandages for the wounded soldiers." From this background Münsterberg developed his faith in the value of a vigorous nationalism, and his years in distant America allowed the idealized Germany of his childhood (and its imperial leadership) to endure in his imagination.[11]

The Münsterberg family also exhibited a division of labor that was typical of the nineteenth century. If Moritz incorporated the masculine virtues of work, duty, and self-discipline, his wife Anna reflected the feminine graces, at least in Hugo's memory. She was an artist, devoted to her painting and drawing in pen and ink, and she implanted in her home "love and respect for the beautiful in art, music, and letters." Years later, when Hugo was to write "the realism of the man and the idealism of the woman supplement each other in every noble home," he reflected his romanticized perception of his own childhood. Anna's ennobling influence on the family, however, was short-lived. She died after a lengthy illness in the spring of 1875, when Hugo was less than twelve, leaving behind her an image of martyred sanctity. "With Anna my sun set," Moritz wrote, "and it is as if I saw nothing but affliction around me."[12]

Throughout his life, but especially after Anna's death, Moritz dedicated himself to his sons, whose success and devotion to him were to be monuments to his virtue. In his journal he persistently relegated his own personal hopes and concerns to a secondary position and discussed again and again the moral upbringing of his sons and their prospects. "In not much time," he wrote shortly after the birth of his first son, "my own feelings will be subordinated, and the feelings which I can awaken in my son will occupy me the most. May I succeed in raising him to be an honest and capable man." A few days later, he repeated the wish: "May God grant that I raise my son so he can, through his own efforts, become a useful member of society."[13]

Moritz's dedication paid off: The Münsterberg sons lived up to their father's hopes, not the least in their strong bonds with one another and their devotion to their father. "All four have a common center of their thought and their love," Moritz wrote a year after Anna's death: "I am that center." His perception was accurate. Otto wrote his youngest brother, Oscar, following Moritz's death in 1880, "My wish is simple: I will be a good man as Papa was."[14] Beyond their familial devotion, which remained throughout their lives, all the sons became "useful members of society." Otto was a leading businessman in Danzig and served for several years as a representative in the Prussian assembly. Emil was the mayor of the city of Iserlohn and later director of public charities in Berlin. Hugo became one of the leading psychologists of his generation and Oscar an authority on oriental art.[15]

Among his four sons, the elder Münsterberg held out the highest hopes for Hugo. Twenty years later William James characterized Münsterberg as "desiring to please and to shine." Apparently the trait developed early. At home, Moritz wrote, young Hugo was "amiability itself," and he showed promise at school. His two older brothers had already disappointed their father. Otto failed promotion in the *Gymnasium* and consequently entered a business academy in Danzig. Moritz commented: "My ideal that Otto pass the *Abitur* and then, if he wished, become a merchant was shattered." And Emil, as a youth, did not exhibit "the material that raised him above the average of the general mass." On the other hand, when Hugo's teachers reported him to be a gifted and exemplary pupil, Moritz was delighted.[16]

Hugo's schooling began with kindergarten, followed by several years at a private school in preparation for the city *Gymnasium*. He entered that institution at age nine and completed its rigorous classical program in the regular time of nine years. On graduation he successfully passed the state-conducted *Abitur,* winning entry into university study and the cultured elite of Germany. Few German children enjoyed such a privilege in the late nineteenth century, for the rigid system of educational promotion presupposed a cultivated family background, and the many years in school involved a considerable financial burden. In 1885, Fritz Ringer has estimated, 7.5 million children attended the compulsory primary schools or their equivalent in Germany. Only 238,000 students, however, were enrolled at that time in secondary schools, and of this number fewer than half attended the elite *Gymnasium*. Of those who entered the *Gymnasium*, fewer than half could expect ever to receive the *Abitur* certificate.[17]

The curriculum of the *Gymnasium* aimed at instilling in its graduates a quality of personal cultivation, or *Bildung,* that might serve as a surrogate for the inherited traits of nobility. The talented student—that is, the aristocrat by nature rather than by birth—acquired intellectual breadth, wisdom, and virtue through contemplation of ancient and contemporary masters. And the student who successfully completed the *Gymnasium* program and continued his studies at the university automatically joined the cultural, social, and political elite of the country. This educated elite, the philosopher Friedrich Paulsen wrote in 1902, "constitute a kind of intellectual and spiritual aristocracy in Germany. . . . They form something like an official nobility, as indeed they all participate in the government and administration of the state." Without the proper academic credentials, Paulsen asserted, few avenues to social status or political prominence lay open. The merchant, the banker, and the rich manufacturer, "no matter how well he stands in other respects," suffered from his lack of academic credentials.[18]

Paulsen wrote at a time when the prestige of higher education was declining. The percentage of academics and academically certified government officials and professionals in the Reichstag and the Prussian House of Deputies had decreased over the previous twenty-five years; reform movements aimed at democratizing the systems of secondary and higher education and directing them toward more practical ends were gathering strength. Critics from Friedrich Nietzsche to popular nonacademicians like Julius Langbehn attacked the university mandarinate for sterility and for betraying the old, true values of the German *Volk*. Paulsen's statements, and countless similar pronouncements by academic spokesmen from the 1890s on, consequently represented as much assertions of how things ought to be as descriptions of how they were. But, whatever the facts, the old middle classes of the nineteenth century accepted the argument: Social prominence and political influence depended upon acquiring an education.[19]

The Jewish bourgeoisie, especially, regarded academic credentials as a ladder to social acceptance. Evidence of personal cultivation belied the stereotype that associated Jewishness with excessive materialism and a lust for profits. The remarkable pursuit of culture among wealthy Jews, at least from the eighteenth century, and their attempts to merge into the Enlightenment and Romantic intelligentsia represented in part the hope of escaping the stereotype. Moritz Münsterberg expressed this tradition when he scorned a practical education for his sons and extolled the humanizing effects of poetry and literature.[20] At the same time, the *Abitur* and a university education were prerequisites for those professional careers outside of business that lay open to Jews: medicine, journalism, and, later in the century, law and academics. Although a businessman without an *Abitur* certificate might earn more money, a professional career held out a far greater prospect for the sort of "usefulness" that Moritz Münsterberg desired for his sons. The surest path to this end for the sons of a businessman and a Jew, with or without conversion to Christianity, was the acquisition of *Bildung* and the academic credentials that testified to it.[21] Consequently, an ideal of education that shunned the purely practical was thoroughly practical for the Münsterbergs, and the ideal of the "cultured man"—whatever its value may have been in personal self-fulfillment—became the ideological bulwark of those who were fortunate and wealthy enough to aspire to it.

The pursuit of cultivation within the *Gymnasium* was autocratic, rigidly intellectual, and self-consciously humanistic.[22] The curriculum stressed mastery of Latin and Greek as well as extensive familiarity with French, history, and mathematics. On the whole, practical subjects were avoided, and recitation and rote memorization characterized the teaching. Frederick Bolton, an American educator investigating German secondary schools late in the nineteenth century, remarked on the absence among pupils of "the questioning attitude we deem most important." In all his visits, he wrote, he "never but once heard a pupil ask a single question." Classroom discipline, in all, "is most perfect from a soldierly point of view." At the same time, recreation did not exist. Outdoor exercise amounted to only about three hours a week, and even then it consisted of strictly regulated calisthenics, the explicit aim of which was to train young men for military service.[23]

Unlike so many of his German contemporaries, however, Münsterberg looked back on the disciplining years of his youth with fondness. The *Gymnasium,* he suggested in an attack on American progressive education in 1899, was neither overly demanding nor oppressive; rather, it allowed its pupils considerable free time. Throughout his teenage years, he wrote, he spent several hours a day "in the fresh air" and, from his ninth year, an hour a day practicing the cello. In addition, he and his classmates formed clubs to fill their vacant time.

> At ten years we played instructive games; at twelve years we read classical dramas, each taking one role; at fifteen we read papers on art and literature; and at seventeen we had a regular debating club. And all the time, at every stage, there were private theatricals, and excursions into the country, and dancing lessons, and horseback-riding, and coeducation with the education left out; for the poor overburdened girls helped us to bear the load by suffering in common.[24]

As if such a schedule were not enough, from the age of seven the young Hugo dabbled in creative literature, a habit he carried into the twentieth century. As a teenager he refashioned classic German myths of Baltic mermaids and of Kunigunde and Kühnhast into ballads and epic poems. He produced a novel as well, which, he modestly recalled, made up in length what it lacked in quality.[25] He also pursued a series of "minor special interests and amusements." In the early school years "botany was all my desire ... every minute I could spare belonged to the plants which I collected and pressed." Then followed for several years a "passion for physical instruments," especially electrical machines, succeeded in its turn by the study of Arabic with a friend. The two boys, the friend "wrote prophetically in my album," were preparing to become missionaries to the Arabs—an unusual aim for a young Jew. An interest in the German past, however, cut this ambition short. Near the end of his *Gymnasium* years, Münsterberg turned to archaeology, spending free afternoons and weeks of vacation in excavations in the Danzig area, finally producing an unpublished manuscript on prehistoric Prussia for his diploma.[26]

Münsterberg's leisure-time activities illustrated the extent to which he, like a good Kantian, had internalized his sense of duty. They reflected a sense of high purpose, a commitment to hard work, and a concern for order. These activities may have been free of adult control, as Münsterberg claimed, but their orderliness was striking. Even their milieu had been tamed and arranged in a predictable order. He spent many of his vacation hours, for example, at the family summer home in the wealthy suburb of Langfuhr. The ordered gardens and the woods cleared of undergrowth stood in sharp contrast to the unkempt nature he was to encounter in America.[27]

Yet these years were less idyllic than Münsterberg later would sometimes choose to remember. As a young student at the University of Leipzig, he offered a view of the *Gymnasium* very different from that of his later reminiscences. "More than ever," he said in a student address,

> the *Gymnasium* today absorbs the energies of the students; we carefully prune out every inclination that leads beyond the school curriculum. We console ourselves through a long period of schooling with the thought that there will be time later for private interests. The result is that the *Abiturient* knows nothing but his few school subjects. So there is nothing left for him to do but tread the beaten path, only to learn too late that his talents and inclinations, left to a free development, would have led him elsewhere.[28]

The *Gymnasium,* in fact, reinforced the elder Münsterberg's separation of duty from immediate interests and desires. In doing so it conformed to an old tradition in Western and German thought that regarded pleasure and natural inclination as antithetical to duty and work. Lutheranism, of course, implied this separation, and Kant's ethical system found morality only in resistance to inclination. Whatever the intellectual pedigree of this system of morals, when the *Gymnasium* applied it to the instruction of its pupils, it failed to meet their needs. The young Hugo Münsterberg dreamed of gold rushes and California during the "leaden hours" of his mathematics class; young Max Weber at about the same time secretly read a forty-volume edition of Goethe at his desk. Whatever, if any, the cost of this strain may have been, the early death of Münsterberg's father in 1880, leaving him an orphan before he had completed the *Gymnasium,* consecrated his sense of duty, his compulsive work habits, and his need to succeed.[29]

The idea that duty involved service and the sacrifice of pleasure followed Münsterberg throughout his life. His father had subordinated his own desires to the future of his family; Hugo came to see himself as a sacrificial victim to science, to progress, and finally to Germany. But in both cases "self-sacrifice" was finally a means to an egotistical end. Through it Moritz hoped to become the center of his sons' lives and Hugo to satisfy personal ambition and achieve personal glory. A young woman whom Hugo met as an eighteen-year-old studying for the summer in Geneva perceived his ambition clearly. "I wish," she wrote in a student album,

> that your desire to be useful to humanity through your literary and scientific works will be crowned with a full success; and I will be very happy if I ever encounter your name among the famous. As for me, I do not seek glory; I simply hope to spend my life at the bedsides of my patients and to ease their suffering.[30]

Neither Münsterberg nor his French friend anticipated a life of self-denying service for him in the future. When he sacrificed himself to the higher ideal of humanity, he did not choose a life of either subservience or obscurity.

A major obstacle, however, stood in the way of Münsterberg's plans: His Jewish faith limited his prospects of serving humanity. Jews had been legally emancipated in northern Germany in 1869, but they continued to face overwhelming difficulties within most branches of the official bureaucracies, including the universities. The tide was turning away from emancipation by the late 1870s, when the founding of Adolf Stoecker's Christian Socialist Workers' Party in 1878 signalled an outburst of anti-Semitism. This development impelled some Jews to reassert their heritage, but more turned in the other direction. Renewed attacks on Jews by Stoecker and others seemed to justify the traditional Jewish reliance on "accommodation, silence, and Christian intervention."[31] Some went as far as converting to Christianity. Among these were the three younger Münsterbergs, Emil, Hugo, and Oscar, who were apparently baptized shortly after the death of their father.[32]

The younger Münsterbergs' decision was not unusual. Between 1880 and 1910, more than 12,000 Jews in Germany entered the Protestant faith and a smaller number, generally in the South, became Catholics.[33] These converts did not represent a large percentage of the Jewish population, but in wealthy and intellectual urban circles their numbers were significant. One Berlin Jew recalled that, at the turn of the century, it was typical in many Jewish families for those sons interested in an academic career to convert and those entering business to remain Jews.[34] It was Otto, the son who inherited Moritz's lumber business, who alone among

the Münsterberg children did not convert. None of the Münsterbergs actively pursued their new faith after conversion, although Hugo was a
member of a Lutheran church in Cambridge,[35] and for them, as for many
other converts, baptism was undoubtedly a practical act. The philosopher
Fritz Mauthner, himself a converted Jew, speculated in 1912:

> It is indeed not impossible that an adult and educated Jew would become a
> Christian out of conviction. It is only that in my life I have not seen such a
> case. In the vast majority of cases the adult convert is brought to profess
> a creed in which he does not believe out of higher or lower reasons of ex-
> pedience.[36]

The converts, or *Taufen,* enjoyed a considerable political and social advantage over those Jews who had not converted. Official Germany regarded Jewishness as a religious rather than a racial trait, and those who
escaped through baptism and conformed politically could expect success
close to that of gentile members of the middle class. Not surprisingly,
converts in civil service exhibited a striking tendency to conform in personality and act. The academician Paul Laband, according to the historian Ernest Hamburger, emerged as "the strongest pillar of the
Bismarckian *Staatsrecht,*" and the state secretary Bernhard Dernburg as a
clever manager of imperial policies. Münsterberg was to assume the role
of an unofficial cultural ambassador in America and, during World War I,
of a German propagandist. "A sort of tacit agreement," Hamburger suggested,

> grew up between the representatives of the government and Jews who were
> willing to see that their ancestry did not stand in the way of a government
> career. The state extended equality to Jews who completed the step to Chris-
> tianity and whose acceptance appeared advantageous to the interests of the
> state.[37]

Early in 1882, slightly more than a year after his father's death, Münsterberg passed his first attempt at the *Abitur* examination. After a summer's study of French literature in Geneva and a lengthy hike through the
Alps with his older brother Emil, he entered the University of Leipzig,
one of the leading German universities at the time and a favorite among
the sons of Prussian businessmen.[38] As he later remembered, Münsterberg
entered wholeheartedly into the life of the German university student. He
helped organize a student club and on several occasions spoke at gatherings, usually on such subjects as the rights and duties of students. His
words at a small celebration inaugurating a new semester were typical:

> Secondary education has laid for us a firm foundation. On it every one of us
> should build for himself that house in which he chooses to work and to cre-
> ate for the rest of his life. . . . But, in building such a house, each stone must

be slowly fitted next to the others. Yes, without diligence and without effort, we can accomplish even less today than we could before.[39]

Münsterberg initially intended to study medicine, the most common choice among Jews, in preparation for an academic career in science. The pathologist and medical anthropologist, Rudolf Virchow, one of the leading figures of nineteenth-century German science, had been an acquaintance of Hugo's father (Moritz, in fact, died shortly after a trip with Virchow to an anthropological conference in Lisbon),[40] and perhaps he communicated an interest in the medical sciences to the younger Münsterberg. Once at the university, Münsterberg pursued his medical studies in the laboratories and lectures of such authorities as the biochemist Karl Ludwig and the anatomists Rudolf Leuckart and Wilhelm His, gaining from them a mechanistic approach to natural science that reduced all phenomena to laws of attraction and repulsion. Ludwig had been one of the famous "reductionists" of the 1840s, and he had devoted his career to the proposition that no special "vital" forces directed the processes of life.[41] He, more than anyone else, developed organic chemistry as an experimental science. Leuckart and His, a generation younger, had made important contributions in working out a mechanistic account of evolution.

By his second year Münsterberg had expanded his concerns. After a course of lectures from Wilhelm Wundt and subsequent work in Wundt's laboratory, he decided to add the study of psychology to that of medicine. At the time psychology was only just emerging as a discipline independent of philosophy, and it carried with it the crusading excitement of a new field of study capable of unraveling problems that had long baffled philosophers. Not less significant for an ambitious young scholar, it offered opportunities that medicine, by then static, no longer could. Advancement for a newcomer in philosophy, the academic field of a psychologist, was twice as likely as advancement in physiology.[42]

It was Wundt especially who defined the methods and scope of the "new" psychology. Late in the 1870s he established the world's first psychological laboratory at Leipzig. When Münsterberg arrived, the laboratory was attracting students from all over the world. G. Stanley Hall, a future rival of Münsterberg in America, already had studied there, and James McKeen Cattell, Münsterberg's counterpart at Columbia, was working there at the time. Wundt argued that philosophy and metaphysics had proved incapable of explaining how the human mind worked. In his experimental work he applied the laboratory methods of physics and especially physiology to the analysis of simple mental states. His position remained traditional, however, on an important point, which was to set him off from younger enthusiasts. He was skeptical that higher mental states—for instance those that involved acts of will or reason—could be analyzed experimentally. He subscribed instead to a voluntarist philosophy, arguing that the will was an active and creative principle that unified the mind and endowed it with purpose.[43]

In the Leipzig laboratory, Münsterberg took up the problem of the will —an ambitious project from which Wundt could have expected little. Münsterberg regarded feelings of will as nothing more than a compounding of purely sensational elements and the mind as a reactive mechanism with no autonomy. He hoped to prove this view experimentally. Münsterberg later claimed that Wundt, who was not known for his breadth of mind in dealing with students, directed his investigations away from his chosen subject.[44] Whether this was true or not, Münsterberg never published any of his work in the organ of the Leipzig laboratory, *Philosophische Studien,* and he presented as his dissertation a nonexperimental critique of the current theories of evolution.

Münsterberg received his doctorate in physiological psychology from Leipzig in the spring of 1885. That summer he became engaged to a distant cousin on his father's side, Selma Oppler. The Opplers, then living in Strasbourg, had been residents of Danzig years before and frequent guests at the Münsterberg summer home in Langfuhr. For Hugo, Selma was no doubt a recapitulation of his mother in certain respects, particularly in her devotion to painting. She would contribute idealism to the noble home that he hoped to fashion. The engagement briefly delayed Münsterberg's career, but at Heidelberg in October he resumed his deferred medical studies.[45]

Two years later Münsterberg received his medical degree on the strength of an inquiry into the visual perception of space. Armed with both a Ph.D. and an M.D., he began his professional career at the age of twenty-four, taking a positon as *Docent* at Freiburg, a small but prestigious university in Baden. *Docenten* occupied the lowest faculty rank in the German university system. Unlike the higher-ranked professors, they were not civil servants and did not receive salaries from the state; their only income came from fees that students paid to attend their lectures. To become a *Docent,* a young scholar applied to a given university for permission to offer a course of lectures. Prior to his appointment he had to pass a *Habilitation* examination, submit a thesis to the appropriate faculty, and deliver two trial lectures.[46] Münsterberg offered as his thesis *Die Willenshandlung,* a challenge to Wundt's theory of the will. In the fall of 1887 he moved to Freiburg with Selma, whom he had married less than a month before.

At Freiburg, Münsterberg's docential lectures reflected his developing interest in philosophical questions. During four years there he talked on the philosophy of the natural sciences (his view was positivistic),[47] on the history of philosophy, on pedagogy, and on Schopenhauer, who was enjoying a revival in Germany. It was his work in experimental psychology, however, that earned him an international reputation. On arriving he set up a laboratory with his own money in two rooms of his house. Within a few years that laboratory was competing with Wundt's at Leipzig and G. E. Müller's at Göttingen, both of which were financed by their respective states.[48] It soon drew students from throughout Germany as well as abroad.

Over the next few years Münsterberg pursued his experimental work in a series of controversial volumes under the general title, *Beiträge zur experimentellen Psychologie.* As in *Die Willenshandlung,* his writing was dogmatic and occasionally polemical in its attacks on Wundt and others. Instead of confining himself to the statistics-gathering activities that then went under the name of "empirical" in Germany, he offered a single theory of mind—viewing it, in the final analysis, as a reactive mechanism and expelling from it any trace of spontaneity—and he proposed to demonstrate his theory's applicability to all the mind's functions. By the early 1890s, after several volumes of the *Beiträge* had appeared, Münsterberg was recognized as the leader of what one authority called the Freiburg School of psychophysics and as an important spokesman of the positivistic and anti-Wundtian wing of experimental psychology.[49]

Münsterberg's work drew immediate criticism from orthodox psychologists in Germany. Wundt himself, and his assistant Oswald Külpe, suggested in the pages of the *Philosophische Studien* that the young Freiburg *Docent* had misrepresented Wundt's work. His approach, they also argued, was excessively intellectualist, stressing the cognitive processes of mind to the exclusion of the affective. Edward Titchener, another Wundt student who would head Cornell's psychological laboratory for many years, attacked Münsterberg in the prestigious British journal *Mind.* Titchener argued, with some reason, that Münsterberg's methods were too inexact and his reporting of experiments too incomplete to justify his far-reaching conclusions. And he contended that Münsterberg suffered from a disability that was serious for a scientist: "Dr. Münsterberg," he wrote, "has the fatal gift of writing easily—fatal especially in science, and most of all in a young science, where accuracy is the one thing needful." Psychological literature, instead, required "dry figures and circumstantial details."[50] It was a curious claim for a science in which experimenters regularly measured reaction times to the thousandths of seconds, yet could not agree on what those times told of mental processes, or indeed what they were measuring at all. But for the young psychological professionals, dry figures and circumstantial details proved that they were scientists.

The strongest attack on Münsterberg, however, came not from a Wundtian but from G. E. Müller, the leading rival to Wundt in German experimental psychology. While Müller expressed agreement with Münsterberg's psychophysical axioms, he found little else in the work to praise. It was "unbearably trivial" in its generalizations and frequently wrong in its details. Its logic was more scholastic than scientific (a complaint with considerable justification). But more than anything else, Müller found its ambitious hypothesizing and dogmatic tone objectionable, especially from so young a man. On reading the third volume of the *Beiträge,* Müller concluded:

> I had to swallow so many hypotheses that I finally earned the right to propose one myself. It is in fact far better grounded than all the hypotheses that the author has us swallow. Specifically, it is the hypothesis that the author, in composing these treatises, is governed by the effort—not exactly very exalted or useful to science—of producing as much printed material as possible.[51]

It was not the last time that Münsterberg would face the charge of excessive verbiage, but he could console himself, perhaps, with the knowledge that such a failing was apparently congenital among many of his colleagues. Wundt, by one calculation, wrote about one word every two minutes, day and night, between the dates of his first publication in 1853 and his last in 1920.[52]

Outside of Germany the reception of Münsterberg's work was considerably different. In England, as Titchener observed, "the subsumption of the whole mass of German results under traditional English theories was a project with which our own psychologists could not but sympathize." Münsterberg's reactive theory of mind was in fact a sophisticated version of associationism, not far from what Alexander Bain and H. C. Bastian were moving toward. G. F. Stout and Croom Robertson, both influential psychologists, welcomed his work enthusiastically in the pages of *Mind.* No one had greater praise for his writings, however, than did William James, who admired his iconoclastic approach and his emphasis on kinetic bases of thought. *Die Willenshandlung,* James wrote, was "a little masterpiece."[53]

James's opinion carried weight in the Anglo-American world, but not in Germany, where Münsterberg had the misfortune of having drawn the intellectual, and perhaps personal, opposition of several leaders of experimental psychology. His family wealth, on the other hand, allowed him to put together a first-rate laboratory, and in some respects it was an advan-

tage to be attacked as excessively literary at a time when many philosophers still looked with some skepticism on the new psychology. He had
his allies, like Alois Riehl, then the leading philosopher at Freiburg, and
Heinrich Rickert, a fellow *Docent* and Danziger, who had made important contributions to the developing definition of the social sciences.
Münsterberg's Jewish background certainly did not help his prospects,
but Freiburg was among the most liberal German universities in its position toward Jews. As a convert who was politically conformist and made
no public identifications with Jewish culture, Münsterberg could enter-
tain reasonable expectations of success.[54]

In 1892 the Freiburg faculty acknowledged Münsterberg's prospects by
electing him, at the remarkably young age of twenty-eight, to the position
of *extraordentlicher Professor*. As "extraordinary" professor, Münsterberg
became a permanent, salaried state official. While advancement to the position of full professor (which carried with it a higher salary, greater prestige, and the right to participate in the administrative affairs of the
university and the faculty) was not guaranteed, it was likely. Most philosophers who reached the level of *Extraordinarius* eventually gained an
Ordinarius.[55] Münsterberg's career seemed set.

Reductionist Science: Biology, Psychology, and Ethics

At Freiburg, Münsterberg was heir to an honored tradition. The German academics—"mandarins," Fritz Ringer has called them—occupied a unique position as the guardians and transmitters of *Kultur.* They held in their hands, so they constantly reminded their countrymen, the education of the nation's elite and, through their search for truth, they advanced the German *Geist* as it unfolded in history. There were Volkist pretenders to their place and Philistines who had little respect for their work, but few among the academics doubted a direct correlation between the vigor of German scholarship and the prestige and power of the state.[1]

These academics, as Karl Mannheim has written, were a bourgeoisie whose sole capital was their education,[2] and, like many property-owners, they worked fiercely to prevent the depreciation of their assets. They had survived the long, rigorous, and expensive German educational system and to show for it they had their *Wissenschaft,* or scholarship, which provided them with a True Method that belonged to them as distinctly as the ritual of the Church did to a rival priesthood. Academics defended careful, disciplined, and logical thought, consistent with the "critical" tradition of Kant, and they rejected direct metaphysical revelation and blind intuition as paths to truth. They stood constantly on guard against *a priori* dogmatism, dilettantism, and intuitionism—all of which threatened to dispossess them of their monopoly.

After the 1840s at least, *Wissenschaft* assumed a special meaning for the natural scientists. Through observation and experimentation they attempted to reduce the phenomenal world to principles of order, law, and predictability. Biologists and physiologists, impressed by the successes of physics, transferred its mechanical model to their studies: They argued that the processes of nature depended solely upon the attraction and repulsion of minute particles. This "reductionism," as it has been called, expelled all teleology from nature. Its proponents, however, never directed it against the Idealists' evolutionary view of history, which assumed that human civilization evolved according to laws of purpose and that the German state represented the culmination of that evolution. Therefore, the radical materialism of a Carl Vogt or a Ludwig Büchner never gained much support from orthodox academics, including Münsterberg, for it called into question the spiritual bases of the nation. Most academics subscribed instead to some sort of Idealism in which the operations of mind determined the structure of physical reality, not the reverse, and in which culture was differentiated from nature and the cultural sciences from the natural.

Münsterberg, however, was unwilling to concede any restrictions on natural law. The laws of mechanics, he argued, applied not merely to organisms in the present but to evolution itself and, even more radically, to the natural and cultural life of man. In this respect he departed from a mainstream of German academic thought that included figures as far apart from each other as Hermann von Helmholtz and Max Weber. But, unlike Büchner or Karl Marx, Münsterberg did not turn a positive science to iconoclastic purposes; he attempted, rather, to demonstrate that the standard ideological pillars of academic orthodoxy were consistent with a reductionist explanation. Reductionist science did not undermine the distaste for mere practicality, nor did it threaten beliefs in the dependence of all morality on self-denial, the organic unity of society and a functional concept of vocation, and the existence of a purposeful trend in natural and human history; it confirmed them. In a sense, then, Münsterberg was to appropriate positivistic science for German Idealism.

Münsterberg went a step further. He subscribed to a fundamental and finally unresolved epistemological dualism: The phenomenal world (including human history) could be considered either as nature or as spirit, either for the purpose of explaining or for that of understanding. Neither viewpoint could dictate its conclusions to the other, and each existed independently as a *Wissenschaft*. By the twentieth century, this dichotomy puzzled Münsterberg's American contemporaries and led him to apparently contradictory positions. He seemed a committed behaviorist in psychology and at the same time a voluntarist in his understanding of historical processes. But this discussion gets ahead of the story, for the voluntaristic tendency of Münsterberg's thought was secondary in the 1880s. It is enough for the moment to trace how he sought to explain teleological events by a mechanistic science.

Münsterberg's scientific work in the 1880s must be understood in the context of a lengthy dispute between teleological and mechanistic approaches to science—a dispute that often assumed political overtones. In his published work in biology, psychology, and ethics, he hoped to discredit the old *Naturphilosophie,* which was creeping back into German sciences and whose traces he found in the works of Ernst Haeckel and even Wundt. *Naturphilosophie* was dangerous not simply because it was wrong. Its mystical tendencies—as Münsterberg read it—might open the floodgates to spiritualists and quacks, undermine *Wissenschaft,* and, to extend his logic, threaten the political order that supported the scholar.

Early in the nineteenth century *Naturphilosophie* dominated German scientific thought.[3] Kant had posited a fundamental and unbridgeable gap between the world of thought and the world of objects. His successors, however, prey to "the metaphysical pathos of the time,"[4] abandoned his unattainable "things-in-themselves" and turned to a world view in which the natural world became a corporeal and progressive manifestation of a higher spiritual unity, or, in the language of Friedrich Schelling, a *Weltseele.* The totality of Nature, in its past and future as well as its present, resulted from neither the random wanderings of atoms nor the mechanistic laws of physics and chemistry. It reflected a final purpose. Man, as part of that purpose, could hope to understand it through his own capacity of intuition.

The *Naturphilosophen* advocated an *"a priori* method of biology,"[5] assuming a correspondence between the real and the intuited, which led to what today seem highly speculative results. They asserted that a special vital force, akin to the force of gravity, pervaded nature and directed life processes toward the realization of the normal whole or perfect organism. These processes—generation, self-preservation, irritability, and sensitivity —differed fundamentally from the motion of physical bodies and the compounding of chemical elements. They expressed instead a teleological development of the individual and the race in accordance with the final purpose of Nature. The individual organism, then, served Schelling's *Weltseele* by "actualizing" itself in much the same way that the Fichtean egoist served a final purpose through "self-actualization." In both cases the individual operated freely and independently, according to forces immanent in it. But in doing so it conformed to its destined role in the development of the universe. "Freedom" and "individuality" for Schelling and Fichte meant neither caprice nor self-determination but, rather, the willing performance of a preordained function.

During the 1840s a group of experimentalists, trained in Johannes Müller's Berlin laboratory, launched a reductionist attack on *Naturphilosophie.* "We attempted," reminisced Moritz Münsterberg's friend Rudolph Virchow, "to shake off the spell which philosophy, nature-philosophy in particular, had for a long period cast over science."[6] Already in the 1830s, Müller's student Theodor Schwann had attacked the notion that the organism was more than the sum of its parts and called for a new mode of explanation that would reduce biology as far as possible to physical and chemical laws. A few years later two other students of Müller, Emil Dubois-Reymond and Ernst Brücke, accepted the challenge of creating a truly "scientific" physiology. "Brücke and I," DuBois-Reymond wrote at the time, "we have sworn to validate the truth that no forces operate in the organism other than the ordinary physical and chemical ones." By the end of the decade the reductionist campaign was well underway, first in the work of still another Müller student, Hermann von Helmholtz, who in 1847 wrote *Uber die Erhaltung der Kraft* (On the Conservation of Energy), and shortly thereafter in the publication of DuBois-Reymond's work on animal electricity and that of Münsterberg's teacher Karl Ludwig on organic chemistry. "The retreat from *Naturphilosophie,*" Everett Mendelsohn has written, "had turned into a rout and the attitude of the new generation was one of revulsion."[7]

The position of the reductionists depended as much on a rethinking of the epistemological basis of scientific explanation as it did on the weight of experimental evidence.[8] It is worth developing their argument briefly, because it was the source of a mechanistic and quasi-positivistic view of science extremely important not only in German biology and physiology, but in psychology as well. Like so many members of the post-Hegelian generation, the reductionists looked back to Kant for an escape from the metaphysical constructions of their predecessors. Following Kant, as they read him, they asserted that scientific explanation, for epistemological and logical reasons, meant the reduction of natural processes to matter in motion, governed by forces of attraction and repulsion and, Helmholtz added, the law of the conservation of energy. Since these forces or laws of mechanics, "whose intensity depends solely upon distance," were both necessary and mathematically calculable, the world of matter and motion became closed and deterministic, absolutely devoid of any higher purpose.[9]

The reductionists found their greatest difficulty in applying laws of mechanics to the natural processes of growth and development. The publication of Charles Darwin's *Origin of Species,* translated into German in 1860, triggered a revival of *Naturphilosophie* and teleological explanations among German scholars.[10] While many scientists in America and Great

Britain believed that Darwin's work eliminated the need for an explicit design in nature, German scientists on the whole reacted quite differently. Opponents of *Darwinismus,* such as the botanist Albert Wigand, as well as its defenders, including Ernst Haeckel, asserted that Darwin reintroduced a concept of purpose into nature. Such phrases as "survival of the fittest" implied to them a preordained pattern that transcended material causation, and the concept of "function" seemed to deny that the universe was totally atomistic and purposeless.

Haeckel, a professor of zoology at Jena, emerged by the 1860s as the major spokesman of *Darwinismus.* Although he claimed to find in Darwin an opportunity to extend mechanistic explanation and physicochemical laws to the problem of development, his mechanism proved of a curious kind, owing more to the romantic than to the reductionist tradition in biology. He borrowed explicitly from that *bête noire* of the reductionists, Johann von Goethe, whom he considered a forerunner of Darwin. He talked of "cell souls" and "soul cells," resolving nature into spirit and turning spirit into substance. He explained the mystery of biological inheritance by arguing that the molecules of living matter possessed a faculty of memory; he accounted for variability by assuming varying mental capacities in these molecules. And he postulated an *innerer Bildungstrieb,* an inner impulse toward development that, together with environmental influences, guided the evolution of both the organism and the species. This notion of inner development was to play an important part in the mechanistic physiologies of Wilhelm Roux, Wilhelm His, and Münsterberg himself. But in Haeckel's hands, at least according to his critics, it depended on exactly that concept of a special force, aiming toward fulfillment, that both Darwin and the reductionists hoped to banish from biology.[11]

Haeckel's controversial theories made the problem of evolution in the 1870s and 1880s "the most popular theme of popular science in Germany," in the words of the visiting American, G. Stanley Hall. In its extreme forms, *Darwinismus* delivered a direct attack on the academic orthodoxy and its exclusive claims to *Wissenschaft.* Haeckel did not fall into the intuitionism of the romantics, but he attacked the reductionist orthodoxy as a cold and sterile philosophy that betrayed the spirit of the German *Volk.* Thus, the challenge had political implications, for Haeckel expressed a Volkist politics that drew support among the lower-middle classes.[12]

In the 1880s the teleological explanation of evolution—although not Haeckel and certainly not his Volkist politics—found an unlikely ally in Wilhelm Wundt. A careful investigation of the history of natural and human evolution, Wundt wrote in the third edition of his *Grundzüge der physiologischen Psychologie,* "forces us to the view that physical evolution is not the cause, but rather is the effect of mental evolution." And purpose, far more than random selection, provided its motive force. Indirect evidence even suggested, Wundt contended, that the *Naturphilosophen* might have been correct when they attributed a mental basis to plant life. The mental evolution of plants might have been cut short in an earlier period of life, leaving behind only the residues of original voluntary actions. He suggested:

> The ancient, animistic view, which Aristotle first summarized in his famous scientific definition of the soul as the first "entelechy of the living body," proves itself to be, in a different form, the only view which promises to throw light simultaneously on the problem of mental and material development. Only by assuming that mental evolution has fashioned matter can one comprehend the undeniable fact of life's purposefulness, despite all the antiteleological tendencies of biology today.[13]

One example of those antiteleological tendencies was the dissertation that Münsterberg wrote in 1885 under Wundt's direction.

In this dissertation, *Zur Lehre der natürlichen Anpassung* (On the Theory of Natural Adaptation), Münsterberg attempted to explain the process of evolution in wholly mechanical terms. He completely accepted the evidence for natural adaptation, but not Wundt's argument that it proved the prior existence of mental evolution. "Biology tells us," he wrote, that "every creature in natural evolution can develop only those characteristics that are of service to its own preservation or the preservation of its immediate descendants." Darwin's contribution lay in recognizing that this apparently teleological process could be explained without the concept of "purpose." Darwin's system was incomplete, however, because it did not account for the rapidity of evolutionary change or the apparent inheritability of acquired traits. At the same time, Haeckel's modifications of Darwin set the science of biology backwards, for they came dangerously close to assuming the existence of transcendental forces. What Darwin needed, Münsterberg argued, was a mechanistic principle of internal development to complement his theory of random variation.[14]

Münsterberg borrowed here, no doubt, from the work of Rudolf Leuckart. One of the three men on his doctoral committee, Leuckart had been attempting for several years to work out a "physiology of the plastic," that is, a physiology that reduced evolution to the laws of attraction and repulsion. But Münsterberg owed his major debt to a study written a few years before by the embryologist Wilhelm Roux, who had been a student at Jena when Haeckel was at the height of his career. Suggestively entitled *Der Kampf im Organismus* (The Struggle within the Organism), Roux's book drew considerable attention when it appeared. Darwin, for example, greeted it with typical generosity as "the most important book on development that has appeared for some time."[15] Roux argued that a Darwinian struggle for survival between individuals could account for the larger bodily forms, such as the type of foot, but not for the fine details of structure that we find in all organisms. To explain these, he posited "an inner struggle for existence between the various elements of the body"—a thoroughly mechanical process that he named "functional adaptation." As the biologist Emanuel Rádl explained it:

> Imagine bone [to be] a homogenous substance, and every part of it equally well nourished. If the weight rests on it, and muscles expand it in certain directions, some parts will be more used, and so stimulated, than others. Those parts grow stronger, and rob neighboring parts of both room and nourishment. They survive, the parts less favourably situated degenerate. Thus the bone gradually evolves a structure, at once strong and well suited to its work. Other organs evolve in the same way.[16]

This explanation, Münsterberg believed, corrected Darwin's overemphasis on the biological organism or "individual." Münsterberg's own description of natural adaptation would avoid the mistake. "When influenced by a complex of conditions that is relatively constant," he wrote, "every organic unit [*Einheit*] always assumes, out of all the possible arrangements of its parts, just that one which . . . is most advantageous for its preservation." The key word in this definition was *Einheit*, which Münsterberg carefully distinguished from the word *Individuum*, used by Haeckel and others. The organic unit was not necessarily individual, much less an individual. Münsterberg imagined instead a scale of increasingly complicated units in the natural world: cell, tissue, organ, organism, and species; or, to follow another line, cell, tissue, organ, organism, sexual pair, family, and state.[17]

Natural adaptation within this system, in Münsterberg's opinion, occurred as a result of two different processes. Every organic unit evolved as its own internal parts interacted with one another, and, in a direct competition between units, those units with advantageous characteristics survived. The second process, when it occurred at the level of the organism, was the Darwinian principle of natural selection. Münsterberg, however, considered the first process, which he called "direct" or "mutual" adaptation (*wechselseitige Anpassung*), to be far more important in the evolution of the organism and its parts. Although its name had been changed, the process was almost identical to Roux's functional adaptation.[18]

Mutual adaptation took place at every level of the chain of being, within cells, tissues, organs, and organisms. Münsterberg's description of the process within the cell was strikingly close to Roux's. To paraphrase Münsterberg, if the environment operated upon a cell in a fashion that favored certain of its parts but harmed others, then the parts not favored would be unable to maintain their metabolism. As a result, they would die out, while those favored would grow and multiply. Finally, the cell would be made up only of those parts that were adapted to outer conditions. At higher levels, where the parts were differentiated, the process became more complicated, but not essentially different. As an example of mutual adaptation within the organism, Münsterberg cited the interdependence of the internal organs of the body. If one were altered in any way, the others had to compensate automatically in order to preserve the organism. In other words, as each organ evolved, it affected the others in a competitive but at the same time cooperative process. "As a result of the struggle of its parts," Münsterberg suggested, "an organic unit will end in a form as advantageous as possible for each individual part."[19]

Münsterberg was in effect offering his theory of mutual adaptation as a mechanistic explanation of Lamarckian evolution. Evidence both in the laboratory and in nature, he claimed, left little doubt that at least some acquired traits could be inherited. A Darwinian principle of random selection could not account for the rapidity of evolutionary change that occurred in some cases. The hoofs of the horses on the Falkland Islands were so reminiscent of the building of calluses, he argued, that "the development must not be a chance one, found here and there and bred through selection, but [it must occur] in the case of every single individual; the special hoof-structure must be stimulated and strengthened repeatedly, until it finally becomes inherited."[20]

Evolution, for Münsterberg, worked toward a universal harmony. Adaptation became a series of adjustments to environmental changes, and these adjustments ensured a perfect balance within the organism and between the organism and its environment. In a state of "completed" adaptation to a stable environment, the organism (and, by implication, the cell, the tissue, the family, and the state) exhibited a harmony of purpose in which all of its individual parts worked toward their mutual benefit. As long as every part fulfilled its function properly, the organism as a whole prospered. It would be a mistake to see this condition as something far off in the hypothetical future, for it actually existed in nature. "Every healthy plant and animal," Münsterberg contended,

> now represents . . . such a condition of completed mutal adaptation. In the general organism, every organ finds its own possibilities for self-preservation in the conditions required for the continuation of other organs. At the same time, out of this cooperation, as the basic condition for the special existence of all particular organs, emerges the life of the individual.[21]

Münsterberg's nature, therefore, differed from the nature "red in tooth and claw" of so many British evolutionists. Darwin, as he himself acknowledged, derived his theory of natural selection from Thomas Malthus's pessimistic views on population. The concept of a struggle for existence in a world of scarcity formed the core of his theory. Münsterberg drew his inspiration from the German Idealists and especially Fichte, who considered history to be progressive. He argued that Darwin misread nature in two ways: first, by overstressing its parsimony; second, by placing too much emphasis on conditions that were favorable to individuals but unfavorable to the whole. Münsterberg did not deny the existence of these factors, and he conceded that they were important in determining the course of evolution. But natural history could not be reduced to a simple struggle for existence because nature offered surpluses as well as deficits. When the means of subsistence were abundant, Münsterberg argued, every individual absorbed nature's excesses in a way that was beneficial to all. The aim of the organism in this case was no longer a *Kampf ums Dasein,* a struggle for existence, but rather a *Kampf ums Bessersein,* a struggle for a better existence.[22]

The course of natural history in fact expressed a dialectic. At one stage in its development nature would be miserly, and the struggle for existence would dominate; at another stage it would be generous, and the struggle for a better existence would rule. Both stages were necessary for evolution. A few years later, Münsterberg was to use a similar dialectic when he wrote of human history: The age of Goethe was an age of cosmopolitanism, when the ethical individual committed himself to a general ideal of humanity; the Wilhelmian era was a period of nationalism, when the ethical individual devoted himself to his nation's purposes. In general, this sort of historical relativism typified Münsterberg's thought, and it adhered to a well-entrenched Idealist tradition.[23] A validation of German Idealism was an odd place for a mechanistic account of natural evolution to end. But that after all was the meaning of Münsterberg's work: to provide an atomistic and mechanistic explanation of both society and the mind that did not jar the traditional world view of the German academic.

Münsterberg did not draw out the social and political implications of his biology, but he did not have to. It reflected the symphonic view of society and the ideal of personal *Innerlichkeit* or "inwardness" central to German social thought. The kidney, when it acted as a kidney should, was expressing its true personality and at that moment playing its part in the survival of the individual to whom it belonged. The vocation of a human individual, in the same way, was determined by his true personality—not by what he capriciously "wanted" to do but by his innate capacities and talents (which in traditional thought generally coincided with social class). The way to ensure a properly functioning society was to guarantee that each of its members had the opportunity and the will to express his individual potential. This position frequently took on an authoritarian air, especially as it was often assumed—by Münsterberg among others—that the individual did not always recognize his own vocation. It was the task of the monarchy, the Idealist historian Leopold von Ranke wrote in 1836, to see to it that "the right man arrived at the right position."[24] For Münsterberg, in the twentieth century, this became the responsibility of the psychological expert.

Münsterberg's speciality at Leipzig was not biology but the new field of "psychophysics"—a term first used by Gustav Fechner in 1860. By the 1880s the most prominent member of the field was Münsterberg's major professor, Wundt, whom he had called "the critical creator and leader of the true experimental psychology."[25] Physiological psychology, as Wundt at first preferred to call his approach, studied the relations of body and mind and attempted to apply exact measurements to mental processes. The subject of this discipline was the consciousness as revealed to trained introspective observers, not the behavior or motivation that psychologists today emphasize. Wundt and the German experimentalists aimed at unveiling the structure of the conscious mind. By analyzing it into its constituent "ideas," they would build up what one of their number, Hermann Ebbinghaus, called a "morphology" of mind. For Münsterberg, as well as for Wundt, the discipline was far more philosophical than twentieth-century psychology. It asked such questions as: What unit-ideas make up our concepts of space and time, and where do they come from? How do unit-ideas combine to form complex emotional states such as fear? What is the place of the feeling of effort and will in the mind?[26]

Leibniz, Kant, and Fichte had stressed the creative spontaneity of mind. It operated upon sense data, they asserted, rather than reacted to it. Both Leibniz and Kant, in particular, described an active and unifying process of mind, called "apperception," which did not lie in the phenomenal world but, rather, was "rooted in the logical unity of consciousness which lies at the basis of everything." In other words, the logical structure of thinking determined perception. The *Naturphilosophen* continued this tradition, bringing to the study of the mind an insistence on "the complete reality and unique peculiarity of the psychical phenomena."[27]

The reductionists responded with a mechanistic and often physiological approach, attempting to explain the human sensory and nervous structure (and therefore the mind) in physicochemical terms. Müller's credo of *"Nemo psychologus nisi physiologus"* pointed to the possibility of investigating mental processes through their physiological corollaries. In the 1840s DuBois-Reymond identified the vitalists' "nerve-force" with common electrical energy, and a few years later Helmholtz successfully measured its speed. But the reductionists refused to go the whole way to an outright materialism or to a thoroughly mechanistic view of mind that would strip it of all activity. If for no other reason, the physiology of the mid-nineteenth century did not permit such a step.[28]

For most of the nineteeth century physiologists had accepted the doctrine of the "inexcitability of the cerebral cortex," the putative seat of the "higher" mental activities. They did not extend the simple reflex arc, which connected stimulus with response in the bodily mechanism, to complicated mental processes. As a result, Müller, like Kant, postulated a will, or active principle of mind, that "played on" the lower centers and could not be reduced to a mechanical reflex. His student Helmholtz proposed a mental process of "aesthetic inference," upon which the *Geisteswissenschaften,* or humanistic disciplines, depended. The products of culture, Helmholtz argued, were inexplicable in the mechanical terms of natural science. In 1870, however, Gustav Fritsch and Eduard Hitzig proved in a famous series of experiments that the cerebral cortex was indeed susceptible to electrical stimulation. In the decades that followed, investigators worked out a detailed map of motor centers in the cortex. While this discovery could not, of course, prove or disprove the reality of a will, it did make possible the extension of the reflex arc into the higher processes of mind. Münsterberg and others used it in the 1880s to deny the existence of any citadel of creativity or will in the mind.[29]

Even as Fritsch and Hitzig were violating the brain's deepest recesses, a revival of voluntarism challenged the reductionist trend in psychology. In Germany, Schopenhauer's long neglected work gained a new popularity, and a Fichte revival (tied to a celebration of the new German state) was well under way in the 1880s. The rise of neo-*Naturphilosophie* in biology expressed the same tendency. So did the philosophy of Eduard von Hartmann and, shortly thereafter, that of Friedrich Paulsen and Rudolf Eucken, all of whom placed the will on an equal footing with the intellect. Abroad, by the end of the century, Alfred Fouillée, Henri Bergson, and William James were moving in similar directions. Wundt, an outspoken opponent of metaphysical speculation, at the same time voiced his own dissatisfaction with the expulsion of the principles of purpose and direction from the life sciences.[30]

American students of Wundt, especially Cornell's Edward Titchener, generally emphasized his role in the formation of a scientific psychology and in pioneering the exact measurement of mind. It should not be forgotten, however, that Wundt espoused an explicit voluntarism and insisted on the primacy of a creative will.[31] To be sure, Wundt did not begin his career as a voluntarist. He was trained in the 1850s as a physiologist and he studied briefly at Müller's Berlin laboratory, where he became friends with DuBois-Reymond. When he first came to psychology in about 1860, he reminisced almost forty years later, "I shared the general prejudice, natural to the physiologist, that the formation of our sense-perceptions was solely the work of the physiological properties of our sense organs." His reading of Leibniz, Kant, and others and his experiments on space-perception, however, changed his mind. Whatever their successes might have been in other respects, he argued, no physiological explanation and no purely physiological experimentation could explain visual phenomena like contrast or glitter. To account for them, Wundt postulated a "creative synthesis of mind," a principle that was to become central to his psychology.[32]

In the years that followed, Wundt stressed the act of "apperception," adapted from J. F. Herbart as well as from Kant. He compared the mind to an eye, before which lay a field of vision (*Blickfeld*) that was the product of passive sensory experience. Through an act of spontaneous, unifying attention, or apperception, the mind could bring that *Blickfeld* into sharp focus, or, in Wundt's words, into a *Blickpunkt*. The mind, then, in an act of will and for its own purposes, compounded out of the raw material of the *Blickfeld* a single, unitary idea (*Vorstellung*). This simple act of apperception lay at the basis of all voluntary actions, from the movement of limbs to complex deliberations.[33]

Wundt explicitly argued, therefore, that the axioms of mechanics, however fixed they might be for the inanimate world, did not apply to the mind. "Laplace's fiction of a world formula," which held that the whole course of nature could in theory be reduced to an intricate mathematical mechanics, "is inapplicable to psychical processes not only because it is shattered by the incalculable complexity of events, but because it is itself in contradiction with the laws of psychical processes." The mind instead operated according to its own special laws, which were just as deterministic as the laws of mechanics but were quite their opposite. In the physical world, matter and energy were static, bound by the law of conservation; in the mental and cultural world, energy expanded according to a scheme of Becoming or "mental causation." In this process, the personality of the individual unfolded through his own life and the culture of mankind unfolded in the course of history.[34]

Münsterberg offered a thoroughgoing critique of this view of mind and culture. He denied the existence of special laws of mental development. All physical events, including human behavior, could be explained in completely reductionist and materialistic terms. Mental events, the subject of psychology, were nothing but epiphenomena; they gave rise to neither physical events nor subsequent mental ones.

In this way, Münsterberg specifically challenged Wundt's concept of mental causality (as well as those of the German *Geisteswissenschaftler*), and he reduced the apperceiving mind to a brain reflex, conditioned by experience. In doing so, Münsterberg reversed Wundt's analogy between the mind and an eye. The analogy held true, Münsterberg explained, only if "the eye is absolutely rigid and immobile. It cannot fixate itself upon anything and it cannot adjust for distances. It cannot shut itself and it cannot open itself to its field of vision." Here was an exact reformulation of Hume's passive sensationism, in which the mind was nothing but a stage upon which the sensations played.[35]

There were other ways in which this view resembled that of the British associationists. In it the mind consisted of nothing more than the sum of its contents (like the reductionists' organism); it was a structure made up, in a Lockean fashion, of building-block "ideas" or percepts. These ideas, moreover, derived entirely from sensations. Each individual sensation was characterized by quality, intensity, and a particular "feeling-quality" (*Gefühlston*). The familiar sensations of pleasure and pain, for example, were nothing more than the feeling-qualities that accompanied the flexing and extending of muscles. To argue his position, Münsterberg developed a motor theory that depended upon the existence of a "muscular sense."[36]

The concept of inner sensation and "muscular sense" had a lengthy history in the nineteenth century. Traditional associationists, whose concerns were generally epistemological, concentrated on how the mechanism of mind recognized the various stimuli that bombarded it. They reduced cognition to the reception and ordering of sensations received from outside the body. In reaction to this passive model, the British philosophers Erasmus Darwin, Thomas Brown, and especially Charles Bell argued for a sense that transmitted the condition of the muscle directly to the brain. Johannes Müller developed this concept into a "full-fledged motor view on associationist lines," and others in Germany followed his lead, especially after the identification of sensory receptors in the skeletal muscle in 1874. The Englishman H. C. Bastian demonstrated in 1880 the importance of the sensation of muscular movement or "kinesthesis" in perception. During the 1880s William James pulled these threads together in his ideo-motor theory: The bodily and motor processes were essential, he argued, in determining consciousness. His *Principles of Psychology* (1890) canonized a view, particularly among Americans, that was strikingly similar to Münsterberg's.[37]

According to Münsterberg, every sensation inevitably brought forth a motor response of one sort or another, expressed perhaps in the muscular structure, the respiratory system, or the internal organs. The sensations produced by these secondary actions, whether the individual was aware of their source or not, colored the perception of the original sensation. The kinesthetic sensation derived from eye motion, for example, contributed to the sense of space. This coloring process, which today might be called "feed-back," allowed the mind not only to perceive abstractions like time and space, but to monitor and regulate its own behavior. A human organism emerged, then, that was much more capable of refined adjustment to its environment. It was this train of thought that John Dewey brought to a fuller development in 1896 in his classic article on the reflex arc.[38]

As Münsterberg saw it (and here he differed from Dewey), this view opened the way in the long run for a physiological explanation of mind. "It must not be overlooked," he wrote in 1891,

> that the source of the elements of consciousness which are most important for our mental life—those which control the make-up of our ideas [*Vorstellungen*], judgments, feelings, and will-acts—do not lie in the particular sense organs, but rather in the internal but peripheral bodily parts—the muscles, joints, glands, blood vessels, tendons, intestines, etc.

It is no wonder that Münsterberg's work impressed James so much. James himself made almost exactly the same point when he wrote in his *Principles,* "our entire feeling of spiritual activity, or what commonly passes by that name, is really a feeling of bodily activities whose exact nature is by most men overlooked."[39]

When this sensory peripheralism was applied to emotional states such as fear or guilt, it became the famous but now discarded James-Lange theory of emotion, to which Münsterberg subscribed. It is perhaps easiest to catch the spirit of this approach to mind through James's own extreme formulation of his theory: "One enthusiast," he wrote, "has even gone so far as to say that when we feel sorry it is because we weep, when we feel afraid it is because we run away, and not conversely." The Swiss psychologist Edouard Claparède offered another example to justify his good-natured claim that he had independently discovered the theory while still a child. "It was in the autumn of 1885," Claparède wrote:

> I was twelve, and was standing for the first time in the playground of the College of Geneva, waiting to go in for the entrance examination. As may be guessed, I was rather nervous, and this caused me to repair frequently to a certain little room. "How scared you are!" said my friends, laughing, when they noticed those oft repeated trips, "It makes you pass water all the time." "Why, no," I answered, "it's not because I am scared that I must do that, but it's this constant need which annoys me and makes me scared." My little friends laughed and thought me paradoxical, but since then I have often repeated the same experience, and that in cases where the emotion I felt could absolutely not be explained by motives of an intellectual order.[40]

Or, to put it in terms closer to Münsterberg's, when I feel "free" to stand up, it is because the muscles of my body are preparing to stand up. My free will then does not cause my standing up; instead, my illusion of having a free will results from my muscular preparations.

A motor theory of mind, therefore, offered Münsterberg a solution to the most recalcitrant problem for sensationism: the apparent existence of a will, or our perceived ability to act as a result of choice and determination. He rejected Wundt's view of the will "as a specific impulse, as a push, as a deed, as opposed to a passive experiencing of ideas." He did not, of course, deny that a feeling of inner efficacy accompanied willed actions, but he disputed Wundt's contention (or more exactly, the contention that he and James imputed to Wundt) that this feeling offered introspective evidence of apperception. A correct introspective analysis, Münsterberg argued, revealed instead that the feeling of efficacy was nothing but the memory of the willed action, performed previously. Willed actions in fact were only complicated, physiologically determined acts of association. When a person willed his arm to grasp something that he desired, his mind contained nothing but certain optical stimuli, certain memory reproductions of previous pleasure that had been called up automatically, and the memory of how moving his arm had felt in the past. It was this latter memory that was mistaken for a feeling of mental activity. Here Münsterberg's theory of the will was close to James's, for he agreed with James that it depended on the anticipatory image "of the sensorial consequences of a movement"—although he would not have added, as James did, "plus (on certain occasions) the fiat that these consequences shall become actual."[41]

From this argument Münsterberg deduced the radical conclusion that all the products of human culture were, when "considered materialistically," nothing but automatic reactions. He wrote in *Die Willenshandlung* that the behavior exhibited in human communication, however rational or ethical it might seem to be,

> is conditioned through the sum of impressions already experienced, together with the sound waves of the last word and the structure of the central apparatus. This conditioning is as exact as the conditioning of the muscular contraction of the brainless frog who jerks his leg from the salt solution.[42]

Positivism this extreme was virtually unique among German academics, and it eliminated the standard distinction between the *Geisteswissenschaften* and the *Naturwissenschaften* that Wilhelm Dilthey, Wilhelm Windelband, and others were explicating. Münsterberg tempered his positivism in subsequent years, and even in the 1880s he indicated that the materialistic world view was more heuristic than real. But he never doubted that a materialistic explanation of all human behavior was possible (even if the scientist might not choose to make it), and in his science he never departed from his deterministic and materialistic assumptions.

It was this argument, finally, that separated Münsterberg from Dewey, James, and the American functionalists. Throughout his career, James somewhat inconsistently sought an escape from the deterministic system that his science had created. At times he found it in spiritualism—which Münsterberg regarded as groundless superstition—but in his more sober moments, as in his *Principles,* he sought it in his theory of consciousness and the will. The Darwinian principle of natural selection, he argued, did not permit the evolution of any characteristics in the living organism that were not functional. As consciousness was an undeniable human characteristic, it necessarily took a part in the adjustment of the human organism to its environment. The sphere of action to which James assigned an active consciousness in this process was, to be sure, very small, but it allowed the severing of the necessary chain of cause and effect: Within the sensory-motor arc, will served the purpose of issuing the familiar "fiat"—a mental order that held the mind's attention to an object or act. In other words, people could choose to concentrate. This argument, in one form or another, became central to functionalism in America.[43]

Münsterberg thoroughly disagreed. James had violated, he believed, the fundamental principles of science when he assumed that the contents of consciousness could influence physical processes. There was absolutely no mental link and no "fiat," Münsterberg argued, between the idea, for example, of grasping an object and the subsequent perception that the object was being grasped. Münsterberg also rejected the argument from Darwin that, because mental epiphenomena had evolved, they were necessarily effective. To take this position, he suggested, was to confuse the epiphenomena with the events that caused them. "For the preservation of the individual," he wrote in *Die Willenshandlung,* "it is obviously irrelevant whether a purposeful motion is accompanied by contents of consciousness or not."[44] In this respect, Münsterberg stood closer to the American behaviorists than to James.

Münsterberg considered himself a disciple of Fichte, and he asserted that *Die Willenshandlung* offered a psychology along Fichtean lines. His claim had a certain precedent. Several decades earlier the reductionist Helmholtz had argued that Fichte's distinction between the Ich and the non-Ich offered the best explanation for the physiology of the sense organs.[45] The basic principle of Fichtean philosophy was the existence of a creative ego that defined the world through its own activity. This was exactly the position that Münsterberg validated, even as he reduced the individual ego to an automaton. By the twentieth century he called his psychology Action Theory, but its outlines existed in the 1880s. In *Die Willenshandlung* and the *Beiträge,* he argued forcefully that a person's actions—that is, his motor processes—determined his perceptions. The acting individual created in a real sense his own world. What Münsterberg had done, therefore, was to verify an Idealist account of mind in mechanical terms.

In a series of docential lectures at Freiburg, *Der Ursprung der Sittlichkeit,* Münsterberg attempted to resolve another challenge that positivist science had presented to academic orthodoxy. If it was irrelevant whether or not consciousness accompanied purposeful motions, then all the cultural past of man could be viewed as epiphenomenon. How, then, did values, and particularly moral values, evolve? The answer was not easy because Münsterberg followed Kant in arguing that ethical behavior by definition involved actions in opposition to utility, natural inclinations, and self-preservation. How, therefore, could a natural history whose only motive power was the attraction of the pleasant and the rejection of the unpleasant evolve a self-denying (and not simply a pleasure-deferring) pattern of behavior?

It is not necessary to trace Münsterberg's complicated reconciliation of mechanistic science with Kantian ethics. His argument suffered from over-fine logic and his morality in the end amounted to little more than conditioned guilt. What is interesting for the moment is the way in which he relativized Kant by depriving morality of any substantive content. Kant had posited a categorical imperative—that man was to be treated as an end and not a means—and he applied it to all humans, regardless of their circumstances. Münsterberg preserved the formal structure of Kant's ethics. He agreed that the moral act necessarily involved obedience to duty and therefore could only be judged on the basis of the actor's intentions and not on the results of his action. Münsterberg consequently opposed all empiricist and naturalistic attempts to construct an ethical system, such as Herbert Spencer's or, later, the American pragmatists'. But, following the post-Kantian Idealists, he defined duty in historicist terms: The moral act was an act performed in accordance with a socially and historically determined commandment.[46]

Münsterberg denied, as a result, that any act could be in itself moral and that any moral code could be universal. He echoed Fichte in arguing that ethical commandments followed social position: the soldier, the laborer, the scholar, the man, the woman, and the child—of each society demanded some special standard. Different societies, furthermore, made different moral demands on their members. The thief who stole or murdered in accordance with the principles of the robber band acted ethically if he acted out of neither inclination nor compulsion. The national citizen acted ethically if, in spite of personal preferences, he lived up to the ideals of his national *Kultur,* even if those ideals might seem to conflict with the aims or rights of other peoples.[47]

Although he did not develop the analogy as extensively as some of his contemporaries, Münsterberg viewed society as an evolving organism. His position was reminiscent of Spencer's: In the natural world, he argued, evolution proceeded from a state that was homogenous but unstructured toward one that was differentiated and organized for efficiency. And, like Spencer, he traced a parallel development in human history toward diversity and *Kompliziertheit,* reflected in the hierarchical structure of society and the world community of national cultures. The laws of evolution—that is, the laws of natural selection and mutual adaptation—assured a harmony among the various segments of society and a progressive tendency in its increasing complication. "If our results are right," he wrote in *Die Willenshandlung,* "then the state, the family, the economy, moral conventions, and the social community harmonize fully in their objective structure. They are held together by one and the same principle—the division of labor."[48]

Among other results, this division of labor meant a biological sanction for existing social roles and arrangements. Family life, for example, allowed a mutual adaptation between men and women. In *Die Willenshandlung* he justified the conventional order with a touch of anatomical fancy:

> The man operates externally, the women internally. That the man is strong, that the woman is weak, follows from conditions of sexual life. But, even if the sexual life has completely disappeared, it remains ever useful that the strong and the weak do not carry out each for themselves all the actions . . . which are necessary for their self-preservation. They should share the muscular contractions that are necessary for their mutual existence in such a way that the strong fights out the challenging battles for both and the weaker carries on the smaller, more delicate, finer tasks for both.[49]

By the twentieth century Münsterberg had expanded his argument to acknowledge a whole range of psychological differences between the sexes.

History progressed, according to Münsterberg, as civilization evolved from "the half-animal *Naturvolk* to today's *Kultur."* He happily anticipated "a continuing enrichment of knowledge, an ever new production in technology and art, religion and science, unlimited modifications in state and society, and more and more complicated forms of cooperative life among individuals and races."[50] He obviously had little sympathy with the pessimistic positions of sociologists like Friedrich Tönnies and the later Max Weber, who feared a loss of community and personal contact in modern society. He celebrated instead the increasing specialization of function. Münsterberg also felt little threat from the emerging technological society. While he did share some of Weber's skepticism for "rationalization," he on the whole stood closer to the optimism of the natural scientists Helmholtz and DuBois-Reymond and to American social scientists like Charles Horton Cooley and engineers like Frederick Taylor, all of whom found liberation in technology. Münsterberg's idea of history, however, did color his view of America, making him sense a crisis in twentieth-century American life. The homogenized and mass society that he saw emerging there, where laborers insisted on the rights of academics, children on those of their elders, and women on those of men, reversed the fundamental principles of development and threatened the fruits of progress.

In a proper divison of labor, the individual citizen, like the individual unit in a biological organism, served a higher evolutionary purpose by fulfilling his function, and from that function he received his meaning. Instinct, habit, self-interest, and conscious morality all conspired to bind the individual to his duty. As Münsterberg concluded his Freiburg lectures:

> The progressive will of humanity organizes itself in a thousand forms: the totality evolves in science and art, in government and economic structure; we all advance the prodigious Becoming, the lofty goals with our insignificant daily work. We all serve the general will insofar as we fulfill our interests; we are all its tools and we do not even know it.[51]

Despite its wording, this passage did not assume a Smithian "hidden hand," coordinating and reconciling the selfish and self-interested acts of individuals. The "interests" to which Münsterberg referred, it must be emphasized, coincided with social function. They stood in contrast to the personal caprice and whim that some mistook to be essential to personal freedom. Duty had been socialized and secularized. The moral act was no longer the means to personal fulfillment, as American rhetoricians of self-reliance often claimed; it had become an instrument of social progress. And conscience was not an inner light leading directly to God. It amounted instead to the internalized demands of society.

Decision for Harvard (1892–1897)

In February 1892, shortly before his promotion to *Extraordinarius,* Münsterberg received an inquiry from his friend William James, the New World's leading psychologist, that was to change the direction of his life: Would he be interested in becoming head of the Harvard psychological laboratory at a salary of three thousand dollars a year? The appointment, James suggested, would be for three years, but he hoped that it would become permanent. Harvard, according to him, "could get younger men here who would be *safe* enough, but . . . we need a man of genius if possible." To fill the position he called upon a man whom he described to his brother Henry as "the Rudyard Kipling of psychology."[1]

Under James's prodding, Harvard had been, for more than a decade, a pioneer in America in the new science of experimental psychology. In the late 1870s James had set up a small "demonstration room" in Cambridge, and his Natural Sciences 2, "Physiological Psychology," was the first course at an American university devoted entirely to the field. Yet in the competitive arena of nineteenth-century university building, Harvard's program soon fell behind those of such rivals as Johns Hopkins, Clark, and Pennsylvania. For James, this decline was intolerable: "We are the best university in America," he wrote, "and we must lead in Psychology." In the late 1880s he began a campaign among friends to raise money to expand and modernize Harvard's outdated laboratory, and he tapped Münsterberg to direct it.[2]

James and Münsterberg had first met in the summer of 1889 in Paris at the International Congress of Physiological Psychology, and in the years that followed the two maintained a sporadic correspondence. As early as 1890, James recommended to his advanced students in experimental psychology (whom he himself felt unprepared to guide) that they go to Freiburg and continue their studies under the young German. In a letter to Münsterberg that same year, he lavished praise on the *Beiträge,* which promised more for psychology, he wrote, "than the work of any one man who has yet appeared." A few months later he added, "I must say that you seem to me to be doing more to open out new vistas in Psychology than anyone today."[3]

When the Müller critique of Münsterberg's work appeared two years later, James sent his friend a letter of "condolence," praising just those traits that Müller and Titchener had criticized. He lauded Münsterberg for his "sense of perspective and proportion of things (so that for instance you *don't* make experiments and quote figures to the 1000th decimal, where a coarse qualitative result is all that the question needs)." Later he complimented Münsterberg on his "broad light touch in writing," so different from the style of most of his German compatriots who "suffocate one under details which have no importance." He considered Münsterberg an energetic and imaginative investigator, "whose sagacity in making distinctions are only equalled by the promptitude with which you devise experiments, and the energy with which you fall to work on them." If he should remain flexible toward his theories and ingenious in testing them, he was destined, James predicted, to beat "the whole army of your critics before you are forty years old."[4]

Germany's influence on American higher education was at its height at the time of James's probe, and it was therefore no surprise that he looked to that country for his laboratory director. "German scholarship had become a fetich," the psychologist James Mark Baldwin reminisced of the period. In all fields of advanced study, he added, "German authorities were quoted, German methods adopted, German approbation courted." In psychology this observation was particularly true. Almost every American psychologist of the period had studied in Germany, and most of the younger generation—including James McKeen Cattell at Columbia, Lightner Witmer at Pennsylvania, James Jastrow at Wisconsin, and Edward Scripture, soon at Yale—had been students in Wundt's Leipzig laboratory. To secure a young and promising German like Münsterberg, therefore, would represent a coup for Harvard.[5]

Münsterberg later recalled that James's offer tempted him with a prospect "that sounded interesting and almost romantic." The narrow academic environment of Freiburg was already confining his restless energies. Here was the possibility of a temporary escape to America, that "land of unlimited possibilities," as one German traveler described it. In popular German literature of the nineteenth century, the New World had come to mean romance, fabulous wealth, and spiritual liberation. Münsterberg himself had daydreamed of California, and as an eleven-year-old he had written a drama, "The Uncle from America," which depicted his future home as "the land from which unnaturally rich people can suddenly emerge." He was a youthful reader of James Fenimore Cooper, then a great favorite among the German youth, and by his Leipzig years he had graduated to Edgar Allen Poe and Ralph Waldo Emerson. At Freiburg he became acquainted with Hermann von Holtz, the celebrated Americanist, who regaled dinner parties with tales of the wonders of the United States. Perhaps, then, a three-year tour at Harvard might sate the wanderlust of a young man, who, in James's words, was "fond of traveling and of all kinds of experience."[6]

Münsterberg's decision, however, was not easy. First among his worries was the problem of language. Although he could read English, he could neither speak nor understand it when spoken. But more important to him was the fear that a sojourn at Harvard might interfere with the direction that his life was taking. He wished to jeopardize neither his promising academic career nor his position at Freiburg, where his laboratory, he claimed, drew more students than any other in Germany. He worried too that the demands of organizing and running a psychological program in the New World would sidetrack his growing interest in philosophical and aesthetic questions. The work might freeze him into experimental psychology, in which he was already losing interest. Finally, like other German academics who emigrated to the United States, he felt toward the German universities, German culture, and the German nation a loyalty that he found difficult to renounce. "The thought," he wrote, "of giving up permanently my native tongue and my Fatherland is . . . unbearable to me."[7]

Despite its reputation for intellectual backwardness, however, America had more to offer an ambitious young psychologist than did Germany. Experimental psychology occupied a marginal position in most German universities, and its popularity among young investigators led by the 1890s to severe overcrowding. Its future in a university system whose rapid growth had peaked, furthermore, was less promising than it seemed to American observers who did not travel beyond Leipzig. Experimental psychology, in fact, received relatively little financial support in Germany. Münsterberg's self-financed laboratory in his own home compared poorly with Johannes von Kries's "large, brilliantly appointed" and state-supported physiological laboratory at Freiburg. The situation was not different at most other universities, where psychologists, lacking state finances, maintained very modest facilities. In America, on the other hand, private and state universities by the early 1890s financed laboratories that were lavish by most German standards.[8] In a sketch of psychology, *Ueber Aufgaben und Methoden der Psychologie* (On the Tasks and Methods of Psychology), published in 1891, Münsterberg recommended that the German governments imitate the New World and establish psychological institutes at every German university. Psychology, he wrote, "should never lack its own particular homesites, and the example of America . . . should not be overlooked in Europe."[9]

Higher education in the New World gained credibility when von Holtz accepted a position at the new University of Chicago in the spring of 1892. As Münsterberg wrote later, "If a former rector [at Freiburg] found it worthwhile, the youngest instructor might risk it." After several months of vacillation, he decided in early May to accept Harvard's call. But he did not cut his ties to Germany. He made his decision only after receiving assurances from German friends that acceptance of the position would not hinder his future career in Germany, and he secured a three-year leave of absence from the Baden government. He informed James that he would remain in America no longer than that period of time. He wished to remain a German, and, as he told James, he looked upon the whole affair as an adventure. "The beautiful, grand field of action and the wide world attracts me mightily," he wrote. By coming to America, "I would see and hear much that is new; I would get out of the muggy atmosphere of the German universities and into the free air of grand affairs and would be able to serve practical ends." *"Gottlob!,"* James wrote in response. "I believe that this has been the best stroke I ever did for our University!"[10]

Münsterberg moved to America, he was to tell a German audience ten years later, "with all the prejudices of the average German and above all the especial prejudices of German university instructors who look down patronizingly on the scholarship of the New World."[11] For the educated German, America stood not so much for romance as for individualism, utilitarianism, Philistinism, and commercialism, all bugaboos of German *Kultur.* Emil DuBois-Reymond, more outspoken than most on the question, even warned of a creeping "Americanism" in German society, illustrated by the move to admit the graduates of the *Realschulen* (technical high schools) to the university. As G. Stanley Hall reported, DuBois-Reymond identified Americanism with the materialistic attitudes of the era, "which are more specifically expressed in making money-getting the prime object of life, in love of display, and in public and private corruption." He contrasted these attitudes to the German ideal of "Hellenism," "or the love of humanistic and scientific culture for its own sake, apart from all considerations of profit or advantage."[12]

Münsterberg, however, found Cambridge in general and Harvard in particular a welcome exception to the general picture. The Boston intellectual community, at least by his own estimate, expressed a genuine American *Kultur,* derived from its Puritan heritage. "Almost everything which is intellectually exalted and significant in this country has come from Boston," he wrote in 1904; "all the best aesthetic and moral and intellectual impulses originate in New England." The Harvard philosophy division, which included Josiah Royce and George Santayana as well as James, was in fact remarkably strong. (In a letter to Wundt, Münsterberg ranked it second in the world behind Berlin's and well ahead of Leipzig's.) One enthusiastic student in the department, C. M. Bakewell, years later traced the "new birth of philosophy" in America to the development of the department under George Herbert Palmer in the 1870s and 1880s. This development, Bakewell modestly suggested, offered "an interesting parallel to that which resulted from the teaching of Socrates in the latter part of the fifth century B.C." DuBois-Reymond's Hellenism had found a nineteenth-century home in Cambridge.[13]

Münsterberg arrived in Cambridge in the fall of 1892 with his wife and two young daughters. He took immediate control of the laboratory and, in the absence of James, who was in Europe on sabbatical, conducted the "psychological seminary" for eleven advanced students. From the first, he placed the same strong personal stamp on the laboratory that Wundt had imposed at Leipzig and G. E. Müller at Göttingen, and he adopted a German model for psychology at Harvard. Specifically, this meant an emphasis on original experimentation in advanced course work, traditional introspective investigation of the normal mind in the laboratory, and tight control of the direction of research. He ordinarily assigned problems to students, and the results of their investigations, described from time to time in the American Psychological Association's new *Psychological Review,* regularly confirmed his motor theory of consciousness.[14] By all accounts he was received well. Royce described him late in 1892 as an immense success; the following year James reported that he was "going really *splendidly,*" and he called the laboratory "a bower of delight." Before long less interested observers, such as Princeton's James Mark Baldwin and Columbia's James McKeen Cattell, recognized Münsterberg's laboratory as the most important in America.[15]

Earlier James had predicted, "With Münsterberg's torrential flow of eloquence in his own tongue, he will have a fearful *Hemmungsgefühl* [feeling of inhibition] when he tries ours," and indeed Münsterberg did hold himself back somewhat at first. In the fall of 1893, only a year after his arrival, George Herbert Palmer tried unsuccessfully to persuade him to teach the elementary course in philosophy with Santayana and himself. "Shut up in your laboratory," Palmer advised, "you seem a little aloof from Harvard tides of affairs." In that year Münsterberg did team up with James to teach Philosophy 2, the introductory course in psychology, and he conducted a course at Radcliffe, but, as he wrote Eliot years later, his German background had ill prepared him for an American university. He found the busy work of grading unappealing, and "I know that I felt it still in my second year as a humiliation to lecture to undergraduates." By all objective measures, however, his teaching was a success. When he conducted Philosophy 2 by himself in 1894, its enrollment increased from forty to sixty, and his psychology seminar drew only one student fewer than James's, Royce's and Palmer's philosophy seminars combined. How much these figures reflected the popularity of psychological studies and how much Münsterberg's personal appeal is unclear, but not important. In either case, Harvard had every reason to be satisfied with its new faculty member.[16]

In the meantime, Münsterberg's experimental work slowed. Criticism of his writings had stung him, and after Müller's "brutal" critique he informed James that he would in the future work more deliberately. None of the projected new volumes of his *Beiträge* appeared, and he published only two experimental studies under his own name in American journals. He devoted his daily writing at home, instead, to "a big work" in German on the foundations of psychology. After all, he reminisced,

> I knew that these three beautiful American years were only an excursion. My life-work would lie in German university, German scholars would be my public, and so I toiled on the book of my hope in order to show my colleagues when I went home that I had not wasted those years of my journey.[17]

Münsterberg came to America not only to serve psychology at Harvard but also to see a new land. During his first winter he and his wife made the obligatory pilgrimage to Niagara Falls. The following summer, after a lengthy bout with diptheria, for which he consulted the homeopathic doctor Walter Wesselhoeft, he visited the University of Chicago and the Chicago World's Fair. Later he journeyed through the Midwest, directing his attention particularly to the new American colleges, and continued on to California. There he saw Berkeley and Stanford, spent "a whole night with the Chinese," and brought home Indian relics.[18]

In the course of his travels, Münsterberg found the New World's version of nature—so different from what he had known in Danzig, the Tyrol, or Geneva—little to his liking. He preferred to spend his vacations in Swampscott, on the coast just north of Boston (he later acquired a summer home in nearby Clifton), and he exhibited none of James's or Royce's predilection for New Hampshire. In the summer of 1894 he followed his wife and children to the Adirondacks, where the itinerant philosopher Thomas Davidson had a summer camp that was popular among Boston intellectuals. Münsterberg's first act on arriving was to remove his family from their rustic accommodations in the woods and install them in a nearby hotel. He described this experience in the wilderness to Cattell as "several weeks in the mountains," which he found "dusty, dry, foggy and disagreeable so that we escaped soon."[19]

Münsterberg's reaction to American "nature" was that of a European raised in a society that invested its tamed environment with a mythic past. He appreciated the traces of Spaniards and Indians in California, but, beyond that, the American wilderness had little to offer him. Nothing in the Adirondacks could rival the romantic grandeur of the Alps or the legendary past of the Baltic. The nature they did offer struck Münsterberg as uncomfortable and inconvenient. He came to oppose the whole "naturist" tradition in American thought, whether in educationists' idealization of the child as a natural creature or in the various "country-life" movements that urban Americans espoused at the turn of the century.[20] These longings were reactionary, in his opinion, for history moved away from the "natural" and toward increasing technology, culture, and civilization.

Münsterberg, however, also sensed that the United States was entering a new phase, which he, like so many of his American contemporaries, interpreted as a rebirth of Idealism. Through a new spirit of purposeful work, America was redirecting its proverbial energy toward its own inner development. Its humanitarianism and concern for social reform, its universities, and its philosophy and art flourished as it outgrew its laissez-faire past. The excessive practicality and the fascination with money for its own sake had been supplanted by a new sense of communal purpose. "Yes," Münsterberg wrote for a German audience in 1893, "America is at work."

> It strips off with restless energy its graceless garments and weaves for itself new ones. That tasteless, that barbaric, that unbridled spirit, which corresponds to the childhood of a *Volk,* and that demon of egoistic mammonism, which fell like an illness upon this young people after the closing of the overabundant West, all that is overcome through marvelous work.[21]

The metaphor was mixed, but it incorporated America and its destiny into a typically German vision of historical progress. In a sense it offered an optimistic version of the view of civilization that Freud was later to expound: America repressed its egoistic urges as it grew out of its childhood, and thereby opened the door to a positive and dynamic *Kultur.*

Münsterberg was attempting to disabuse his compatriots, and perhaps himself, of their prejudices against America and to convince them that it indeed possessed genuine ideals. He did not intend, however, to make his home in the New World, and he remained firm in his decision to return to Germany. Both James and Harvard's president Charles W. Eliot encouraged him to accept a permanent position. But, after the Baden ministry had refused to extend his leave, he declined Harvard's offer. Securing an appointment as a German *Ordinarius* was still his ambition, and he believed that a call to a German university was unlikely as long as he remained in America. "I take it as my duty, to go back to my fatherland," he wrote James in 1894. "That is my unchangeable decision."[22]

Without a full professorship in hand, however, Münsterberg kept his options open. He asked for and received two years leave from Harvard, after which he promised a final decision. "I shall return to Germany and if I return then after two or, as maximum, after three years, then I know that I have done my duty." In the meantime, he could run the laboratory from a distance through the mails. Harvard, which still considered him "far and away, all things considered, the best man in the field," granted the leave, and Münsterberg set sail for Germany in the summer of 1895.[23]

For the next two years Münsterberg resumed his post as *Extraordinarius* in philosophy at Freiburg. His interest in the laboratory, however, continued to wane, and he modified his aggressive materialism of the 1880s. "I am working now myself a little experimentally," he wrote James in 1896, "as five men pressed me to offer them some opportunity ... but I sing there with half voice." He also expressed regret that Royce was using his *Ueber Aufgaben und Methoden der Psychologie* in a psychology seminar. The first part of the book, concerning the basis and goals of psychology, he wrote, was "quite antiquated, as my new book will show clearly. I become more and more idealist without changing my position in empirical psychology."[24]

In his letters to James and Eliot, Münsterberg indicated that his return to Harvard was likely, but he clearly hoped for an appropriate position in Germany. Late in 1896, after a fruitless year of looking, he seemed on the verge of securing such a place. On the recommendation of Wundt and others, a faculty search committee at the University of Zurich named him to fill a vacant professorship. The chair, which was responsible for systematic philosophy, the history of philosophy, and pedagogy, had for years been occupied by "genuinely universal minds," and it had served as a stepping stone to a place in a major German university. Richard Avenarius, the leading spokesman of the positivistic "empirio-criticism," had occupied the position since 1877, receiving a call to Freiburg just before his death in 1896. Preceding him in the chair had been Friedrich

Lange, the celebrated author of *Die Geschichte des Materialismus* (The History of Materialism), Wilhelm Wundt, and Wilhelm Windelband. Short of an appointment at a university like Leipzig, Heidelberg, or Berlin, no offer from the German-speaking world could have been more attractive.[25]

Exactly what happened at Zurich is unclear, but Münsterberg's nomination was overruled by the cantonal government, which had the ultimate say in appointments. As Münsterberg described the affair to Eliot, the position was reduced to an *Extraordinarius* for financial reasons, and he as a result refused it. But this account was at best incomplete. In a letter to Zurich at the time, Münsterberg bitterly ascribed his setback to anti-Semitism.[26] Years after the fact, he suggested that Hermann Cohen, the neo-Kantian at Marburg (and a Jew), had intrigued in the interest of his own candidates and brought about the retraction. Whatever the case, Münsterberg asserted that "to be pushed around is not my style," and he refused to talk of a lesser appointment. The position, by then an *Extraordinarius* for experimental psychology and pedagogy, went to Wundt's assistant Ernst Meumann.[27]

The significance of this incident lay on two levels. It delivered a blow to Münsterberg's hopes for advancement in Germany, just as did Carl Stumpf's inability to secure for him a position as *Docent* at Berlin and Freiburg's unwillingness to promote him "because," he wrote Eliot, "the clerical party desires since years a new philosophical professorship for a man of catholic ideas." More important at least in personal terms, it was a very real and public insult to an ambitious young scholar. Although Münsterberg's reaction to his setbacks at Zurich and elsewhere was unfortunately self-righteous, these failures in fact added up to a serious rebuff, and he understandably took them as a spurning of the talents that he had so dutifully offered to his country. As Münsterberg wrote to Wundt at the time, he resented his "not being able to place [his] talents at the disposal of the German fatherland, but having once more to go to America."[28] His explanation for his failures—that he had been rejected as an outsider (in this case, as a Jew)—anticipated his response to later difficulties at Harvard.

A year earlier Wundt had offered a considerably different explanation for Münsterberg's unfortunate situation. It is worth quoting at length because Wundt so neatly echoed Münsterberg's own rhetoric of self-discipline and self-sacrifice:

> But it is also in this case my conviction [Wundt wrote] that it is *not* Antisemitism—as bad as it may otherwise be—which is the cause of this regrettable outcome. I have rather the conviction that, if you yourself had been able to decide to apply in your intellectual development a stern and even at

times renouncing self-discipline, without which nothing enduringly valuable can be accomplished, things would stand very differently today.[29]

Wundt's critique may have reflected his own disappointment at the heresy of a promising student and a potential successor. But he had caught a fundamental ambiguity in Münsterberg's personality: For a man who preached self-discipline and will, Münsterberg indulged his own intellectual fancies to an extraordinary extent.

In the meantime, Münsterberg's reputation remained strong in the New World. When the Zurich position was still open, the Princeton psychologist James Mark Baldwin wrote him, *"You must not go to Zurich."* "Come back to America" he implored:

> We need your *large ideas* in opposition to the near-sighted men who can see only one idea or part of an idea at a time! I especially feel it a great personal loss if you should not return: for we have so much in common both in common doctrine and in intuition. . . . Then you must also consider the demands of our growing American life: the need of a strengthened idealism; the need in our universities of the blood and methods of your country.

After the Zurich incident, Baldwin held to his opinion. "I think the victory was yours in any case . . . ," he wrote Münsterberg. "I think you have reason to feel very proud that such men of all schools stood up for you."[30]

As the Zurich question dragged through the winter of 1897, Münsterberg hedged on a permanent commitment to Harvard. He requested from Eliot an additional year of leave and, after refusal, a half-year appointment for the fall of 1897; he bickered over salary—to such an extent that James offered to the Harvard corporation to renounce part of his own salary in order to balance the departmental budget; he complained of his nervous troubles, which might not stand up to the "rather moist Cambridge climate." The latter concern impelled Eliot, a little annoyed at Münsterberg's indecision, to offer some valuable advice:

> I am very sorry to hear that you have had any return of nervous disorders. Would not you be less liable to such attacks if you too settled down upon a fixed and definite course of life, settling once and for all the great question of the country in which you will pass your prime, and your children will grow up?

Eliot went on to warn, "I ought to say frankly that the University will not be content to have you return hither without 'burning your ships.' " Harvard would require of him, just as it did of its other professors, "the definite intention of spending his life in all probability at Harvard."[31]

Without the option of an equivalent place in Germany, Münsterberg accepted, but he informed Eliot that he could not of course "give up the possibility that other universities wish me and the realization of that possibility will depend on my wire-pulling." Although badly expressed, it was a reasonable position—especially considering Eliot's willingness to raid other universities—but it could not have pleased a college president who placed institutional loyalty high on his list of qualifications for his faculty. Harvard in fact remained a way station for Münsterberg, and his partial commitment was to lead to nearly two decades of friction with his employers and contribute to a growing sense of estrangement from his New World milieu. America, at least in 1897, was also a sacrificial mission. In a letter to Eliot, Münsterberg pointed out that he was not obliged to come to Harvard in 1892, "as few men had such brilliant careers" ahead of them. Borrowing directly from Baldwin's metaphor, he continued:

> I came to Harvard not *in spite* of the fact that I am foreigner, but *because* I am foreigner. I take it that in your opinion it is good for the organism of the Harvard Faculty that a transfusion of some drops of German university blood may be made, just at the critical time when the College is so splendidly growing into a university.

At times the mission seemed more of an exile. "But after all," Wundt had consoled him earlier, "America is not the end of the world."[32]

Social Idealism and the Social Organism

Münsterberg recrossed the Atlantic in the fall of 1897, "burning his ships" at Eliot's request. He resigned his position at Freiburg and sailed to the New World with his family, his household furniture, and his entire library. At the same time, he drew his German youth to a symbolic close, publishing under the name of Hugo Terberg a volume of poems written over a period of fifteen years. With him also, he brought a new outlook. Between 1892 and 1895, he wrote later, "I had only tried to observe and to understand my surroundings." When he returned in 1897, "my new aim was to influence them." During his two-year interlude at Freiburg he had become "aware that the greatest failure and deficiencies of American civilization resulted from a lack of that social idealism which gave meaning to German life." He would bring German ideals to America—a "life-task," as he called it, that "would not interfere . . . with my professional calling as a scholar and teacher, but . . . would give to it a deeper and wider significance."[1]

Despite his setback at Zurich, Münsterberg returned to America as a German scholar of some standing and automatically assumed a leading place in a discipline that was thriving in the academic struggle for existence. The recently founded American Psychological Association recognized his prominence when it chose him its president in 1899, an honor that passed yearly from one luminary in the new profession to another. A year later he confirmed his position with the appearance of the long-promised first volume of his *Grundzüge der Psychologie,* a massive discussion of the epistemological foundations of psychology. To be sure, few in America read the volume, and its English-language reviews were generally critical. But it was a major work, and German scholars of the stature of Heinrich Rickert, William Stern, and Max Weber recognized its importance.[2] In the same year, Münsterberg assumed the chairmanship of the Division of Philosophy at Harvard, a position that he occupied until 1906.

Münsterberg had established himself in the meantime as a popular and successful teacher. Years before, Wundt and James had testified to his ability to teach, and in 1907 Cattell called him "one of the best speakers we have." Opinion of course was not unanimous: Some found his mechanistic approach to mind unappealing, and the psychologist Henry Murray later recalled, "At college a bud of interest in psychology was nipped by the chill of Professor Münsterberg's approach. In the middle of his second lecture I began looking for the nearest exit." But his flair for showmanship won others over, especially undergraduates. His courses, even during the war, were always large and popular, and, like other members of the philosophy department, he attracted a coterie of admirers.[3]

Münsterberg also had firm supporters among his advanced students and younger colleagues, despite his increasing distance from the laboratory. Mary Whiton Calkins, the Wellesley psychologist, considered him to be "a man of deep learning, high originality, and astounding versatility." Knight Dunlap, who became chairman of the Psychology Department at Johns Hopkins, particularly remembered his seminars, where, he reported, Münsterberg was at his best. "Never did any loose conclusion or faulty method get by him," Dunlap recalled. Robert Yerkes, a pioneer in comparative psychology and mental testing, spoke of Münsterberg's "almost paternal interest and solicitude," as well as "his rare generosity." "I seriously doubt," Yerkes wrote, "whether I should have remained in Harvard more than one or two years except for his influence and encouragement."[4]

Münsterberg soon became "a kind of permanent part of the landscape in the east side of the Yard." "His appearance was striking," George Herbert Palmer reminisced.

> In no company could he be overlooked. A tall figure, neither stout nor lean but carrying no superfluous flesh; as it were trimmed for action. The roving, observant blue eye, the springy step, the slight bend in the body in a kind of forward lunge, all suggested an alertness which characterized him throughout.

Despite his Jewish heritage, he conformed to Harvard's Teutonic stereotype: Above all, his imposing air, his heavy accent, which never mellowed, and his waxed "Prussian" mustache lent him a celebrated

character of "Germanness." One former student, Gordon Allport, referred to him as Wotan. The psychologist Frank Angell observed several
years after his death that "twenty-two years of residence over here . . .
wrought no fundamental change in the Germanism of his nature." His
Cambridge house attracted an incessant stream of visiting German dignitaries and it became known as an island of Wilhelmian *Kultur* in Puritan
Boston. Max Weber, a former colleague at Freiburg, visited that home in
1904. Münsterberg's hospitality and advice, he reported, were welcome
offerings to the German traveler, and he found it admirable that his Cambridge host still "felt himself above all German"—especially considering
his failure to secure a post in the Fatherland.[5]

Münsterberg's accent and physical appearance, his extreme self-importance, and his prodigious output—all of which were taken as typically
German—made him at times the butt of student jokes. Rollo Brown, a
student during Harvard's "golden age," remembered that "when he was
piqued he had a look of ferocity that students said he had acquired by
trying to look like the Kaiser." And, "when he read in a deep voice to
represent God," his Radcliffe students had to hide their faces and laugh.
His imitations of God apparently achieved a certain notoriety. When
Phillips Brooks House was under construction, one student joke had the
inscription over its door read: *"Ein Münsterberg ist unser Gott."*[6]

This humor was for the most part good-natured, but Münsterberg's
personal style at times became a real source of aggravation. He stood out
as one of the more difficult members of a profession—both the psychological and the academic—that was beset by feuds and extraordinary child-
ishness. Baldwin, Hall, Scripture, and Titchener were notoriously
cantankerous. For this reason, perhaps, it was easy at first for Münsterberg's contemporaries to dismiss his quirks as merely annoying, as Palmer
did when he wrote, "Often one had to think of him as a big boy who had
never grown up." Yet in the course of twenty-five years, he fell out with
one after another of the men in his own department, including Herbert
Nichols, Dickinson Miller, William James, Edwin Holt, and finally Josiah
Royce.[7]

By the time the more difficult aspects of Münsterberg's personality had
become obvious, he was already working hard toward instilling in
America the values of social idealism. The basis for this undertaking lay
in a specifically German view of society as an organism, but it had paral-
lels in American social thought at the time. Münsterberg was in fact not
far from those thinkers who at the turn of the century sought through a
"quest for community" to mitigate the effects of what they considered an
increasingly disintegrating society.[8] For, even where the communitarian
model of thinkers like Royce, Baldwin, or Edward A. Ross was egalitar-

ian (which it generally was not), community meant, in addition to a sense
of belonging, a surrender of the atomistic self and a rejection of the nineteenth-century ideal of self-reliance. In it the centrifugal and wasteful tendencies of the capricious individual had been rooted out.

Münsterberg did not come from a static society—indeed Germany's industrialization occurred at a rate perhaps even more rapid than America's
—but he shared the outlook of a German class that valued order, authority, and a rigid differentiation of social function. His sudden transfer to a
rapid-paced, heterogeneous, and by German standards egalitarian New
World heightened his own confrontation with modernity and if anything
reinforced the conservative implications of his thought over the next decade. Like so many Americans of the period—for instance G. Stanley Hall,
Royce, and even John Dewey in a way—his social vision was essentially
nostalgic, although unlike them he did not long for a sense of place in a
democratic village past. His ideal was a society, like Germany as he
remembered it, in which all citizens knew their place and the place of the
academic was at the top. The chaos of America suggested more than ever
the need for order.

The crucial failing of American society, as Münsterberg saw it, lay in
too much freedom and too much equality—the obverse, in his terms, of
community. Individual initiative and independence of mind had tamed a
wilderness for pioneer America, but the complex conditions of the twentieth century demanded a renewed commitment to social purpose and the
application of German principles of efficiency. The individual had to
learn to subordinate his own interests and goals to those of the society as
a whole and to assume his proper role in the social organism. This meant,
above all, an increased respect for authority, whether represented by parents and teachers, political leaders, academic scholars, or scientific experts. "Everyone," Münsterberg wrote in 1901, echoing a common theme
of the time,

> feels himself lawmaker and authority; the immediate result is the tendency
> to disregard every other authority but one's own self. A lack of reverence
> pervades the whole community and controls the family, the school, the pub-
> lic life.

The American, he continued, learned "too late that it is a great thing to
command, but a greater thing to obey, and that no one can sign early
enough the declaration of dependence."[9]

This lack of reverence for authority translated itself into a failure of
will—an American ailment that men as different as Theodore Roosevelt
and William James had diagnosed. Münsterberg's social and metaphysical thought elevated will to a central place at the same time as his psy-

chology reduced it to an automatic compounding of sensations. In his Fichtean universe, will meant the regulation of self for higher purposes, which he considered synonymous with society's purposes. Yet the faculty of social and self-discipline was just what Americans seemed to him to lack. To meet this crisis of the will, therefore, Münsterberg proposed a focusing of energy and a disciplining of self, and during his American years he became an outspoken advocate of character-building.

In the years that followed his return, Münsterberg hoped to import the institutions that he believed were responsible for will, or social idealism, in Germany: the family, the school, and the universities. Especially in the beginning, he argued that education and respect for education in the broadest sense might rehabilitate the principle of authority. He agreed, therefore, with progressives on the centrality of education, but his profoundly conservative outlook was opposite theirs. Where progressives attempted to use formal schooling, at least in theory, as a lever to unseat the traditional sources of socialization in society (especially the family), Münsterberg employed it to reinforce them. And where progressives attempted to bring *Wissenschaft* down to earth by justifying higher education through its usefulness and its ability to serve the public, Münsterberg hinted that scholarship was society's reason for being.

Münsterberg's agenda for strengthening the will in America consisted for the most part of exhortation, which he did with enthusiasm. As early as 1895, he confronted G. Stanley Hall, the leader of the "child-study movement" in a debate in Boston. Soon after his return to Harvard, he published *Psychology and Life,* a contorted attempt to reconcile Idealism with scientific positivism, but he delivered his clearest and most effective blow for social idealism in a series of essays from 1899 to 1901, collected together under the appropriate title *American Traits from the Point of View of a German.*

Like most conservatives, Münsterberg made the family, which he called the "natural unity," the bulwark of social order. The school trained the child in mental discipline and taught him the classics, but the family instilled in him a conscience and a sense of morality. It socialized him, in other words, so that he accepted society's demands as universals and its symbols of authority as final, and it strengthened within him the will to perform his duty. It did so through a careful division of parental labor between fathers, "who feel the responsibility to be the ultimate moral guides of the youth," and mothers, "who through all their love and indulgence steadily insist on the seriousness of duties."[10] Siblings apparently did not have a place, despite their importance in Münsterberg's own life. The parents, instead, in a one-sided and authoritarian manner, indoctrinated the children in society's standards.

Münsterberg offered a sketch of moral education in 1889 in *Der Ursprung der Sittlichkeit*—before his own daughters were old enough to put it to the test. Moral principles, he argued, did not grow naturally, but they "must be bound directly to the emotions, to the idea of weal and woe." The child had to be punished for transgressing and rewarded for obeying. To do so over time would develop a well-conditioned conscience and a willingness to act correctly without compulsion. To be more specific, if a child were punished for lying, he would refrain from it in the future because he feared further punishment. That fear eventually dropped away, and in its place remained a revulsion at even the thought of lying. That revulsion, which amounted to a free-floating sense of guilt, prevented any future acts of lying. Correct or socially useful behavior was no longer compelled externally; it had become tied to an internal sense of duty.

Effective moral training might require a certain amount of deception. Parents could not always know when a child was transgressing, and therefore a consistent administration of rewards and punishments was difficult to achieve. But the traditional teachings of religion, even if untrue, might assist in the process of education. As Münsterberg put it, "If the subjective origin of the idea of God is forgotten," or, to paraphrase, if we pretend that God exists, then warnings about his powers of retribution become "the most valuable aid imaginable in securing obedience to social commandments and their translation into ethical maxims." The fiction of a God "who sees all and knows all" and who punishes sooner or later, if only in the after life, facilitated the disciplining of a conscience, and it ensured moral behavior, even when a belief in a personal God had vanished.[11]

Münsterberg found the American family in disarray. One of his favorite stories, which he repeated on several occasions, involved an incident that took place when he was visiting a Buffalo school-room. The teacher asked her class, "What do you think is the greatest difference between the life of the old Romans and our modern American life?" A young boy in the class answered: "With the old Romans the father was head of the family."[12] For Münsterberg this scene summarized much of what was wrong in American life: The normal order of the family and much of society had been reversed; women, who were assuming an increasingly dominant role, lent a soft-headed, undisciplined tone to the home and the national character.

At the same time, Münsterberg contended that women were deserting their familial duties—a development that he contrasted to the German experience. In an *Atlantic* article subsequently published in *American Traits*, he argued that "the aim of the German woman is to further the interests of the household, and that of the American woman to escape from the household." In Germany "the average girl attains to the fulfillment of her hopes only in marriage"; but for the American woman, marriage signified "a period almost of resignation." Especially for those women who had enjoyed the stimulating atmosphere of an American college, it seemed "an awakening from a lofty dream." After marriage, therefore, they attempted to perpetuate that dream in activities that drew them away from their families: They tended to "attach themselves, not to a husband and children, but to clubs and committees, to higher institutions and charity work, to art and literature." "The whole situation . . . ," Münsterberg asserted, "militates against the home and against the masculine control of higher culture." The result, on the one hand, was "pert and disrespectful children" who made ineffectual adults and, on the other, "an effemination of the higher culture, which is antagonistic to the development of a really representative national civilization."[13]

To stem this development, according to Münsterberg, America had to accept two principles long enshrined in German life. The first was that "it must remain the central function of the woman to be wife and mother." And the second that "public life and culture, including politics, public morality, science, art, higher education, industry, commerce, law, literature, the newspaper, and the church," had to be "produced, formed, and stamped by men." Without such a differentiation of function, a progressive and vigorous national life was impossible.[14]

Münsterberg's argument was at one level inconsistent—he pictured a family undermined simultaneously by the wife's flight from it and by her usurpation of all powers within it—but it expressed an emotionally consistent reaction to what he might have called the "self-assertion" of women. It was a common reaction, for it had become almost a cliché of the period that American civilization was becoming feminine. The often discussed "emasculation" of society was in fact nothing but another name for the crisis of the will that James and Roosevelt sensed, for maleness was associated with self-discipline, efficiency, and the ability to work. As a feminine principle came to dominate American culture, the nation lost its virility, the argument went. Not suprisingly, the foremost proponent of national virility offered Münsterberg his congratulations on the *Atlantic* article. "I agree entirely with what I take to be its general trend," Vice President Theodore Roosevelt wrote to him. For women and indeed for men, he continued,

the home in its widest and fullest sense should be the prime end of life. The first requisite in a healthy race is that a woman should be willing and able to bear children just as the men are willing and able to work and to fight.

The alternative was race suicide.[15]

Münsterberg and Roosevelt agreed on a secondary point: that higher education for women was valuable in the modern world and that, as Roosevelt put it, "the really able, intellectual, cultivated women" made the best wives. For Münsterberg, however, this meant neither university education nor professional training. He did support and encourage the exceptional few in their postgraduate work: Several of his best students at Harvard were women and he vigorously backed Mary Whiton Calkins of Wellesley in her unsuccessful bid for a Harvard Ph.D.[16] But he argued that most women could not endure the rigors of advanced work, and, where they could, it lured them away from the home and toward the careers for which they had been trained. The best American women's colleges, including Radcliffe, where Münsterberg regularly taught, offered instead a liberal education. In his Freiburg years Münsterberg recommended the establishment in Germany of an institution for women along such lines. But he was careful to emphasize, "Its goal would *not be an academic vocation, but a deepened level of cultivation [Bildung].*" It would nourish the spiritual and intellectual life of its students, but always in reference to their mental and physical organization and their purpose in life. "The woman," Münsterberg asserted, "should not strive for intellectual cultivation to do away with marriage but to ennoble it."[17]

The purpose of women's education, then, was to socialize them to a male-dominated social organism. In this way, it was no different from any other social arrangement. "Every system of public spirit," Münsterberg wrote, "which in its final outcome raises the individuals, but lowers the families, is antagonistic to the true civilization of the people." He conceded that a surface contradiction might appear between society's demands and the "individualistic, brilliant achievements" of women, but he assumed that the real interests of the individual always coincided with those of society, and that society therefore could require obedience from its members without violating their true selves. "We have the right to demand from the community," he wrote, "that the woman be taught to consider, as the really best for her, what is in the highest interests of the whole of society, even if it be second best for the individual."[18]

One of the symptoms—and one of the causes—of the feminization of culture was the number of women working as elementary and secondary school teachers. In the 1880s and 1890s American public school systems replaced men by women in teaching positions. School boards often argued that women were more "natural" teachers than men, but the compelling reason for most was the willingness of women to work for less. Münsterberg deplored the development. He wrote that even if women were able to teach as well, which he doubted, they offered a poor model for young boys. "Can it be without danger," he asked, "that the male youth of this country, up to the eighteenth year, is educated by unmarried women?" Could it be doubted that " 'nascent manhood requires for right development manly inspiration, direction, and control?' " The predominance of women in the classroom reflected the trend away from all principles of authority at school, and it paralleled the submission of the father at home. Progressive reformers only aggravated the situation.[19]

By 1900 a movement for reform in education, associated with such figures as John Dewey and G. Stanley Hall, was in full swing. Its story has been told often and needs no retelling, but several points should be made in order to put Münsterberg's writings on education in context.[20] It is not easy to characterize a movement so broad as progressive education, but as a minimum the reformers shared a belief that the school should make concessions to the natural development of children and should allow, at least up to a point, a place for free activity by the students. The more radical of the reformers, who borrowed heavily from a romantic tradition of continental thinkers, including Rousseau, Froebel, and Pestalozzi, hailed the natural goodness of the child and saw in him the potential for social regeneration.

The progressive school, therefore, was "child-centered"—even if its goals remained adult-defined. It became in theory a cooperative and experimental enterprise, with children, teachers, parents, and pedagogues working together to produce the independent-minded, responsible citizenry allegedly so necessary to a democracy. At a more tangible level, reformers recommended learning by doing and the free choice of courses, and they emphasized a principle of utility, which led them at times into an uneasy alliance with advocates of vocational and manual training. Educational reform also carried with it the aura of science. Many of its leaders, including Hall and Dewey, were associated with the new psychology, and the latest advances in the science of the mind seemed to sanction their pedagogical methods.

As early as 1895, Münsterberg declared his firm opposition to this modernizing trend, and in the decade that followed he published a series of popular articles that drew praise from educational conservatives, including the U.S. Commissioner of Education William Torrey Harris and Columbia's Nicholas Murray Butler.[21] On almost every issue his views were diametrically opposed to those of the progressives. He harshly criticized the participatory aspects of their reforms; he championed rote learning, classical subjects of study, prescribed curricula, and teachers trained in their specialties rather than in pedagogics; above all, he rejected all naturist tendencies. "Is it not savage life to follow merely the instincts and natural desires?" he asked rhetorically in 1900 in an *Atlantic*

Monthly article entitled "School Reform." The goal of schooling was to restrict and overcome the natural inclinations of the child rather than indulge them. "Is not all the meaning of education just to discriminate between good and bad desires? to suppress the lower instincts, and to reinforce the higher; above all, to awake new desires, to build up new interests, to create new instincts?"[22]

As Münsterberg viewed it, America's school methods epitomized its commitment to laissez-faire, and the waste of human resources that they encouraged rivaled any in the economic or political spheres. The foreigner looking at America, Münsterberg later wrote, could not "help feeling the lack of accuracy and thoroughness, the superficiality, the go-as-you-please character of the work." Such a condition, he argued, had resulted from the systematic indulgence of childish whims in the schools. The child, Münsterberg asserted in "School Reform," might "learn a thousand pretty things, but never the one which is the greatest of all: to do his duty."[23]

Education, therefore, taught the child to work, and it did so by forcing him to do what by inclination he preferred not to do. Only in this way could it overcome the tendency of the mind to fix on the superficial and the eye-catching and could it teach the student not to become bored. In later essays Münsterberg expanded this point in a fashion reminiscent of James's famous discussions of habit and attention. "The real development of mankind," he wrote in 1909, "lies in the growth of the voluntary attention, which is not passively attracted, but which turns actively to that which is important and significant and valuable in itself." Children had to be taught to attend by forcing them to do so, not by cajoling them to learn isolated facts through the use of attractive teaching devices. To do so would only further weaken their will. "Whoever is allowed always to follow the path of least resistance," Münsterberg suggested, "will soon find any work drudgery and any effort tiring and a torture to his nerves." Education, in other words, meant the formation of good work habits.[24]

Münsterberg's emphasis on "voluntary" attention suggested that he shared Dewey's and James's belief that education should lead to independence of mind. But independence for him meant only the ability to do what one ought to do without external compulsion. He later offered as his model of independence and freedom the soldier who performed his duty even after the death of his commander. Will therefore implied choice only in the sense that it allowed people to choose to do their duty, to choose not to be distracted. The right to define duty was removed from the individual and imposed upon him. Münsterberg often talked of human interaction in education, calling it an art rather than a science, but his educational model bypassed completely the conscious interests and demands of the child. Its aim was to link the will of the child to the historic will of society as a whole.

The crux of Münsterberg's program of social idealism lay in higher education and universities, for he brought with him to the New World the cultural baggage of the typical German academic. The dedication of the scholar to *Wissenschaft,* in Münsterberg's mind, set an example of selfless commitment to an ideal, and the scholarship he produced reflected the vigor of the nation that supported it. The essence of university work was productive scholarship—research that advanced the world's fund of knowledge—and the students enrolled in the university were apprentices in the *Gelehrter's* craft, not candidates for a liberal education or general cultivation. The university in this way differed significantly from the *Gymnasium,* but to that institution, which was lower down the academic (and social) hierarchy, it passed a reverence for the authority of scholarship and a respect for the scholar.

The situation in America, Münsterberg quickly discovered, was very different, and in consequence, he believed, America's scholarly record was poor. "Why has Germany's productive scholarship attained the power to mould the thoughts of the world, while America's, so far, has not?" he asked in 1901. The answer, he suggested, was that America failed to value the work of its scholars and the American college stressed the teaching and transmission of learning rather than the advancement of it. Consequently, university work in the United States attracted second-rate men, and the whole structure of the American educational system drew competent scholars away from scholarship.[25]

Münsterberg's initial distaste for the American college moderated over the years. In 1904 he wrote that "the college is to-day, more than ever the soul of the whole nation," and he advocated the establishment of its equivalent in Germany. But for him the college was a broadened and liberalized *Gymnasium.* He considered its domination of American higher education to be another example of the emasculation of American civilization, for it incorporated a "passive, receptive, uncritical attitude toward knowledge." "The historic development of the American college," he wrote in his *Atlantic* essay on American women, "has brought it about that the whole higher study bears far too much the type of the feminine attitude towards scholarship." Just as the university ideal seemed to be gaining ground, movements toward coeducation endangered it. "What a calamity for the country," Münsterberg asserted, "if this great epoch in the life of the universities were ruined by any concessions to the feminine type of thinking!"[26]

Almost from the first, Münsterberg worked to transfer a "masculine"

German model to Harvard. During the school year 1893–94, the Harvard faculty considered instituting a *Docent* system, according to which young instructors would be free to give specialized instruction to advanced students. Münsterberg, unlike his fellow German on the faculty, Kuno Francke, strongly supported the proposal, which, he assumed, would protect and nurture the ideal of scholarship. Only through a system of *Docenten,* he wrote Eliot, could the university become "something else higher than a college only" and the Graduate School "something higher than an appendix of the College, controlled by the college spirit." How Münsterberg believed it could do this revealed much about his attitudes toward the university and society in general.[27]

Münsterberg's reasoning was simple (and, as a full professor, self-serving). At the present, he complained to Eliot, the graduate school "contains just the poorest men who graduate from the College." He amplified this point several years later:

> Our graduate school students stand on a by far lower level than the average member of the college and the law school. On the one side they belong to a socially lower class, men mostly without manners, without means and without connections, on the other side men with limited intellect.[28]

The American system of paying relatively high wages to young instructors did not reward established scholars adequately and it attracted men who were looking for quick and easy money. A *Docent* system, on the other hand, would draw the strongest young men and "especially those of independent means who are ready to serve for a long while without honorarium but see high premiums and great distinctions ahead." At the same time, Münsterberg's scheme called for more money and honors at the top. "Give to the scholar's life here the splendor which it has in Germany and your best men will rush towards scholarship."[29]

Harvard, however, proved unreceptive to Münsterberg's fifteen-year campaign to close scholarship to all but those of good breeding and independent wealth. It did flirt briefly with a limited *Docent* system after 1897, when the university allowed any Ph.D. with faculty approval to teach four months without payment or for a fee that he raised himself. Münsterberg claimed to "expect much" from this development, and he believed it would arrest the drain of his best students into business and law, but it never caught on. Harvard and other universities instead attempted to support their graduate students through scholarships and fellowships and continued to reward their young instructors with salaries. These were systems, Münsterberg complained, that attracted "the weaklings" and drew "more strongly than before the unoriginal cheap man into the Graduate School." Such sponsorship of the mediocre had ruined the ministry in Europe, he claimed, and it would do the same to American scholarship, for "no great science can be built up by philanthropy."[30]

In 1901 Münsterberg broadened his attack on American higher education and brought it to the public in an article entitled "Productive Scholarship." In this essay he criticized not only how the universities drew men into teaching but also how the nation treated men who were already there. Much of Münsterberg's argument was well taken, but the article often read as a personal lament, close in language to his private requests for increases in salary. "After the student days," he wrote, "everything militates against scholarly production, in this country." The young instructor found himself overburdened with administrative and teaching duties, and he faced an insuperable temptation to prostitute his science by lowering it to the beginner's level. But even the position of a tenured professor at a good university was unsatisfactory. In a passage that no doubt described his own feelings, Münsterberg noted that not only was the salary of the dedicated scholar low, he also

> sees himself, perhaps, in a faculty where real scholars mingle with men who have not the slightest ambition to advance human knowledge, but who have simply done on a great scale all that the men in his fresh-water college did on a narrow scale. He feels as if his productive scholarship were merely tolerated, or at least considered unessential, as no one demands it from the others as an essential condition of their presence.

Scholarship remained nothing but "a professional luxury, relegated to the scarce leisure hours of an overworked man who has little to gain from it."[31] Shortly before, Münsterberg had published his magnum opus, *Die Grundzüge der Psychologie,* to a generally unappreciative academic public in America.

Münsterberg's prediction of how the low state of scholarship in America would influence the work of the individual scholar proved accurate in his own case: Indeed, one of the ironies of his writings was the extent to which his criticisms of others applied to himself. America's scholars, he wrote, were "so poorly paid that they feel everywhere pushed into pursuits antagonistic to scholarship." In a nation that defined its aristocracy by income, the problem was not simply one of dollars but of social status. Scholars therefore did little for free: They wrote popular books here and articles for encyclopedias there; they offered expert testimonials; they lectured before audiences whose judgment they despised. Münsterberg characterized these activities as "self-destructive," yet he was engaged in most at the time and within a few years he would have done them all.[32]

Münsterberg's advocacy of productive scholarship struck a responsive chord. The sociologist Edward A. Ross cited with approval his argument in *The Americans* that "the most important factor in the aristocratic differentiation in America is higher education and culture." And in May 1901, a month before his letter on "American Women," Theodore Roosevelt wrote Münsterberg complimenting him on his argument in "Productive Scholarship": "I have always felt uncomfortable over our very small output of really serious scholarly work, but I have never in the least understood where the trouble lay—or, to speak more accurately, I felt it, but I have not been able to formulate it even to myself." He had never before appreciated the need for the complete divorce of the work of "teachers of history to ordinary classes in an ordinary college" from "the work which we ought to expect from a serious historian" who received his appointment because he was likely to do "the kind of work which would add to the sum of national achievement."[33]

But Roosevelt's words did not mean much in a nation that granted little acclaim to its leading scholars. Several years later, after his scholarship had failed to attract a large American readership, Münsterberg offered a general lament on the position of the scholar in America. "The other day," he wrote in 1909,

> we mourned the death of Simon Newcomb. There seems to be a general agreement that astronomy is the one science in which America has been in the first rank of the world, and that Newcomb was the greatest American astronomer. Yet his death did not bring the slightest ripple of excitement. The death of the manager of the professional baseball games interested the country rather more. Public opinion did not show the slightest consciousness of an incomparable loss at the hour when the nation's greatest scholar closed his eyes. And if I compare it with that deep national mourning with which the whole German nation grieved at the loss of men like Helmholtz and Mommsen and Virchow, and many another, the contrast becomes most significant.[34]

Münsterberg's observation was an apt one, and he had indeed put his finger on a weakness of higher scholarship in America. But he was also testifying to his own failure: His ideal of *Wissenschaft* had translated poorly to the New World and it seemed as alien there as his phrase, "the manager of the professional baseball games."

Values and Science:
A Search for
Philosophical Order

When Münsterberg campaigned for social idealism in America, he reflected his more general goal of restoring philosophical Idealism to its presumed former position of eminence in Western thought. He was not alone in this enterprise. An "idealistic reaction against science," to borrow the phrase of the Italian philosopher Antonio Aliotta, swept European and even some American philosophical circles late in the century. For men as diverse as William James, Josiah Royce, Henri Bergson, and Wilhelm Dilthey, the central intellectual problem of the age became identifying a transcendental source of values and purpose in a world where science had transformed nature into the blind interaction of atoms and where history had relativized all cultural standards of beauty, morality, and truth. Dilthey lamented in 1903:

> The historical way of looking at things has liberated the human spirit from the last chains which natural science and philosophy have not yet torn asunder. But where are the means of overcoming the anarchy of convictions which threatens to break in on us?[1]

For Münsterberg, the "anarchy of convictions" was of a piece with the weakened state of social idealism. The mechanistic, historical, and pragmatic world views, in his opinion, all undermined the sources of authority in society, just as they threatened belief in absolute values. He did not, however, abandon his youthful enthusiasm for a reductionist science in which the laws of mechanics could account for all appearances, both in nature and human society. Instead, after his return to Harvard, he took as his general philosophical aim, as he wrote in a diary of 1900, "the harmonization of a positivistic study of human life with an ethical idealism in the direction of Kant's and Fichte's philosophy."[2]

I have already suggested that Münsterberg found a solution to the challenges of scientism and historicism by radically divorcing Kant's realms of the sensible and the intelligible, or, in his own more Fichtean language, of "perceiving" and "willing." This dichotomy had important implications for Münsterberg's applied psychology, for it suggested the virtual abdication of critical values in questions of practical affairs, and it exiled ideals, values, and purpose to an insubstantial neverland. It also reflected a dualism in Münsterberg's psyche that was often observed but never resolved. The youth who wrestled between a career in science or art developed as an adult a philosophy that compartmentalized "science" from "life" and "causative" from "purposive" psychology. He "struggled most earnestly with the problem of a Weltanschauung," his friend William Stern wrote of him in 1917.

> That he did not always achieve a full unification and harmony of its manifold features, that two souls often fought within him, forms the tragedy of his personality.[3]

Before his first tour at Harvard, and again between 1895 and 1897, Münsterberg came under the influence of the Sud-Baden, or Southwestern, School of neo-Kantianism. At Freiburg and nearby Heidelberg, Wilhelm Windelband, Heinrich Rickert, Paul Hensel, and others were working out a philosophy that viewed the world as a construct of rational consciousness. In the process they hoped to validate an absolute Idealism in which the norms of truth, beauty, and morality, like Kant's modes of thinking, depended on the structure of the mind rather than on the forces of history or nature. Their defense of absolutes, rooted in Kantian principles of the universality of thought, therefore aligned them with "that direction of German philosophy which, in reaction to Nietzsche, sharply rejects the relativization, transformation, and variability of the values of life." "Relativism," Windelband wrote, "is the dismissal and death of philosophy. Philosophy can live only as the science of values which are universally valid."[4]

Among this group, Rickert especially exerted a lasting influence on Münsterberg. Only a week older than Münsterberg, he was the son of a prominent Danzig journalist and liberal politician known for his steadfast opposition to anti-Semitism. He may well have known Münsterberg from Danzig, but, in any case, after Rickert's arrival at Freiburg as *Docent* in 1891, the two became close friends and lifelong philosophical allies. It was from Rickert, according to Max Dessoir, that Münsterberg derived his interest in the epistemological foundations of science and especially psychology, his distinction between realms of the "is" and the "ought" (the *Sein* and the *Sollen*), and his belief that the question of value was central to philosophy.[5] Münsterberg was to bring these positions back to the New World with him.

When he returned to Harvard in 1897, Münsterberg launched an offensive against what he considered to be the pervasive American habit of "psychologism"—at the time a favorite target of the Sud-Baden group. At least in the early stages of his argument, for instance in his 1895 talk to Boston schoolmasters, Münsterberg divided the operations of mind into "perceiving" and "willing," the equivalents of the *Sein* and the *Sollen*. The former was the sphere of cause and effect, of scientific explanation, and of psychology—all artificial mental constructs that stood distinct from the experiences of "real life." These constructs made possible a consistent system of explanation and even guidelines for action, but, Münsterberg argued, they were wholly inappropriate as a working outlook on real life. When the scientist or the layman violated this distinction, when he applied psychological principles to his relations with fellow human beings, he committed the sin of psychologism. In this sense, psychologism was a sophisticated version of positivism. Where positivism attempted to reduce the phenomena of life as it was experienced to the laws of mechanics, psychologism reduced it to those of a mechanistic psychology.

In his talk to the Boston schoolteachers, Münsterberg derived from this argument a warning that he applied throughout the practical arena of life. "That overwhelming movement towards psychology among elementary teachers," he intoned, "seems to me a high tide of confusion and dilettantism." In fact, *the individual teacher, for his teaching methods, does not need any scientific psychology.* Münsterberg agreed that the teacher ought to teach some psychology, since it was such an important part of human knowledge, and he conceded that a scientific pedagogy might gather suggestions on the methods of teaching from modern psychology. But he argued that it would be a disaster if teachers viewed their pupils in a psychological fashion, if they considered them to be bundles of sensations and motor actions to be manipulated. In no case should the teacher apply his own cursory knowledge of the science to the instruction of his pupils. *"Tact and sympathy and interest,"* he proclaimed, *"are more important for him than all the twenty-seven psychological laboratories of this country."*[6]

Münsterberg sharpened his attack on psychologism in subsequent years, first in an intemperate review of Edward Scripture's *The New Psychology,* and then in a series of articles on the relation of psychology to physiology, art, history, and mysticism, which were published in 1899 as

Psychology and Life. In each his argument was the same: The systems of psychology and the natural sciences were divorced from each other and from the experiences of real life. They had nothing in their pure state to say, therefore, to the artist, the teacher, or the historian, all of whom had to understand and appreciate human values. Yet laymen in America were rushing to psychology for answers to life, and professional psychologists encouraged them in their mistaken enterprise. The two groups conspired, in Münsterberg's view, to propagate the false belief "that the full reality can be understood as a phenomenon"—a belief that he called "the disease of our time."[7]

Münsterberg's attack on the spread of applied psychology—which carried with it many of the *Gelehrter's* prejudices against utility—drew criticism from leaders of the profession. Cattell and the educational psychologist Edward Thorndike defended Scripture, and John Dewey argued that psychology could not be divorced from social practice. Joseph Jastrow explicitly rebutted Münsterberg's arguments in his presidential address to the American Psychological Association in 1900. "Psychology and life," he asserted, "are closely related; and we do not fill our whole function if we leave uninterpreted for practical and public benefit the mental power of man."[8]

Münsterberg later reversed his position on applied psychology. It should be pointed out, however, that his separation of psychology from real life, which he considered a corrective to a particularly American fallacy, was in an important way consistent with his subsequent position. He aimed his criticisms primarily at the democratization of science and the breakdown of the proper cultural division of labor rather than the application of psychology *per se*. The fad of experimental psychology among laymen in America threatened academic control of the discipline.

Münsterberg did not spell out the cultural division of labor, but its outlines were clear. At the highest rung were the philosopher-academics, men who were committed to a fundamental Idealism that subordinated the individual to the whole and who spoke for the national *Kultur*. Their work was no idle enterprise of ivory-towered scholars. "The more abstract its language, and the more technical its system," Münsterberg wrote in 1909, the greater a source of "new life-energies" was philosophy. Next to religions, philosophies were

> the most powerful factors in the history of the last two thousand years; they have made revolutions and they have brought reforms. . . . Only the laborious self-consistent systematic thought can give us the full truth, and only the full truth can make us free.[9]

At a more pedestrian level, the philosopher arbitrated between the various *Wissenschaften* and defined for each specialized scholar what his sphere of operation was to be.

Below the philosopher stood the various specialists, one of whom was the psychologist. Through his own particular methods of introspection and experimentation, this specialist analyzed the structure of consciousness. His goal was to derive a special and secondary truth that allowed him to predict future states of mind. Very different from him was the applied scientist—for example, the pedagogue, who derived practical rules of operation from the data of psychology, physiology, and other disciplines. At the bottom rung were those functionaries, such as the teacher, who applied the rules daily in their professions and derived consolation from the knowledge that their work was an "art."

Münsterberg's separation of psychology from real life, therefore, was deceptive. In theory, it freed humanistic arts like teaching and writing history from the technical model of the physical and psychological sciences. For this reason William James regarded his early essays on education favorably.[10] But "tact," "sympathy," and "interest" were vague terms and offered no meaningful guidelines. When it came to the actual defining of methods and curricula, the trained educational psychologist had the final say. In practice, therefore, Münsterberg's dual view of experience protected the monopoly of the expert, and it deprived the teacher or the historian of any say in the conduct of his art. Münsterberg's epistemology returned *Kultur* to those whom he considered its proper owners.

Münsterberg explicated his epistemology fully in 1900 in his *Grundzüge der Psychologie,* the "big book" upon which he had been working since his first years at Harvard. Despite its generally cool reception in America, this massive, 600-page contribution to the *Methodenstreit,* or discussion of methods, which dominated German thought at the turn of the century, drew considerable attention in Germany. Rickert greeted its appearance enthusiastically and praised Münsterberg as "a psychologist who far from overestimates the importance of his science for the totality of spiritual life." Another reviewer expressed the view, "It is a joy once again to encounter a book like this one, which has the courage and the energy to undertake the greatest task of philosophy: synthesis." The psychologist William Stern, who disagreed with some of the volume's particular formulations, called it "a necessary step in the evolution of the scholarly Weltanschauung of our times." Max Weber, who had more extensive doubts, devoted a lengthy portion of his *Roscher und Knies,* an analysis of the methods of social science, to a careful criticism of its arguments.[11]

In his *Grundzüge,* Münsterberg began from the position that he had expounded to the Boston schoolteachers. "We will start," he wrote, "from the primordial Reality," from the realm of pure experience. This reality for Münsterberg—and here he followed Fichte and Rickert—did not consist of the flux of atoms, but rather the attitudes and judgments of the active ego (*Ich*).

> In preferring and not preferring, in loving and hating, in using and shunning, in admiring and detesting, in striving for and abandoning, in affirming and denying, in brief, in the decisions of Willing and not-Willing, shaded in infinite variations, the Ego fashions for itself reality as a free act.[12]

The individual ego sought in the flux of will-motives a special sort of self-consistent, interconnected logical system whose result was knowledge (*Erkenntnis*). To take a simple example, in order to create a world of predictable objects, a person had to affirm intuitively the identity of the clock that he saw in front of him (or, rather, that abstracted segment of experience that he identified as a clock) with the clock that he saw several moments before. This act of identification was absolutely free, and no one was under any compulsion to perform it. It was at the same time value laden because the creative will had made it and because failure to make it would leave the world a meaningless chaos. But it was not done for any trivial utilitarian reasons: The transformation of pure experience satisfied the will in its needs for order.[13]

Knowledge and the value of Truth, therefore, depended upon a normative act: the affirmation of identity in a world of flux. From this affirmation the scholar went on to systematize Truth by extending observed identities into complicated principles of connection. He could do this from two distinct viewpoints: He could find one object identical to another, as in the example of the clock; or he could find one purpose identical to another, as when he studied the career of a historical personality. In the first case he regarded experience as a compounding of objects whose causes he could identify and whose future he could predict. In this fashion, he constructed a *Naturwissenschaft,* an "objectifying" science, for example physics, chemistry, and, in a complicated way, psychology. Like the reductionists, he explained the world as a system of atoms moving in conformity with the general laws of mechanics. In the second case, which Münsterberg considered to be the more natural, the scholar treated experience as a compounding of subjects, and he constructed a *Geisteswissenschaft,* or "subjectifying" science like ethics or history. In this type of science, the scholar analyzed the intentional actions of other subjects in such a way as to allow him to understand their meaning and to assign them value.[14]

A few examples from Münsterberg's English writings might make his distinction more clear. Socrates' refusal to escape from an Athenian prison, Münsterberg wrote, could be attributed to the absence in him of those muscle processes that would have brought about an escape. This absence reflected a specific brain-state, which in turn was produced by "sense-stimulations and dispositions, associations and inhibitions, physiological and climatic influences." In other words, Socrates' decision to remain could be explained in wholly behavioristic and even (potentially) physicochemical terms. But the scholar could also assert that "Socrates remained in the prison because he decided to be obedient to the laws of Athens unto death." This obedience was a "will-attitude," which "we must understand by feeling it and living through it, an attitude which we cannot analyze, but which we can interpret and appreciate."[15]

Or take the case of a man who had committed a crime. "We might," Münsterberg suggested,

> ask ourselves from what causes this criminal deed arose in this man. How far are his education, his life habits, his surroundings, his state of health responsible for the development of these impulses? How far did the fatigue of his brain, or the influence of alcohol, or a disease produce the abnormal impulse? What causes interfered with the mental resistance of will? From what source did the ideas or the memories and the hopes or fears arise, and how did they come to result in that criminal deed?

On the other hand,

> we may be interested in understanding the motives and aims in his mind, and, if we are to judge his deed, we certainly must try to think ourselves into his mind, in order to understand his actions from the inside. His emotions and his volition, his crime, everything is to be understood as the expression of his personality.[16]

The distinction between cultural and natural science had been a central theme of the German *Methodenstreit* for two decades. In general terms Münsterberg's version was not far from the Idealist systems of Dilthey and Windelband, and it modified the positivistic view that he outlined in *Ursprung der Sittlichkeit*. His scheme, however, was distinctive not only because of its extreme rigidity, but because he located the source of the duality within the intentions of the scholar. The differences between the study of culture and of nature, he argued, did not lie in the nature of the objects studied or the methods by which they were studied, as Helmholtz, Dilthey, Windelband, and Weber had in different ways argued. Rather, they depended upon the scholar's point of view. Did he wish to explain and to predict? Then he was a *Naturwissenschaftler*. Did he wish to understand and to appreciate? In that case, he studied the cultural sciences.

Münsterberg assumed that any object of nature or fact of culture could be considered from either the natural-science or the cultural viewpoint, but not from both simultaneously. His approach permitted, therefore, an absolutely mechanistic and deterministic view of mind to exist side by side with, but unconnected to, an affirmation of creative, purposive activity. In such studies as physiology and psychology, the *Naturwissenschaftler* objectified; in biography and history, the *Geisteswissenschaftler* subjectified. But they both dealt with the same material. Münsterberg believed that most of his contemporaries failed to understand this distinction and therefore confused the two viewpoints, ending up with bad scholarship. Positivists like Auguste Comte and Henry Buckle attempted to arrive at understanding through scientific explanation. They sought to reduce morals, logic, and beauty to principles of cause and effect, but through their relativism, they stripped values of their real, immediate meaning. Wundt, on the other hand, wrote bad science because he allowed purpose to slip into his explanations through his concept of apperception. James committed the same sin when he espoused mysticism. The problem for all these men was not their evidence, or even their argumentation; their epistemology was at fault.

In the *Grundzüge der Psychologie,* Münsterberg asserted that psychology was a natural science (a controversial issue among German philosophers), and he devoted the bulk of the volume to explaining its unique relationship to the other natural sciences. According to his system of knowledge, each branch of *Wissenschaft* could be divided into two parallel subcategories: the study of phenomena accessible to any number of observers and of phenomena accessible to only one. Among the *Geisteswissenschaften,* the normative sciences, such as logic and ethics, dealt with "over-personal" questions: Everyone could derive the logical rules of Euclid or the ethical system of Kant. The historical sciences dealt with the individual; only Caesar experienced his motives for crossing the Rubicon. Among the *Naturwissenschaften,* the physical sciences were the over-individual, the psychological were the individual. As Münsterberg explained it, and as Figure 1 illustrates, psychology, like chemistry and physics, was a natural science because it approached the phenomena that it studied as objects, analyzing them into simple elements bound together by regular and predictable patterns. But the objects of its study were very different from those of physics or chemistry: Any given sensation, feeling, or volition could by definition be known immediately only to the person who experienced it. Psychology, therefore, was a science involving "knowledge given to individual consciousness," and it was the equivalent in the *Naturwissenschaften* of history in the *Geistewissenschaften.*[17]

In Münsterberg's scheme, as a result, psychology was an "objectifying" science. it should be noted, however, that Münsterberg's method of objectification gave his psychology a curious unreality and, since Münsterberg depended on traditional methods of self-analysis, his science of the mind

Figure 1
Münsterberg's Classification of the *Wissenschaften*

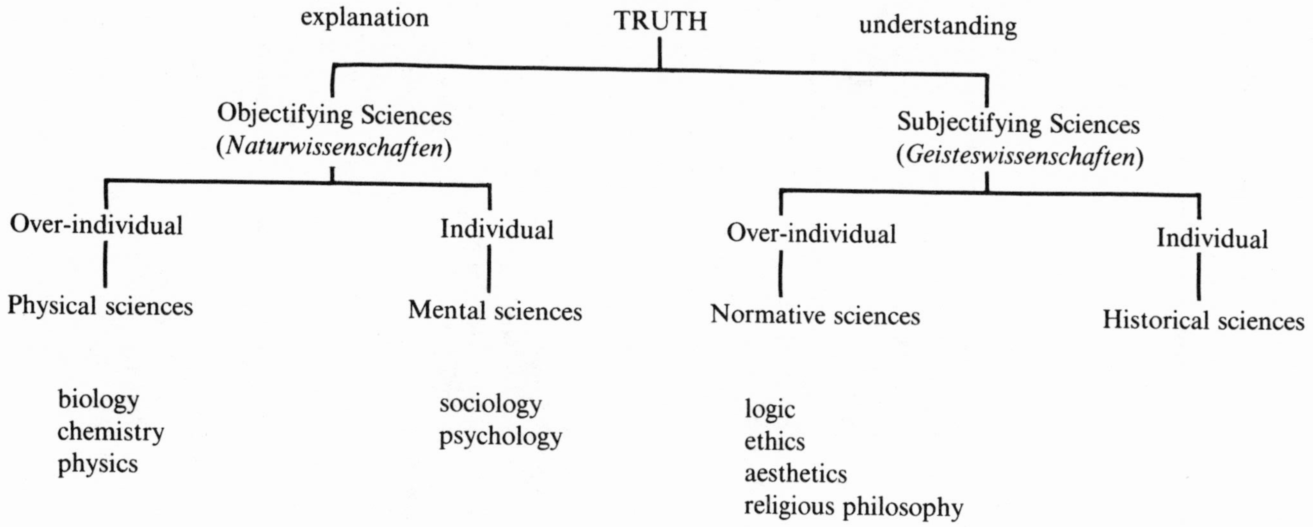

TRUTH

explanation   understanding

Objectifying Sciences   Subjectifying Sciences
(*Naturwissenschaften*)   (*Geisteswissenschaften*)

Over-individual   Individual   Over-individual   Individual

Physical sciences   Mental sciences Normative sciences   Historical sciences

biology   sociology   logic
chemistry   psychology   ethics
physics   aesthetics
                                        religious philosophy

Adapted from Hugo Münsterberg, "The Position of Psychology in the System of Knowledge," in *Harvard Psychological Studies*, ed. Hugo Münsterberg (New York: Macmillan Co., 1903).

obscured his own mental states. During his Freiburg years, Münsterberg once wrote, he had the habit of "experimenting whenever daily life brought me into a characteristic mental state, such as emotion or interest or fatigue or anything important to the psychologist." He attached to the bottom of his coat a small measure on which, without looking, he could record estimates of four and eight inches. After half a year he came up with a set of figures correlating emotional states with muscular actions. When he was excited, he consistently overestimated; when he was depressed, he underestimated. He found other correlations for the states of pleasure, displeasure, gravity, and mirth.[18] (This from a man who refused to perform psychological experiments on his daughters because it would hinder the interaction of human wills.) In a very real sense, then, he observed his subjective states "objectively," but in doing so he defused them of their immediate impact, and he deprived the consciousness studied by the psychologist of purpose and indeed personality.

Why should the psychologist take such an admittedly abstract and artificial view? For Münsterberg the answer was simple: It allowed him to predict and, he hoped, to control the immediate reality of experience. "The objectifying of reality," he wrote, "is . . . an abstracting act by the subject [that is, the scientist], whose goal it is to determine the expectation of future experiences based on present experience." Science also could shape that experience. "Our personality," he went on, "would be robbed of its best meaning if we only passively directed our attention to a mechanism that pushed ever new forms into existence, but were unable to influence the unfolding reality." The scientist, through his ability to supply causes, could assist man in transcending the role of passive observer and allow him to influence experience directly. Psychology in particular could determine the exact mechanism by which the individual consciousness was formed and could reveal how one individual came to influence another.[19] Hence Münsterberg's early interest in the phenomena of suggestion and hypnosis and his later commitment to applied psychology.

Psychology went about its explanation in a unique fashion, according to Münsterberg. He argued that, because ideas did not possess properties of quantity, dimension, and time, psychology could not measure or quantify its objects. And because ideas had no physical reality, psychology could not speak of mental causation or law. Most of Münsterberg's American colleagues found this position baffling in a "new psychologist," particularly one who aggressively defended psychological atomism. Cattell, for example, asked, What was Münsterberg doing in his laboratory if not quantifying and measuring mental phenomena?[20] Münsterberg, however, considered his point crucial to his critique of psychologism, and he went to considerable lengths to justify it. In an argument that the English philosopher Alfred E. Taylor called "a wonderfully subtle deduction ... from philosophical first principles," Münsterberg asserted that the science of psychology was possible only because of the fact of psychophysical parallelism. Every mental event was accompanied by a physiological corollary, which could be measured, analyzed, and explained. The psychologist, by a process of "introjection," superimposed the mental phenomena upon the physiological. He could, as a result, derive patterns and regularities in the flow of ideas by examining the physiological organism and its behavior. But he never measured ideas, only physical events.[21]

The patterns in the flow of ideas, Münsterberg emphasized, were not causal laws in any scientific sense, and psychology's "laws" were only predictive generalizations derived empirically. For example, the psychologist could say that, in accordance with the laws of association, idea A always (or usually) called idea B to mind, and therefore he could predict the appearance of B on the basis of observing the presence of A. But such a formulation was not a law, according to Münsterberg; it did not have the necessity of mechanics. Like Darwin's theory of evolution, it amounted to a teleological shortcut to a true mechanistic explanation and would disappear when replaced by an atomistic determinism. The processes of association would be truly explained only when they were reduced to necessary physiological terms.[22]

Psychology, therefore, became for Münsterberg a shortcut for physiology. Some day, he indicated at times, a thoroughly consistent neurophysiology might explain all mental events in mechanical terms and allow their complete prediction and manipulation. In the meantime, psychology could examine only those mental traits that had a conceivable physiological correlate. In the *Psychological Review* of 1900, Münsterberg asserted:

> If we see now that explanation in psychology must always be indirect, based ultimately on the causal connection of physical processes, it is clear that psychology has no reason to investigate elements which have merely a psychological interest and no bearing on the psychophysiological explanation.[23]

In taking this position, Münsterberg eliminated the immediate reality of mind from the range of his psychological vision.

At the conclusion of his *Grundzüge,* Münsterberg moved from a discussion of the epistemological foundations of psychology to a theory of consciousness that could explain the observed facts of mind. His problem was essentially the one that he had set for himself in the 1880s: How could he account in psychophysical terms for the Fichtean principle that the "real" world depended upon the will-act of the subject, that the mind, through its activity, created the world that it perceived.

Münsterberg offered his Action Theory as a solution. In it he departed from the peripheralism that characterized his early work, and, because he stressed the influence of preparation and training in determining the contents of consciousness, he sounded at times very much like the American functionalists. But because consciousness remained an epiphenomenon in his theory, Münsterberg's work lent itself easily to a behaviorist account of mind. His assumption of a strict parallelism betwen mental and physiological events and his assertion that all mental events could be explained exclusively as brain events allowed his students, at least, to ignore the mental side of the mind-body equation. At the same time Münsterberg's identification of psychology with prediction and control, however theoretical this identification was in 1900, led to a practical interest in manipulating behavior. It should come as no surprise, therefore, that the Harvard laboratory under his direction, with such men as Robert Yerkes, Knight Dunlap, Floyd Allport, and Edward Holt working there, assumed by 1910 a practical and behavioristic flavor.

As he had in *Die Willenshandlung,* Münsterberg argued in his *Grundzüge* that sensationist theory was inadequate, for it told only half the story. The intensity of an idea, in the Lockean sense, depended on the strength of the sensory stimulus. Its quality (that is, whether it was hot, red, or loud), as the German physiologist Johannes Müller had years earlier proved in his law of specific energies, depended on the location of the nervous track leading from the sensory organ to the brain. But, Münsterberg argued, sensationism could not account for the degree of vividness or clarity of particular ideas or the shading of value (*Wertnuance*) that accompanied them—for instance, their feeling-tone, the degree to which they were surprising, or the degree to which they seemed valid. Only by considering the motor portion of the sensory-motor arc, could the psychologist explain these phenomena.

Münsterberg based his argument on the principle that "every sensation and therefore every element of consciousness is associated with the process by which an incoming excitation is discharged in the cortical area." Its character depended on where and how it was discharged. If the tracks of a particular motor discharge lay open, for example as a result of training, then the sensation became vivid. If they were closed, it was inhibited. The vividness of an idea, therefore, depended on the strength of the discharge. Its value, at the same time, reflected the location of the discharge-track.[24]

It should be emphasized that Münsterberg derived his theory *a priori* and sought no confirmation for it in the facts of brain structure as they were known in 1900. He explicitly rejected the need for any histological or neurological investigations to confirm it.[25] He believed instead that his physiological speculations, which in fact reflected the same concern for

order and balance that characterized his system of knowledge, were theoretically necessary. The neatness of his formula was extraordinary: The
strength of the stimulus determined intensity, the location determined
quality; the strength of the discharge determined vividness, the location
determined value. This sort of reasoning, removed as it was from functional and practical issues, failed to strike a responsive chord among most
American psychologists. Yet it hid a concern for preconditioning and
preparation that brought it much closer to the American mainstream than
many of his contemporaries suspected.

The central tenet of American psychology was that action determined
perception and habit determined action. James had made habit critical to
his theories of attention and will. His student Edward Thorndike offered
the classic formulation of the problem in his law of effect, which held that
any act that produced satisfaction became associated with the circumstances under which it arose and was more likely to recur if those circumstances recurred. In other words, purposive behavior was a compounding
of learned reactions. Habits took the part in the mind formerly reserved
for will, and character-training became a question of habituation. John
Dewey made the point explicit in 1922. "Concrete habits," he wrote, "do
all the perceiving, recognizing, imagining, recalling, judging, conceiving
and reasoning that is done." In his view they constituted nothing less
than the self: "In any intelligible sense of the word will, they *are* will."[26]

Münsterberg had arrived at much the same point from a very different
perspective. Consciousness, he wrote in the *Grundzüge der Psychologie,*
was "just as dependent on the dispositions for action that are already
present as it is on the peripheral and associative input." By 1914, when he
published an American textbook, *Psychology: General and Applied,* he had
come to express himself in the language of pragmatism. "Our ideas," he
asserted, "are the product of our readiness to act." Like the mother who
slept through thunder, but who awoke when her child cried, we

> perceive the world just as far as we are prepared to react to it. *Our ability to
> respond is the true vehicle of our power to know,* and all training and habit
> formation in the sphere of our actions shape and stamp the perceptions and
> memories and thoughts in our mind.[27]

By this time Münsterberg was immersed in the application of psychology
to social issues. His Action Theory—that we perceive what we are prepared to act upon—informed his work in therapy, law, business, and
propaganda.

Unlike his American colleagues, Münsterberg insisted that the mind as
object and the world as cause were only mediated abstractions of reality.
"Modern philosophy, since the days of Fichte and Schopenhauer," he
wrote,

has never lost sight of this fundamental fact that the true reality of our life lies in our free creative will and that the thought forms in which this world of will appears as a causal universe are the creative evolution of the will itself.[28]

Yet this Fichtean vision of a free and creative will proved irrelevant: In stripping the "world of will" of the power to predict and control events, Münsterberg consigned it to oblivion.

Eight years after the appearance of his *Grundzüge,* Münsterberg outlined the contours of the world of will in his second major philosophical work, *Philosophie der Werte* (Philosophy of Values). It is not necessary to trace here the details of his argument, which modified Kantian Idealism along the lines of Windelband and Rickert. Suffice it to say that Münsterberg, in answer to those who asserted that values were relative, affirmed the absolute demands of the True, the Beautiful, the Good, and the Holy. But he did so in a way that only confirmed their relativity and reduced them to cultural norms. Specific truths—for example, Ptolemaic astronomy or Newtonian physics—varied with the historical situation. What was absolute was the process or form: the seeking of identity over time, as Münsterberg described it. In the same way, particular standards of beauty or morality depended on factors essentially social in nature. Only their form—respectively, the expression of "agreement" and the "realization" of historical function—remained constant from age to age.[29]

Münsterberg's position here was very close to Rickert's, for, like him, he finally reaffirmed what Georg Iggers has called "the German Idealistic faith in the meaningfulness of history and the validity of the diverse values to be found in history." As Rickert put it:

> A system of cultural values that lays claim to validity can be found only in meaningful historical life and can only gradually be elaborated *from* it by our asking what general and *formal* values underlie the substantive and constantly changing multiplicity of cultural life and its individual complexes of meaning as it manifests itself in history.[30]

In much the same way, Münsterberg also, in the name of absolute values, eliminated any substantive higher truth that transcended history or society; his value philosophy offered little more than a metaphysical, and indeed religious, gloss to the social organism.

Several years later, in *Psychology: General and Applied,* Münsterberg conducted another foray into the realm of values. In 1900 he had argued that psychology could only be a natural science, but by 1914 he had changed his mind. In his textbook he divided psychology into two branches. The first was "causal" psychology, a *Naturwissenschaft* in which the psychologist treated mind as object and the law of the conservation of energy was paramount. The Action Theory, of course, belonged to this branch. The second branch was "purposive" psychology, a *Geisteswissenschaft* in which the psychologist studied mind as subject, in which he understood it "as a system of meaning."

The purposive approach, as Münsterberg described it, was not only immediate and natural; it was "the most significant way of looking at man." Its central concept was the self—a consistent set of purposes—which was underlaid by a theoretical soul. Its task became to address the question, "How can we think of the self so as to understand every act as identical with other acts in the self?" In other words, the psychologist understood and appreciated the motives of another individual as consistent with that individual's personality. To return to the examples given earlier in this chapter, he understood "from the inside" the motives of Socrates or the criminal.[31]

Münsterberg made it clear that he was speaking of a rigorous scientific method and not some vague process of sympathy. "Purposive psychology," he wrote, "is not controlled by faith or imagination or intuition, but depends upon a thorough study and analysis of actual facts." What he had in mind, apparently, was very close to *Verstehen* or understanding, a process that Dilthey and Weber, among others, had promoted as the basic method of the *Geisteswissenschaften* in order to preserve for them a teleological core. For Weber it meant "the 'inner,' imaginative reproduction of the motive" behind an action; Dilthey described it as "the rediscovery of the I in the Thou." A person's own basic insight into himself allowed him to understand the motivations of others. But in Münsterberg's hands, despite his protestations, it degenerated into an amorphous and uncontrollable sort of empathy, with no possibility of confirmation. He suggested that laboratory work in purposive psychology in the near future would unveil the regularities of thought and emotion. But he offered not the slightest hint as to what the experiments would involve or how they could give insight into the "self" and the "soul." He apologized lamely, instead, "At present it would be a vain undertaking to present even in outline the facts of purposive psychology."[32]

Münsterberg was not alone in his understanding that "a psychology which is only an analysis of consciousness does not do justice to the value of personality." By the twentieth century, the concepts of purpose and personality had become increasingly prominent in psychology, even as the behaviorists expunged them. Mary Whiton Calkins, Münsterberg's student and friend, developed a psychology of the self early in the century; the English psychologist William McDougall, later Münsterberg's replacement at Harvard, expounded the importance of purpose and "instinct." The trend was even more pronounced in Germany, as William Stern, Oswald Külpe, and the early Gestalt psychologists emphasized the unity of perception, the holistic character of personality, and such nonele-mentary and purposive processes as insight. But Münsterberg differed from these men and women in an important respect: He radically sepa-rated the purposive from the causal, robbing the "self" of any real influ-ence. The "personality" operated in neither time nor space, and the principles of cause and effect did not apply to its actions. For this reason, he asserted, the individual ego was absolutely free and indeed immortal. But it was also impotent. "It would be entirely wrong," Münsterberg wrote, "to think that the soul is the cause of the movements of the body." "Nor have we a right," he continued, "to ask how one soul can become the cause for actions of another soul."[33]

The split between causative and purposive psychology recapitulated the battle, in Stern's words, between Münsterberg's two souls. Münster-berg completely failed to integrate the two psychologies, just as he failed to integrate so much of his own life. He could not find a meaningful place for purpose or an appreciation of personal goals in his causal and applied psychology, nor could he give the personality a part to play in the real world. When he came therefore to develop a psychotechnology—a psy-chology that served "cultural goals"—he ignored the purposive viewpoint, for only a causal psychology could predict or manipulate behavior.

When they bothered to discuss it, most Americans were critical of Münsterberg's philosophical work. He provided an important link be-tween Royce and the Sud-Baden neo-Kantians, but for the most part American philosophers found that his technical philosophy represented the sort of formalism in thinking against which, as Morton White has ar-gued, they were revolting.[34] His *a priori* methods and his architectonics of knowledge, his pigeonholing of the data of experience, and his habits of "making distinctions sharp, hard and fast," in Dewey's words, struck them as misguided.[35] The roots of his philosophy in Kant and Fichte seemed equally foreign. Münsterberg's discussion of a transcendental "Over-Soul" in *Philosophie der Werte* (and its English version *The Eternal Values*), and his insistence that the individual be completely absorbed into the purposes of the whole, suggested the world view of *Naturphilosophie,* despite his rejection of it in his science, and his work shared few concerns with the pragmatism of a Dewey. In psychology, however, Münsterberg's Action Theory, freed from the constraints of ex-plaining motive and purpose, resembled and even anticipated much of American theory.

Not the least of Münsterberg's problems was language. By the twenti-eth century he had a good command of idiomatic English, and, except where they showed signs of excessive haste, his essays on social questions on the whole read well. He never succeeded, however, in translating his philosophical ideas into adequate English. His *Psychology and Life,* a preliminary sketch of the main themes of his *Grundzüge,* was virtually unreadable and prompted James to observe that "his English *qua* English is pretty fearful." *Eternal Values* was almost as obscure, for in it Münsterberg transferred the complicated syntax and sentence structure of German directly into English. Only at the most popular level—in inspirational talks to students and social clubs on eternal values and immortality—did Münsterberg achieve much success, but here the process of over-simplification stripped his thought of any philosophical value.[36]

Münsterberg's difficulties in English and the failure of his philosophical work in America led him to assume a literary "double personality," as he described it. Following a scathing attack in *Mind* by James's British friend, F. C. S. Schiller, on his use of English in *Psychology and Life,* Münsterberg pronounced that in the future he would publish his scholarly work solely in German. In English he would write only popular essays on social themes.[37] Positing this double personality helped Münsterberg rationalize, both to Americans and himself, his lack of success as a scholar in the New World. But it was as much a conceit as a reflection of fact, for Münsterberg failed to live up to his intentions. Despite his earlier protestations, he began work on an English translation of *Grundzüge der Psychologie* four years after its appearance.[38] This project was never completed, but he did publish an English version of *Philosophie der Werte* in 1909. The conceit, nevertheless, pointed to a psychological truth. By the first decade of the century, Münsterberg considered himself to be a productive German scholar in an alien environment.

Cultural Diplomacy (1900–1908)

In his poetry Münsterberg occasionally set up a dichotomy between the scholar's cramped garret and the grand field of action of men of affairs. Yet his dichotomy was as misleading as his claim to a dual literary personality. He in fact never considered the roles to be mutually exclusive, at least not outside his poetry. Early in his life, as he wrote Eliot in 1908, he took as models men like Virchow, Haeckel, and Adolf Harnack, "men who divided their efforts between scholarship and public affairs." "The ideal of my life," he asserted, "has been Leibnitz, whose work belonged equally to psychology, philosophy, international politics and international academic administration." (He did not mention, however, that he regarded these concerns as serving the interests of "German cultural world power.")[1] His years in America offered him the opportunity to pursue this ambition.

As German rivalry with Great Britain increased during the turn-of-the-century years, the Kaiser and his government cultivated friendly relations with the United States. One of the Reich's more potent weapons, at least in the minds of some, was the prestige of its *Wissenschaft,* which had done so much to shape the nature of American scholarship and the American university. Responsibility for the export of *Wissenschaft* fell to the Prussian Ministry of Education, and by the twentieth century the famous head of its division on higher education, Friedrich Althoff, actively promoted a *Kulturpolitik* in America. Münsterberg joined enthusiastically in Althoff's cultural offensive and occasionally dabbled in more exclusively political concerns. He sought, in the words of the historian Alfred Vagts, "to harmonize the imperial rivalry of Germany and America," and he soon became a spokesman in America for "Wilhelmian *Gelehrten-Nation-alliberalismus.*"[2]

Münsterberg came to see his position at Harvard as that of a semiofficial ambassador from Germany to American academia, and, unlike his colleague Kuno Francke, he never considered naturalizing as an American. In the decade after his return in 1897, he participated in an array of cultural events, including Prince Henry's reception at Harvard in 1902, the International Congress of Arts and Science at St. Louis in 1904, and the Harvard-Berlin exchange professorship begun in 1905—all of which were meant to increase the prestige of *Kultur.* His activities won him several medals from the Kaiser, and Adolf Harnack, Wilhelm's favorite academic and a leading architect of Germany's cultural diplomacy, hailed him in 1908 as "the true 'pontifex' between both countries."[3] But the conflicts within Münsterberg in his triple role of scientist, professor, and cultural ambassador led to increasing difficulties at Harvard, and his persistent "Germanism" in style and accent isolated him from the generally Anglophile Cambridge academic community. His resulting sense of estrangement was to color the rest of his career in America.

Half of Münsterberg's life's task, as he defined it, involved promoting American virtues to a somewhat skeptical German public. Beginning with an 1893 article on the Chicago Fair in Berlin's *Vossische Zeitung,* he published countless essays in the German press in which he explicated America's confusing politics and defended its genuine dedication to transcendental ideals. His major effort in interpreting American culture for Germany was his two-volume work, *Die Amerikaner,* published in 1904. This study, which went through four editions in eight years, proved a success in Germany and remains Münsterberg's best-known book. In it he attempted what he called an exercise in social psychology, tracing American ideals of "self-direction," "self-initiative," "self-perfection," and "self-assertion" back to their historical roots in Puritanism and the frontier experience. He hoped to show the German reader that so much of what he saw in the New World as self-interested—for instance, a blatant interest in making money, corruption in politics, and utilitarianism in philosophy—actually expressed a historically valid commitment to ideals of self-expression and self-fulfillment.[4]

In *Die Amerikaner* Münsterberg frankly tailored his message to achieve an effect on his audience, and he produce a work very different in tone from *American Traits.* "What I write in Germany to counteract the prejudices against American," Münsterberg wrote in *American Traits,* "would sound on American soil like cheap flattery."[5] The "truth" of his study, instead, lay not so much in its fidelity to the whole of American life as in its ability to move its German readers in a proper direction and to lay the groundwork for a grand Teutonic alliance between German efficiency and idealism and American energy. This approach might seem strange from a man who spoke of absolute verities and attacked the American pragmatists for their relativistic view of truth, but it proved consistent with his later views on propaganda.

The more important half of Münsterberg's life's task, however, was to promote German culture and Germany in America, among both German-Americans and the public at large. He announced his availability for this project early. He met Friedrich Schmidt-Ott, a civil servant in the Prussian Ministry of Education, at the Chicago World's Fair of 1893, and the following year he sent Schmidt an article on America that he had written for a German-American newspaper. In 1895 he helped raise money in the United States for a memorial to Helmholtz, who had died shortly after returning to Germany from the fair.[6] Two years later, after finally committing himself to Harvard, Münsterberg cultivated a friendship with the German ambassador in Washington, Edmund von Holleben, another enthusiastic advocate of *Kulturpolitik,* who had described scholarship to the German Foreign Office as "almost the only sure way left to us on this side of the water gradually to bridge over the opposition." Holleben readily accepted Münsterberg's friendship, and he wrote optimistically back home that the Harvard professor would prove to be "a good lever" for influencing American votes.[7]

Over the years Münsterberg assisted Holleben in his efforts to raise the prestige of German culture in American society and especially in its universities. Following the first meeting of the two men, Münsterberg published several articles calling for mutual understanding between Germans and Americans;[8] he wrote speeches for the ambassador on a number of occasions; and he advised him on the academic and German-American communities in the United States. Münsterberg also provided Holleben an entree into the world of American academia, and he lobbied hard to persuade Harvard to grant him an honorary degree. When his efforts failed in 1899 and a degree went instead to the French ambassador Jules Cambon, Münsterberg warned Eliot that Holleben had received a serious rebuke that would probably lead to his recall. Holleben survived, however, and two years later he received the degree for which Münsterberg had worked so hard.[9]

Münsterberg also introduced Holleben to his German-born and educated colleague, Kuno Francke, whose own life's work had become to communicate the values of German art and literature to America and especially German-America. Toward this end, Francke had since 1896 been working to establish a Germanic museum at Harvard, which, he suggested to a German audience, would permit a merger of German and American culture and promote a "great pan-Germanic union, on which the continued efficiency of the Teutonic race depends in the struggle for world supremacy." One of the major purposes of the museum was to reinspire Boston's and America's German-American community in the ideals of *Kultur*.[10] The Foreign Office and the embassy had on the whole little respect for that community, and they considered its members, in Münsterberg's words, "below the level of the average German at home."[11] Such a museum, coupled with German-American cultural events, exhibits of German art, and occasional visits of German dignitaries, might lead the wayward back to an appreciation of the Fatherland. Holleben, Francke, and Münsterberg successfully attracted the interest of the German government and secured the aid of the Kaiser. Wilhelm donated a set of plaster reproductions of German art, illustrating "the cultural development of the German race,"[12] and he named his brother, Prince Henry, to present them officially during his visit to Harvard in the spring of 1902.

The Kaiser had conceived Henry's tour of America as a grand public relations gesture that would allay the growing American hostility toward Germany after the Spanish-American War. One of Henry's stops was to be Harvard, and before his arrival Münsterberg offered Eliot his views on the sort of reception that would be appropriate for a German prince. Münsterberg's initial program called for the granting of an honorary degree before cheering students in Memorial Hall. A second version was more elaborate:

> 1.20 Memorial Hall. Sanders Theatre. The hall is filled when the prince arrives. The centre of the balcony for ladies and so in the second balcony; the whole wings of the first and second gallery for the senior class and graduate schools. The floor taken by the Boston Symphony Orchestra . . . .
> 2 o'clock. The lower college classes form an espalier from Memorial Hall to the Faculty Building; the President and the prince walk with the professors in procession to the Faculty room through the rows of students.

Eliot, who was reluctant to receive the prince at all, must have gagged at these plans, and years later he admitted that he questioned the wisdom of Münsterberg's actions and in fact distrusted his role in the whole affair.[13] These feelings resurfaced, strengthened, in a few years.

In the end, Harvard received the prince with considerable ceremony. He arrived in a triumphant procession of carriages from Boston; he was granted an honorary degree in Memorial Hall, the first time in seventy years that the university had bestowed such an honor other than at the June commencement; and he turned over photographs of the Kaiser's gifts to Harvard at a special ceremony in Münsterberg's home.[14] But the whole affair was markedly less grandiose than Münsterberg had hoped. The low-key protocol of the degree-granting ceremony, for most of which Eliot and the prince remained seated, reflected Eliot's concern about the propriety of "this democratic University" honoring a foreign prince. Eliot also took the opportunity of a banquet speech in Boston to lecture Henry on the virtues of democracy, pluralism, and self-government. Moreover, in granting the degree, he introduced the German prince with a reference to Queen Victoria as a friend of America. "The grandson of that illustrious woman is sitting with us here," he concluded. It was a backhanded compliment to the representative of England's major political rival.[15]

The prince's visit to Harvard and America as a whole was not a resounding success. "American opinion almost unanimously, upon the departure of the Prince, regarded his mission as 'futile.' " Local satirists had a field day with the pomp that attended the tour, which was marred by several gaffes. A minor scandal developed over the question of whether the Kaiser's new yacht, commissioned in New York, had been christened with French champagne. And Henry's attempt to give the American government a statue of Frederick the Great threatened to burden the Republican administration with a symbol of militarism. In a German essay, however, Münsterberg exulted that "Prince Henry came and saw and conquered."[16] The claim to be sure was a self-serving one, but it also reflected Münsterberg's assessment of the visit and exhibited his distance from the environment in which he lived. He had failed, furthermore, to recognize how his activities excited the "distrust" of Eliot and others. That distrust would have been much greater had they realized the extent of his diplomatic maneuvering.

In the months that followed Prince Henry's departure, an international incident long brewing in South America came to a head. For several years Venezuela had failed to pay back debts to European nationals, and Americans from Roosevelt on down feared that the English, and especially the Germans, might use this as an excuse to extend their influence in Latin America. Holleben, with the encouragement of Münsterberg, who by this time recognized the extent of anti-German sentiment in the United States, recommended caution to Berlin. In December 1902, however, Germany, England, and Italy blockaded Venezuela, and early the next year the Germans bombarded a Venezuelan village and fort. Popular hostilities ran high in both the United States and Germany, as American politicians hauled out the ancient Monroe Doctrine. The American press joined the chorus, attacking the shelling as a "wantonly reckless act." By spring the Kaiser had backed down, apparently before vigorous threats from Roosevelt, and agreed to submit the question to arbitration. But for a short period the crisis was real.[17]

In the midst of the affair, the German Foreign Office replaced Münsterberg's friend Holleben with Speck von Sternburg. To bridge the interregnum, Münsterberg sent a lengthy report to the Kaiser describing the political mood of America and the views of his acquaintance Theodore Roosevelt. On the basis of a long private conversation with Roosevelt, Münsterberg assured Wilhelm II—completely inaccurately—that the American president had no worries about German intentions in Latin America. Roosevelt, Münsterberg reported, recognized that the Monroe Doctrine was "no rigid dogma" and he looked forward to imperial cooperation between the United States, Germany, and Great Britain. As Münsterberg saw it, this cooperation would lead within three to five years to the demise of the Monroe Doctrine, America's annexation of Canada, and Germany's "winning" of South America.[18]

Münsterberg wrote that only the defeat of Roosevelt in the 1904 elections could forestall such a development. But the German-Americans, especially in the West, unfortunately failed to recognize how much their interests coincided with Roosevelt's policies. "Very silly of the Germans," the Kaiser wrote in the margin. Münsterberg therefore offered to work in America for Roosevelt's reelection ("We will of course also work here to the same end!" Wilhelm noted). And, in case of Roosevelt's defeat, Münsterberg claimed to have set in motion a plan that would preserve his national prominence: Behind the scenes he was paving the way for Roosevelt's assumption of the Harvard presidency after Eliot's retirement.[19]

Münsterberg also emphasized his own loyalty and willingness to serve:

> I am . . . sure that I cannot make more effective the trust with which the leading men in politics, intellectual life, and business honor me than by placing everything unreservedly, as in these lines, in the service of your Majesty.

"Bravo," Wilhelm wrote. Münsterberg continued, referring to defenses of the United States that he had made in the German press:

> However much I seem to work for the honor of America, in truth my actions remain at every moment in service of my Fatherland; and if I apparently broadcast America's praise too loudly in Germany, that is only because I know that Germany's success would be that much greater, the less it underestimates its American rivals.[20]

The new ambassador Sternburg, who was a friend of Roosevelt, threw a damper on Münsterberg's plans. Roosevelt's adherence to the Monroe Doctrine, he assured the German government, was as firm as it had ever been. He attributed Münsterberg's report "to the pursuit of selfish goals on the part of the German professor," and he doubted that Roosevelt ever made the alleged remarks. Others in the Foreign Office, which generally was skeptical of such forays by professors into politics, were more charitable. They suspected that Roosevelt was using Münsterberg to gain votes in the forthcoming election. Whichever the case, the Foreign Office chose to ignore Münsterberg's offer of aid and returned only a formal letter of acknowledgement. Almost at the same time, Roosevelt politely rejected Münsterberg's suggestion that he attend a gala German-American theatrical performance in New York. During a period of tension between Germany and America, the Germans-for-Roosevelt movement that Münsterberg anticipated could not tempt the President.[21]

As if these rebuffs to his politicking were not enough, Münsterberg also paid a price in rumors. He made no secret of his close relations with Holleben and he was generally known in Washington political circles as an advisor to the ambassador. At least some newspapers interpreted Holleben's summary recall in 1902 as an indirect rebuke to Münsterberg. More serious, rumors occasionally cropped up, apparently first in 1901, that Münsterberg was a German "spy." He had been sent to the United States at the direct request of the Kaiser "to blind public opinion to the true policy of Germany toward the United States," asserted an American in Berlin in a letter to the *New York American*. On Münsterberg's arrival in the United States, the correspondent claimed, he and Holleben had established a "far-reaching spy system." In the same vein, Emil Witte, a notoriously unreliable press agent formerly attached to the German Embassy in Washington, circulated and finally published the claim that Münsterberg received five thousand dollars a year from Berlin for his propaganda activities. Münsterberg denied the charges, which were untrue, but his tendency to trumpet his own importance, his predilection for dabbling in politics, and his ties to figures within the German government lent them credibility.[22]

Only a few months after the prince's departure, Münsterberg began work on a project that was in some respects the high point of his career: the International Congress of Arts and Science, which was held in St. Louis in conjunction with the Louisiana Purchase Exposition of 1904. The idea of a scholarly congress tied to the St. Louis Fair apparently began with William Rainey Harper, president of the University of Chicago. It soon became popular among American university leaders, who hoped to gain recognition for their nation's scholarship. Scholarly congresses had accompanied each of the recent nineteenth-century fairs, but the American version would be the biggest and best, surpassing all others in its scope and organization. In the fall of 1902, the task of devising a plan fell to an advisory board that included Harper, Columbia's president

Nicholas Murray Butler, and Frederick Holls, a German-born diplomat who had recently served as an American emissary to the Hague Peace Conference and to whom Münsterberg had dedicated his *American Traits*.[23]

The board soon farmed out the planning to Münsterberg, who entered the affair at Holl's suggestion, and Chicago's sociologist, Albion Small, both of whom were to draw up schemes of organization for its consideration. The outlines submitted by the two men illustrated the distance between Münsterberg's thinking and the main tendencies of thought in America. Münsterberg based his scheme on the demands of logic, dividing the topics of discussion at the conference into the same categories that he had outlined in *Grundzüge der Psychologie:* the Normative, Historical, Physical, and Mental. Small assumed *"that human interests not logical categories make the world,"* and among his groupings were the Promotion of Health, Production of Wealth, and Harmonization of Human Relations.[24] The two plans, however, shared an outline that transcended their "idealist" and "pragmatist" forms, for they reflected a commitment to the unity of knowledge and a distress at its fragmentation in the nineteenth century. Both offered arbitrary schemes for connection and unity; both attempted to force the specialist to connect his work to higher principles; both sought an organizing principle for knowledge in which every item had a niche and played its part in the fulfillment of the whole. Münsterberg and Small, in different ways, attempted to construct bureaucracies of knowledge; each man hoped to eliminate the accidental, the irrational, and the unpredictable. When pragmatists like Dewey criticized Münsterberg's plan, they did so not because it sought a unified system of knowledge but, rather, because it used *a priori* logical categories instead of the needs of mankind as organizing principles.[25]

Throughout the winter the Committee on Plan and Scope, to which Münsterberg and Small by then belonged, debated the virtues of the alternatives. Münsterberg asserted that his plan was essential for ensuring European participation. Small's scheme, he claimed, undermined his long-term attempts to correct the Europeans' impression that American science was excessively practical-minded, and, he warned, if it were adopted, he would be forced to resign from the planning committee. By spring his entreaties had won over the committee chairman Simon Newcomb, and the acceptance of his plan was assured. Münsterberg and Small, who by then had conceded, were elevated to vice-presidencies of the congress and in the year that followed they joined Newcomb in its promotion.[26]

With the aid of colleagues, the three drew up a list of approximately three hundred speakers, including slightly more than one hundred foreigners, and they devoted the summer of 1903 to recruitment efforts in Europe. The initial response encouraged them, but, as the congress date of September 1904 neared, problems mounted. Any attempt to put together an academic all-star team creates difficulties, and the International Congress of Arts and Science had its share. Well over half of the original foreign guest list was German-speaking, and many Germans viewed the predominance of their representatives as a vindication of German scholarship and of the German nation. The French objected. In mid-March, six months before the opening of the congress, they threatened to withdraw all their delegates unless the committee increased French representation to match the German. Newcomb successfully defused the "French bombshell" only when he granted the French permission to fill available vacancies with any scholars whom they deemed appropriate.[27]

The rate of refusals and cancellations by speakers in the meantime was running high. The sea voyage to the New World was long and the heat of St. Louis in September uninviting. Helmholtz had died shortly after his return from the Chicago World's Fair in 1893; older scholars and those in bad health did not relish repeating his experience. The German government as a result found it necessary to encourage participation as a patriotic duty. Even so, by August withdrawals were coming in at twice the rate that the organizing committee had expected. Newcomb observed to Münsterberg: "I doubt whether any plague recorded in history ever attacked the population of a city in such proportion as sickness has attacked our foreign speakers."[28]

Given these problems, as well as the inevitable logistical difficulties associated with an undertaking of the dimensions of the congress, the affair came off remarkably well. According to the historian A. W. Coates, it represented the coming of age of American scholarship; George Haines and Frederick Jackson called it "one of the most unique gatherings of scholars and scientists in modern history." The impressive list of speakers included James Bryce, Henri Poincaré, Ernest Rutherford, Woodrow Wilson, and Wilhelm Windelband. Max Weber, recently recovered from a prolonged nervous breakdown, gave his first public lecture in six and one-half years at it. The ten-volume work that collected the nearly three hundred speeches given in the conference, in the words of Coates, still conveys "a vivid impression of the vigor and complexity of early twentieth-century scholarship."[29]

The congress nevertheless failed as an advertisement for American scholarship. Despite generous public testimonials by participants and nebulous claims of friendships formed and ties made, German scholars did not come away on the whole impressed by America's commitment to culture. When Münsterberg attempted to attract scholars to an international psychological conference in Boston six years later, he recognized the bad impressions St. Louis had left. To a philosopher who had been there, he wrote, "I only ask you not to let yourself be influenced by the disagreeableness of your first American trip when you consider an American congress of this sort."[30]

Particularly galling to German visitors was the sparse attendance at almost all the speeches given by foreigners. Kuno Francke, who headed the section on German literary history, had a particularly unhappy experience, his account of which deserves to be quoted. His section, he remembered, had been assigned to one of the conference's largest halls, much larger, for instance, than the small room allotted to Bryce. As he neared the conference room with his two distinguished Austrian guests, the silence made him nervous.

> I tried to persuade myself that the public was probably already completely assembled in the hall. What happened when, as the door was opened and we stared at a completely empty room, can only be compared to a mine explosion, and can be fully appreciated only by those who have personal knowledge of the explosive power of both Austrians. After some time, we started again on our way to the speaker's platform, took our places on it, and waited. After several minutes we could hear something at the entrance. I thought, now the audience is going to come streaming in. The door opened and there appeared—a photographer, commissioned to immortalize the opening of the German literature section of the International Congress of Arts and Science of the World's Fair for the St. Louis evening paper.[31]

Münsterberg had in fact anticipated most of these difficulties. As early as the fall of 1902, he expressed the wish that the whole thing would never develop. He questioned the value of cultural extravaganzas in promoting scientific relations and he warned of the notorious vanity of the German professor, especially the Berliner, whose self-importance did not make him a good ambassador (a reflection he did not turn upon himself). He recognized the disastrous results that low attendance would have, and he campaigned vigorously in the summer of 1904 against Newcomb's plan to send out only a limited number of special invitations.[32] Münsterberg's doubts were often justified, but the most interesting thing about them was the extent to which they reflected his own difficulties in America: One of the more curious aspects of Münsterberg's life was his inability to follow his own advice—or even to see that it applied to him.

In the case of St. Louis, Münsterberg's compulsive sense of duty and his personal ambitions had impelled him to the forefront of an organization about which he repeatedly expressed reservations. "Since the money is ready," he wrote Cattell, "something will be done and I am anxious that it is at least something in the noble style."[33] An affair like the congress, he assumed, would not be done right without his efforts, but after contributing those efforts he could and did blame the congress's difficulties on its failure to adhere strictly to his recommendations. At the same time, however, his participation ensured for him a continued hand in academic politics and he could associate himself with any public acclaim his projects might receive. Over the years this pattern led to unfortunate results.

Whatever its difficulties, the International Congress did confirm the prestige of German scholarship. Of the 106 foreign speakers, 41 were German, compared with 21 English and 17 French, even after Newcomb's concession to French demands. And it was a German scholar, Münsterberg, who had devised the congress's scheme of organization and had done as much as anyone to promote it. William James could write of the affair, "To me the whole Münsterbergian Circus seems a case of the pure love of schematization running mad." But in Germany Max Dessoir criticized the event while praising its organizer. "The result . . . ," he wrote in 1918, "did not fully correspond to the expectations; only the framework of the congress, as I can testify, was admired in sincerity by most of the participants." In the spring of 1905, no doubt partially in recognition of his services at St. Louis, the Prussian Ministry of Education offered their man in Cambridge an *Ordinarius* in philosophy at Königsberg.[34]

Here at last was the long-desired full professorship. Königsberg, a small provincial university in East Prussia, was certainly no Berlin, but the chair had been Kant's. Several German friends advised Münsterberg to take the position, including Heinrich Rickert, who telegraphed, "Accept in the name of German science." Münsterberg did accept, but, won over by Royce, Cattell, Francke, and others, he retracted two weeks later. In 1916 he recalled Royce's advice that "others might fill that German chair . . . but here I was needed for more than mere professional work." The future of Idealism in America depended upon him; it was his higher duty to stand by his Harvard post.[35]

The explanation that Münsterberg offered to Althoff, the "enlightened despot" of the Prussian university system, however, was considerably different:

> My intention of accepting Königsberg arouses a strong ill feeling here, because the acceptance of a small university gives the impression of a disparagement of Harvard. Must unfortunately therefore in the interest of German-American relations take back the conditional acceptance.

A month later the Heidelberg philosopher Paul Hensel offered his congratulations to Münsterberg on his decision to remain in America. Hensel correctly perceived the logic of Münsterberg's choice:

> Here [in Germany] you would once again have had to accustom yourself to the conditions of a small German university, and these conditions would offer nothing to a man who enjoys the incomparably grander conditions—scientifically, socially, and also politically—where you are, and in which you have worked.

Acceptance of the Königsberg offer would have meant consignment to political and perhaps academic oblivion. For the same reason, no doubt, Münsterberg discouraged probes by Althoff about positions at Breslau and Göttingen, although he left no doubt at the time that he would have accepted a professorship in Berlin.[36]

Münsterberg's public and, one suspects, private view of his decision to remain at Harvard tells much of his attitude toward work, duty, and self-sacrifice. His position at Harvard, at least in 1905, was advantageous for him and, as Hensel pointed out, preferable to an appointment at Königsberg. Yet, both to his American colleagues and to Althoff, he couched his decision for Harvard in terms of self-sacrifice, as if it went against his personal wishes and inclinations, as if he had made it out of a sense of duty. For Münsterberg, all life was duty and service, both for himself and for others, but he had neither the confidence nor the self-awareness to acknowledge how entwined his duty, as he perceived it, was with his own interest. This gap in personal perception reflected a general gap in social perception, for he also did not understand the extent to which his version of social order and absolute values reflected his interests first as a German and then as an American academic.

Münsterberg in the meantime was proving himself a sometimes difficult member of the Harvard faculty. He became the center of a minor controversy in 1901 when the university offered him an honorary A.M. As a holder of an earned Ph.D., Münsterberg considered the award below his station. The complaint had some justice—he was apparently the first Ph.D. to receive the A.M. instead of the more honorific L.L.D.—but his reaction was out of proportion to the unintended slight. "I feel this," he wrote Eliot, "as if all my work here was in vain." When, to avoid a public issue, he went ahead and accepted the honor, James consoled him with the observation that the academic value of the degree was its least important feature. What it meant was that he had been made "*son* of the family" (a distinction that James himself, to his regret, had not attained, since he did not consider his Harvard M.D. a sufficient pedigree).[37]

Despite this consolatory note, relations between James and Münsterberg had been cooling. Münsterberg dedicated his *Grundzüge der Psychologie* to James in 1900, but their philosophical differences were becoming increasingly obvious. James advocated a pluralism that made room for spontaneity, Münsterberg a deterministic monism. More important, how-

Münsterberg and students in his Freiburg laboratory in about 1891. Münsterberg is seated in the center; the American psychologist Edmund Delabarre is second from the left. Courtesy of Harvard University Archives.

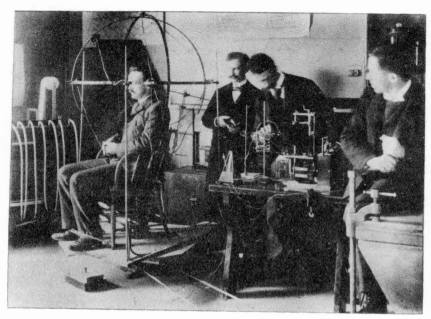

An experiment on the effects of dizziness on the localization of sound in the Harvard Psychology Laboratory in about 1892. From Hugo Münsterberg, "Psychological Laboratory of Harvard University" (Cambridge, Mass.: Harvard University Press, 1893), which accompanied an exhibit at the Chicago World's Fair in 1893.

A profile of Münsterberg in Every Week, *May 8, 1916. By courtesy of New York Public Library.*

LITTLE Hugo Münsterberg looks weary in this picture. "I was a great reader at four years of age," says the psychologist. "At four years also I began playing the piano, but gave it up at nine for the violoncello." His literary and musical habits established, he early plunged into the business of applying psychology to the problems of every-day life. For example, he invented the dread sphygometer. They bind it round your arm and ask you questions. As long as you tell the truth, the sphygo behaves quietly. But start to fabricate, and up shoots the indicator to 140! The doctor will tackle any problem and solve it by psychology.

Puck *introduces Münsterberg to Truth shortly before his death. From* Puck *80 (November 25, 1916): 15.*

Münsterberg interviewing movie actress Anita Stewart in 1915. From Hugo Münsterberg, "Why We Go to the Movies," Cosmopolitan *60 (December 1915): 23.*

ever, were less philosophical issues. James was particularly sensitive to Münsterberg's repeated attacks on spiritualism, for instance in an 1899 article in *Atlantic*. To his friend and fellow psychic researcher, H. N. Gardner, James wrote that he intended to decline all further *a priori* discussion of the question and "so leave M's rot lying in the gutter to decay with similar garbage." Not one to mince his words, when Münsterberg wrote him in the fall of 1899 for aid in censuring F. C. S. Schiller, who had publicly ridiculed Münsterberg's work on spiritualism, an extremely ill James commented, "Your mysticism article, to speak with perfect candour, seems to me a monumentally foolish performance . . . and I think it was a great compliment that he [Schiller] should have discussed your paper at all."[38]

Münsterberg's enthusiastic promotion of higher education and his pursuit of honors and awards also annoyed James, who had declared himself an enemy of the "Ph.D. octopus." In the summer of 1901, James wrote his younger colleague:

> The greediness of the Germans for titles of distinction—the whole *Rath*-business, e.g., conferred by majesty, seems very non-democratic to an American, and quite like the English knighthood, which is so paltry a thing. But the french are almost as bad, and we are making a beginning *with our* Ph.D.[39]

This remark, coming shortly after Harvard granted honorary degrees to Münsterberg and Holleben, must have displeased a man whose commitment to "the whole *Rath*-business" was unbounded.

At the end of 1905, the growing coolness between the two men broke into an open confrontation over the dedication ceremonies of the Philosophy Division's Emerson Hall. For several years Münsterberg had campaigned for a new home for the division that could house its philosophical and psychological wings in comfort. His efforts finally culminated in the completion of Emerson Hall in 1905; as chairman of the division, and at the suggestion of Eliot and Palmer, he presided over the dedication of the new building in December. From the beginning James had doubts about the project, and he took Münsterberg's participation in the ceremony as another example of his colleague's vanity and self-importance. Afterwards he wrote Münsterberg, criticizing his lengthy speechifying and suggesting that it was inappropriate for a German to take such a prominent part in an American assembly. Eliot, acting as mediator and attempting to mollify James, underlined the extent to which Münsterberg's Germanisms were alien to the community. "Of course Münsterberg has a German way of doing things," he wrote.

> For instance, his introduction of me on that occasion would have been absolutely impossible for any born Yankee, and it grated on the ears of all the

Yankees. But when you recommended Münsterberg for an appointment here you must have expected that he would be different from us.

In the heat of controversy, Münsterberg submitted his resignation as division chairman. The crisis blew over in the short run, but James and Münsterberg were never again on close terms. A few years later Münsterberg wrote Eliot that the incident totally changed his attitude toward the Harvard community.[40]

Not long after the Emerson Hall affair, a series of controversial events threw Münsterberg into the public spotlight. It was as if he sought among the public the appreciative audience that he had found lacking at Harvard. In the summer of 1906 he became embroiled in a Chicago murder controversy in which he had suggested from a distance that the accused had made a false confession. The following spring he caused a sensation when, as invited representative of Germany, he defended the German draft and militarism at Andrew Carnegie's National Arbitration and Peace Congress in New York. No sooner had the controversy died down than he appeared once again in the headlines, this time because of his involvement in the murder trial of the radical labor leader, Big Bill Haywood. Popular articles on psychology, in the meantime, were beginning to appear with increasing frequency under his name in such muckraking journals as *McClure's* and *Cosmopolitan.*

Münsterberg's public activities made Eliot and his Harvard colleagues uneasy, but it was his continued work in German-American cultural politics that led to a serious break with the Harvard administration. The first indication of difficulties occurred in the spring of 1908. Münsterberg had been soliciting funds from regular Harvard donors to set up a German-American student exchange program. Eliot saw little benefit to Harvard in the project and grew increasingly annoyed as he learned of Münsterberg's role as a cultural entrepreneur. In April he sent off a sharp reprimand, ordering Münsterberg to cease his solicitations.[41] In the following fall Eliot's annoyance, this time over Münsterberg's part in the Harvard-Berlin exchange professorship, blossomed into undisguised hostility.

The exchange program was originally the idea of several visiting German professors at the St. Louis Congress, and it took shape primarily through the work of Francke and Althoff. Beginning in 1905, a scholar from Harvard taught a semester at Berlin and a German—generally not from Berlin—taught at Harvard. The following year Columbia set up a competing exchange with Berlin under similar arrangements, and soon the exchanges became a pet concern of the emperor. Both he and Althoff considered them cornerstones of *Kulturpolitik.*[42]

Münsterberg publicly supported the Harvard program, and he served as Harvard's representative in Berlin for the year 1910–11. Privately he took credit for its existence. But from the first he had for very good reasons been skeptical of the arrangements. He recognized that many German professors would find Harvard undergraduate course work too elementary, and he appreciated the dangers of mixing diplomatic and scientific missions. He was also unhappy with the work of some of the individuals involved. As an unofficial consultant to Althoff and Friedrich Schmidt, also in the Prussian ministry, he sent back unfavorable reports on several of the Germans at Harvard. And he made known his dissatisfaction with the performance of certain Americans in Berlin.[43]

In Eliot's mind the benefits of the program outweighed its drawbacks, and he lent it his wholehearted support. He had little patience with Münsterberg's negativism, which, he worried, was being taken as the official position at Harvard. The final straw was an article of 1908 by Münsterberg, in which he mentioned that the German exchange professor Eugen Kühnemann lectured before only twenty students at Harvard. Eliot expressed his irritation first in a private conference and then in writing. "For three years," he wrote Münsterberg in November 1908, "I have received clear indications from Germany that such influence as you exerted there was adverse to the continuance of the present arrangement." He continued with a clear-cut rebuke:

> I wish to tell you, and to leave on record in writing, that I believe your influence on the whole subject has been injurious to the exchange, and therefore to the promotion of cordial relations between the men of letters and science in the two countries.[44]

The charge devastated a man who considered the promotion of "cordial relations" to be his life's task. Münsterberg's distress became greater when, a week later, he received a more official communication from Eliot, who in the meantime had brought the matter up before the Harvard Corporation. "What I wish, and what the Corporation wish," Eliot wrote,

> is that you should give over your efforts as a special agent or advisor of German authorities about American affairs, or of American authorities about German affairs; that you should limit your activities to your professional and literary work, and trust your influence and your reputation to your teaching, the conduct of your laboratory, and your published writings. They would be relieved if you ceased to communicate on your own initiative with German officials—high or low—or with American officials—high or low—concerning the affairs of Harvard University. In academic life on this side of the water we are wholly unused to such activities with political officials as you seem to find your most interesting functions. . . . Therefore, we should be glad to have you alter your conception of "the one great task for which I stayed in this country," as stated in your last letter.[45]

A good civil servant, Münsterberg acceded to Eliot's order, but not without a barb at what he considered Harvard's demand for conformity. "I acknowledge fully," he wrote, "the right of my employers to demand from me a line of action in harmony with their own views." But he suggested that Eliot's version of the facts was incorrect. No one had done more to promote the present level of international exchange than he. None of the programs, whether at Harvard, Columbia, or elsewhere, could have existed "without the political pressure of which I made use." Moreover, Münsterberg asserted,

> if the history of the relations of America to the European continent shall ever be written from true sources of which many are not yet accessible, it will be clearly recognized how much of it which seemed to grow of itself was due to my systematic labor and organization. I have all the material at hand and I know that history will do me justice.[46]

Münsterberg's extraordinary combination of defensiveness in these letters reflected the degree to which Eliot's rebuke affected him. He had always had a high opinion of his own worth, yet he had never approached such a level of self-importance. In his own mind, he had taken up his role as *Kulturpolitiker* to serve the true interests of Harvard, as well as those of international harmony. The overwhelming sense of duty that he had inherited from his childhood, where his purpose in life had been to bring glory to the name of his father, transferred itself to Harvard and to the man who in his mind incarnated its ideals, Charles Eliot. His offerings, however, had been rejected and his motives impugned.

The affair especially disturbed Münsterberg because he interpreted it as an attack on him as a foreigner and a German. It complemented his philosophical isolation and confirmed his general estrangement from the American academic environment. But by this time—driven in part by his difficulties—he was already carving out a broader station for himself in American society. In 1908 he was well into a second career that was to make him the best-known psychologist in America.

Psychologies of
Measurement

"We live in the day of the scientist and the expert," Münsterberg wrote in 1916, "and he who closes his ears to their advice will never dig the finest potatoes from his acre." It was a position that Münsterberg had championed for more than a decade, and it expressed a familiar sentiment in Progressive America. A truism of the period, after all, was that scientific intelligence (and the intelligent) had to replace America's tradition of laissez-faire and order the social, political, and economic structure according to principles of efficiency. Münsterberg joined a growing chorus when he elevated the specialized expert, whom in *American Traits* he had called the "pride of Germany," to the forefront of those who served social progress and order.[1] Specialists in psychology, law, economics, medicine, and the other newly emerging social sciences agreed that conscious, rational planning offered an antidote to what Herbert Croly called "the great American drift."

Nineteenth-century developments, appearing first in Germany, made possible the systematic application of science to social ends. Long before 1900 a complicated and symbiotic network between the universities, the state, and industry had emerged in Germany, and, in the final quarter of the nineteenth century, thousands of German chemists and physicists worked in industrial laboratories and at state institutes. Their success in synthesizing fertilizers, tars, dyestuffs, and similar products helped make possible the remarkable growth of an economy that was far more limited in natural resources than the American.[2] This model of scientific progress contrasted sharply with the image of the inventive Yankee, tinkering alone in his shop, but it was not long before American rivals adopted it. And it was not long before psychologists—Münsterberg among them— suggested that an applied science of the mind might prove as effective in harnessing human nature as chemistry and physics had been in organizing the natural world.

For nearly two decades psychologists had been studying such questions as learning, mental testing, and fatigue, all of which carried practical implications. But, above all, applied psychology depended upon a relatively new interest among investigators in human variation. Early experimental psychologists, as Münsterberg put it, "had for decades searched for ever new interesting details of the mind's mechanism," hoping to find "that which is common to all," but they ignored differences between individuals. By the 1890s the focus had shifted: Francis Galton in England, James McKeen Cattell in the United States, and Alfred Binet in France applied the methods of experimentalism to the measuring of various individual traits. In Germany Emil Kraepelin claimed to be able to determine "the basic characteristics of the individual" through a set of simple tests, and William Stern, the founder of "differential psychology," issued in 1900 his widely circulated maxim, "Individuality: problem of the twentieth century." "Our time," Münsterberg wrote several years later, "has just made a new discovery. It has found out that men are not alike."[3]

By the second decade of the twentieth century, an increasing number of psychologists had come to acknowledge the potential of their discipline as an applied science. Particularly in America, where, according to at least one observer in 1912, academic psychology was on the decline, university courses in various aspects of applied psychology proliferated.[4] Psychologists generally found promises for the future easier to come by than actual successes, but they occasionally applied and institutionalized the new techniques—for instance, in Cattell's measurements of Columbia students, in Lightner Witmer's Psychological Clinic at Pennsylvania, and in Walter Dill Scott's studies in advertising. Cattell's clichéd proclamation at the St. Louis Congress illustrated the high hopes that he shared with many of his colleagues: "I see no reason," he announced, "why the application of systematized knowledge to the control of human nature may not in the course of the present century accomplish results commensurate with the nineteenth-century applications of physical science to the material world."[5] "The historian of the future," Carl Seashore proclaimed several years later in a presidential address to the American Psychological Association, "will probably characterize the period upon which we are now entering in psychology as the period of the rise of the applied psychological sciences."[6]

In Germany the tradition of *Wissenschaft,* especially among philosophers, checked "mere practicality" in psychological experimentation and discouraged *ad hoc* methods. But it also encouraged a more systematic attempt to develop an applied psychology as an independent discipline, with its own experimental goals and its own body of facts. For Münsterberg, the attempts of William Stern to define the new field and lend it academic respectability were particularly important. Stern's brief study, *Uber Psychologie der individuellen Differenzen,* published in 1900, and his subsequent essay, "Angewandte Psychologie" (Applied Psychology), anticipated many of Münsterberg's themes: Applied psychology was a neutral and value-free discipline that determined means and not ends; it had the functions of prediction (or measurement) and control; it considered the "whole" personality in its "individuality"—a concern often lost in application; and it aimed at constructing a "symptomatology" that would allow psychologists to rank individuals experimentally according to their gifts and capabilities. Stern also understood the need to institutionalize his experimental and theoretical work. In 1903 he established the periodical *Beiträge zur Psychologie der Aussage* (Contributions to the Psychology of Testimony) as an organ for work in legal psychology, soon broadening its scope under the title *Zeitschrift für angewandte Psychologie* (Journal for Applied Psychology). And with Otto Lippman he founded in 1906 the Institut für angewandte Psychologie in Berlin.[7]

Ironically, Stern's article on applied psychology challenged Münsterberg's *Grundzüge der Psychologie* for rejecting "the possibility of application on a broad scale." Only a year before, Münsterberg had refused as too practical an offer from a leading advertiser to finance a study on the psychology of advertising, and he had argued in *American Traits* that psychology was a sphinx when it came to real life.[8] But his stance had never been entirely consistent. As early as 1891 he devised a set of mental tests for school children, and, much like Stern, he cited the need for a rigorous and scientific applied psychology—potentially an independent *Wissenschaft,* although of a lesser order than its theoretical counterpart. On one position, however, he was consistent: Any psychology, applied or theoretical, belonged in the hands of trained psychologists. The fanciful constructions of faith healers and spiritualists, on the one hand, and the prescientific, common-sense views of rival professionals in law, vocational guidance, and education, on the other, caused only confusion and brought true psychology into disrepute.

Within a few years this negative message had become positive. After years of active participation in psychology's *Methodenstreit,* Münsterberg called in 1914 for an epistemological cease-fire. The psychologist, he wrote, had to give up "the battlefield of psychological theories" and accept the practical tasks of the world. A few years later he expanded the point in a letter to Harvard's president, Lawrence Lowell, who had reprimanded him for straying from the laboratory. "The period of pure theoretical psychology is closed," he wrote; "I should neglect my duties if I were not to join and try to lead in the movement toward applied psychology."[9] That movement, as he saw it, had much to offer society. Social organization required more than scientific management, political organization, and a revolution in communications, for all of these affected only externals. America needed mental efficiency to complement its technical prowess. And only an applied psychology, with its understanding of the "human factor," could achieve it.

By 1906 Münsterberg was working in psychotherapy and legal psychology. The following year he published a series of popular essays on law, and during the next decade he churned out articles on advertising, prohibition, vocational guidance, spiritualism, women, and popular culture, among other subjects, and he published full-length books on psychotherapy, education, industrial psychology, and the psychology of the film. He wrote correspondence courses on learning, business, and vocation, and he put together a series of mental tests on film for cinema audiences.[10] In the interest of "social efficiency," he and his students served as consultants to private industry as well as to such progressive and trade organizations as the Boston Vocation Bureau, the American Association of Labor Legislation, and the National Electric Light Association. Moreover, in both Germany and the United States, he campaigned for the establishment of "neutral" governmental institutions to foster research in industrial psychology.

More strictly within an academic framework, Münsterberg helped organize an official program of applied psychology in the Harvard laboratory in 1908, and over the years he urged his students into areas that touched on industry, law, mental testing, and aesthetics. As an exchange professor in Berlin for the academic year 1910–11, he offered what he claimed was the first comprehensive course in applied psychology anywhere. Three years later, he expanded his lectures into the massive study *Grundzüge der Psychotechnik*—the first full-length book "to view the whole field from a single perspective," he asserted. In a letter to its author, Cattell called the volume "epoch-making," on a level with Wundt's *Grundzüge der physiologischen Psychologie* and Helmholtz's *Handbuch der physiologischen Optik.*[11]

Münsterberg's pugnacious nature and his unerring instinct for the sensational made his work controversial, both within the profession and without. He drew criticism from legal experts and socialists alike for his role in the murder trial of Big Bill Haywood. His spectacular exposé of the Italian medium Madame Palladino in 1909 enraged William James and upstaged the more careful and conclusive work of Joseph Jastrow and others. Feminists attacked him in 1913 for his public assertion that tests on judgment proved women unsuited for jury duty. One of the more explicit public critiques of his work came in 1909 from Lightner Witmer, whom Münsterberg had recommended more than ten years before as a replacement for him at Harvard. "The clarion voice of Münsterberg which has been . . . heard crying his psychological wares in the marketplace," Witmer wrote in his new *Psychological Clinic*, had cheapened the profession of psychology. Münsterberg's therapeutic work, he charged, differed little from that of the faith healers, especially in

> the jaunty way in which the professor of psychology at Cambridge goes about the country, claiming to have treated in his psychological laboratory hundreds and hundreds of cases of this or that form of nervous disease.

Witmer, too, was committed to the principle of applied psychology, but, like others, he found fault with Münsterberg's over-blown claims, his premature airing of laboratory results, and his self-advertising popularizations. These tendencies placed professional psychology, he argued, on the same level in the public's mind as such pseudoscientific charlataneries as phrenology and spiritualism.[12]

Whatever the validity of these charges—and Münsterberg was only the most flagrant of the sensationalizers in psychology—the assumptions behind Münsterberg's work paralleled those of his more sober colleagues. They expressed the challenge of twentieth-century social science to the traditional American faith in individual responsibility and self-reliance. In his work on vocational psychology, testing, and propaganda, Münsterberg developed his position fully, but its outlines were already clear in his legal psychology. His treatment of suggestion, testimony, and lie detection emphasized the fallibility of the human mind and its high susceptibility to illusions. Consciousness was a subjective state, in the makeup of which nonrational factors played a major role. The individual was an unreliable judge of his own perceptions and capacities, and the reasoning power of ordinary men and women offered an unsure path to truth. In the modern world, it was time for the chronoscope, the plethysmograph, and the galvanometer—and the experts who administered them—to replace everyday common sense in the reconstruction of the facts of experience.

Psychology and Law

Shortly after the Emerson Hall affair, a sensational murder trial in Chicago launched Münsterberg's public career in applied psychology.[13] Under interrogation, an apparently retarded Chicago man, Richard Ivens, had confessed to the brutal murder of a young housewife. In a highly charged atmosphere, he was convicted and sentenced to death. The police, however, had obtained his confession under questionable circumstances, and Ivens retracted it long before he came to trial. J. Sanderson Christison, a local specialist in criminal and abnormal psychology, took up Ivens's case, claiming that he was innocent of any wrongdoing and that the confession had been induced by hypnotic suggestion. To support his argument, Christison solicited the opinions of several leading experts, including Münsterberg and James. The respective answers of the two men illustrated their difference in style.

James recommended to Christison that the case be reopened and he tentatively judged that Ivens was innocent. "Reprieve necessary for thoroughly investigating mental condition," he telegrammed. Münsterberg, on the other hand, had no doubts; his reply was dogmatic and assertive. After scrutinizing "the written record" supplied by Christison, he concluded:

> I feel sure that the so-called confessions of Ivens are untrue, and that he had nothing to do with the crime. It is an interesting yet rather clear case of dissociation and auto suggestion.

Münsterberg then attacked the public atmosphere that permitted the conviction. "The witches of the seventeenth century," he lectured, "were burned on account of similar confessions and the popular understanding of mental abberations [sic] has not made much progress since that time."[14] The charge may have been justified, but it did not aid Ivens's cause.

Christison published the communications from the two psychologists. Münsterberg claimed, characteristically, that he had not expected this development, but it was more likely that he had not anticipated the hostility of the public's reaction to it. The city prosecutor scoffed at the charge of hypnosis, and local papers ran such headlines as "Harvard's Contempt of Court." One announced:

> This crime itself, no matter who may be the criminal, was one of the frightful fruits of a sickly paltering with the stern administration of law. We do not

want any directions from Harvard University irresponsibles for paltering still further.

Psychology had become simply "another way of possibly cheating justice." The state supreme court and its board of pardons were equally unimpressed by the experts. They refused to accept Ivens's retraction, and they upheld the sentence. With crowds of record size outside the jail, Ivens was executed on schedule near the end of June.[15]

For Münsterberg, the failure of his and James's intercession involved more than a personal rebuff; it amounted to an attack on psychology itself. Not one to allow such an affront to pass unanswered, he devoted the following fall to a series of popular articles on psychology and law, most of which appeared in such journals as *McClure's Magazine* and *Metropolitan*. These essays, which discussed the questions of hypnosis, psychopathology, the prevention of crime, and especially the psychology of testimony and the detection of deceit, presented a brief to the public on behalf of the psychological expert. Münsterberg argued that for years the courts had accepted the psychiatrist as an expert qualified to judge the sanity, and therefore the legal responsibility, of the accused and that they had made "the fullest use of all the modern scientific methods when, for instance, a drop of dried blood is to be examined in a murder case." Yet the same courts were "completely satisfied with the most unscientific and haphazard methods of common prejudice and ignorance when a mental product . . . is to be examined." They failed to recognize that recent experimental work on perception, memory, suggestion, and judgment could expedite legal processes and insure justice.[16]

Naive and common-sense psychology, Münsterberg argued, had routinely hampered the administration of justice in America. Courts assumed, for example, that the good will of the eye witness and his reputation for honesty were sufficient guarantees of his accuracy. When a witness stated that he was "sure" that something had happened, however, he testified only to his "subjective feeling of certainty," not to the reality of the event. Such a feeling, which was close to the illusory sense of *déjà vu*, stood "in no definite relation to the attention with which objects are observed," and therefore had to be treated with caution. Courts were also misguided in their reliance on oaths. The fear of retribution, earthly or otherwise, was of little help in ensuring accuracy in cases of genuine illusion. The process of oath-taking lent solemnity to the court proceedings, but it did not significantly increase the likelihood of discovering the truth. Modern psychology, on the other hand, could.[17]

Münsterberg also pointed out that a psychology useful to the jurist was emerging from both theoretical and applied work in Germany and

France. For decades French psychologists with experience in hypnosis had emphasized a continuity between the normal and the abnormal and had stressed the ease with which emotion and suggestion led perception astray. By the 1890s similar views had infiltrated German psychology, especially among psychiatrists and renegades from the Wundtian orthodoxy. Willy Helpach, a former student of Wundt, asserted early in the twentieth century that "dissociation is not something so completely strange and extraordinary that it does not have its analogues in normal lives."[18] The Munich psychiatrist Emil Kraepelin spoke of "normal processes of error," which he hoped to reduce to lawful explanation. Albert Schrenck-Notzing, a specialist in hypnosis and telepathy who had worked with Münsterberg several years before, spelled the issue out clearly in 1896: "In the life of normal men, there are also very particular forms of error and deception, to which we are all more or less exposed." As a result, "one definitely does not have to be hysterical or a pathological liar to fall prey" to the suggestions of one's environment. Even the educated were not immune.[19]

Schrenck-Notzing made his remarks as an expert witness in a trial of a Munich man for the murder of three women—apparently the first courtroom use of a psychological expert, as opposed to a psychiatric one. He testified that a sensational press campaign against the accused, Johann Berchthold, had, through a process of suggestion, led numerous witnesses to "retroactive memory-falsification."[20] Berchthold was convicted on good evidence, but this direct application of the psychology of suggestion to court processes impressed a number of German jurists and psychologists.

Two years later the Prague criminologist Hans Gross considered the questions of testimony and judgment in his classic *Kriminal-Psychologie,* and, early in the next century, Stern took up these problems experimentally in Breslau. Among other projects, Stern attempted to define a factor of "suggestibility" and to answer the question, What kinds of people were best at testimony? Age, sex, intelligence, and education, he argued, were important. Children, for instance, were highly suggestible and therefore unreliable; women forgot less than men, but they falsified more. In the foreseeable future, according to the man who was to pioneer the concept of an intelligence quotient, scientists would be able to construct a scale on which to rank individuals according to their reliability. The pedagogue and the judge would find this scale of inestimable value.[21]

By 1906 legal psychology had established a secure foothold in French-speaking areas. Alfred Binet and Edouard Claparède summarized the work of the Germans and called for a "science psycho-judiciare" in the pages of the *Année psychologique.* In America there had been a spotty history of similar appeals. In 1878 the physician George Beard described in *Popular Sciences Monthly* the limitations of the senses and the memory, and he complained: "The great advances in science have not been made in the courts of justice." Nearly two decades later, Cattell suggested in *Science* that "the probable accuracy of a witness could be measured and his testimony weighted accordingly." On the whole, however, psychologists in the United States expressed very little interest in the new field. As late as 1909, an American expert on testing, G. M. Whipple, observed that English-speaking investigators were conspicuous in legal psychology by their absence.[22] No American experimentalist took up the field before Münsterberg in 1907, and none advertised its potential more aggressively.

Münsterberg's popular essays on law extended the work of the Europeans to the American public. Central to the essays was an attack on the common-sense view that people perceived an exact representation of the outside world and that the memory faithfully repeated past perceptions. Instead, Münsterberg argued, how men and women perceived reflected as much the operation of their minds as the nature of the stimuli. According to his Action Theory, perception depended on muscular preparation. Therefore, we tend to see what we are prepared to see, and we hear what we are prepared to hear. Memory, too, was selective, picking and choosing from a mass of data according to its own rules. To understand and evaluate these processes, the psychologist had to know the laws of their operation: In what ways did normal processes of association lead memory astray? What was the effect of emotion on perception? Or of crowds? How accurate was the perception of time? Of numbers? Or the memory of colors?[23]

Beyond the simple limitations of the senses, according to Münsterberg, the major factor in illusions and memory-falsifications was the process of suggestion. Following Stern, he argued that "suggestibility" was a trait that varied from individual to individual and from time to time. It could also be measured. In his 1907 essay, "Nothing But the Truth," Münsterberg described how this might be done. In a classroom experiment he asked several hundred students to judge whether a gray or a blue square of paper was darker. Although the blue one was objectively much darker, one-fifth of the men chose the gray because "the mere idea of greyness gave to their suggestible minds the belief that the colourless grey must be darker than any colour." In a subsequent experiment Münsterberg asked his class to note all his actions carefully. With his right hand he turned a color-disk, toward which he "eagerly" directed his eyes. With his left hand he simultaneously took from his vest pocket a series of objects—a pencil, a watch, a cigarette box, and so forth. When he asked his class to write a description of what he had done, he found that one-fifth failed to mention the action of his left hand. Comparing the results of the two tests, he discovered that those who failed the first were almost to a man the ones who failed the second. He concluded that a simple color test "can pick out for us those minds which are probably unfit to report, whether an action has been performed in their presence or not." With the aid of such a test, the courts might assess the general reliability of witnesses.[24]

Most legal specialists were not receptive to Münsterberg's suggestions. They resented the intrusion into their field of an outside expert, especially one who adopted such a didactic tone and sensational approach. Indeed, Münsterberg did not understand many aspects of the American legal system, for instance that the state was a prosecuting agency in criminal cases. And he ignored the extent to which common-sense skepticism toward testimony had long been incorporated into standard legal texts. Above all, critics attacked his attempt to replace what they considered the practical wisdom of experience with arbitrary guidelines. In an article in *Law Notes* entitled "Yellow Psychology," one vocal critic, Charles C. Moore, charged:

A Northwest Passage to truth has been discovered by no less a personage than Dr. Hugo Münsterberg, professor of psychology in Harvard University. He found it in his class room, and has mapped and charted it.

"A judge's class room," Moore went on, "is the court room." The experimental psychologist, locked up in a laboratory, had little to tell the practicing jurist about real human behavior.[25]

Despite such criticism, Münsterberg's work in legal psychology and the psychology of testimony gained a wide audience, and *On the Witness Stand* became one of his most popular works. It went through numerous reprintings in the United States and Great Britain, the most recent appearing in 1976. Following its initial publication, lawyers throughout the country solicited Münsterberg's advice on questions of insanity and testimony, and on at least two subsequent occasions he appeared as an expert observer at murder trials.[26] The legal profession as a whole, however, proved reluctant to abandon the standard of common sense. As late as 1974, a psychologist, Robert Buckhout, recalled Münsterberg's work and remarked:

It is discouraging to note that the essential findings on the unreliability of eyewitness testimony were made by Hugo Münsterberg nearly 80 years ago, and yet the practice of basing a case on eyewitness testimony and trying to persuade a jury that such testimony is superior to circumstantial evidence continues to this day.[27]

Buckhout's dating was wrong, but his judgment indicated that the dispute between proponents of laboratory science and the lessons of everyday practice endured.

The courts faced other impediments besides the faulty perceptions and inaccurate memories of well-intentioned witnesses. One of the most obvious was the problem of lying. The examination of entrails was long out of fashion, and the third degree had its limitations. But since the 1880s European criminologists, beginning with Angelo Mosso at Turin, had been exploring the possibility of detecting falsification through physiological and psychological measurements.[28] When *McClure's* commissioned Münsterberg late in the spring of 1907 to write an essay on the Idaho trial of IWW leader Big Bill Haywood, he took the opportunity to bring this work to the public's attention.[29]

Frank Steunenberg, a former governor of Idaho and a well-known opponent of organized labor, had been assassinated in a bombing earlier in the year. The authorities quickly arrested a one-time IWW organizer, Harry Orchard, who initially denied his guilt. But, prompted by Steunenberg's widow, Orchard converted dramatically to Seventh Day Adventism, and, contrite, he confessed during a four-day interrogation conducted by James McParlan, a notorious Pinkerton specialist in labor violence. Orchard claimed to have committed this crime and many others at the behest of an "inner circle" of radicals, including Haywood. On the strength of this confession, which saved Orchard's life, the Idaho authorities spirited Haywood and two colleagues, Charles Moyer and Richard Pettibone, by a special night train from Denver to Boise, where Haywood was brought to trial for conspiracy to murder.

The trial brought almost a decade of industrial violence in the West to a climax and immediately transformed Haywood into a symbol of international labor protest. American unionists rallied to his defense, and demonstrations occurred in almost every major American city. Eugene V. Debs ominously proclaimed, "If they attempt to murder Moyer, Haywood, and their brothers, a million revolutionists will meet them with guns." The Russian novelist Maxim Gorky expressed support for Haywood, and Clarence Darrow, already a prominent criminal lawyer, offered his services as defense attorney. On the other side, Theodore Roosevelt pronounced Haywood an "undesirable citizen" on the eve of the trial, and William E. Borah, just elected to the U.S. Senate from Idaho, acted as an attorney for the prosecution. "Hardly ever before an American court," Münsterberg wrote afterward, had there been "a question of wider social perspective. The whole country wanted clearness as to whether Western socialism was really working with the means of an anarchism that overshadows the nihilism of Russia."[30]

To address this issue—and to fulfill the *McClure's* commission—Münsterberg traveled late in June to Boise, where he immediately established a comfortable relationship with state officials. He observed Orchard's final, thirty-minute testimony from the prosecutor's desk, and Idaho's "courageous" governor, as he described him, personally drove him to the penitentiary. In the prison he conducted nearly one hundred tests on Orchard in the course of seven hours. In Münsterberg's mind, the most important of these tests involved word associations. This technique had been applied to the detection of lies only two years before in two independent investigations, one by Max Wertheimer and Julius Klein, two students of Gross, and the other by Sigmund Freud's future rival, Carl Jung. The procedure, which remained a respected technique into the 1930s, was simple (or simple-minded, some critics claimed). The suspect was given a series of words, some of which were related to the crime. He was to respond to each with the first word that came to mind. In the Orchard case Münsterberg threw in such loaded words as "revolver," "blood," and "pardon." The idea was that, if Orchard were lying about either his accusation of Haywood or his conversion, his feelings of guilt and fear would interfere with his associations. He might react slowly, or he might react slowly to the following word. Armed with a chronoscope, the psychologist could detect the slightest retardation. Or Orchard might give himself away by the meaning of the associated word. For example, to "confession," he might reply "humbug."[31]

Orchard passed the tests admirably. Shortly after Münsterberg's return to Cambridge, he wrote in an unpublished article that he had confirmed beyond all doubt that Orchard was "true in every word of his confessions." "No witnesses for the prosecution," he asserted,

> and no outside evidence could have such convincing character as the results of the tests, and no witnesses for the defence and, of course, no opinion of twelve jurymen could have shaken this scientific finding. . . . As far as the objective facts are concerned my few hours of experimenting were more convincing than anything which in all those weeks of the trial became demonstrated.[32]

In Boise, Münsterberg had the good sense to express his conclusions only privately. After his return home he permitted an interview in the Boston press, which quoted him as saying, "Orchard's confession is every word of it true." Münsterberg's revelation and subsequent clarifications created a sensation. The concept of a "lying-machine" caught the journalistic imagination, and the press in Europe and the United States played the incident for all it was worth, one newspaper, for example, publishing a fictitious interview with "Prof. Hugo Monsterwork of Harvard." Most serious, the disclosure, which occurred before a verdict had been delivered, threatened the impartiality of the trial.[33]

Despite the controversy that his interview raised, Münsterberg held firmly to his claims for his science. In response to his critics, he asserted:

> To deny that the experimental psychologist has indeed possibilities of determining the 'truth-telling powers' is just as absurd as to deny that the chemical expert can find out whether there is arsenic in a stomach or whether blood spots are of human or of animal origin.[34]

When he later published an amended account of the Haywood trial in *McClure's,* he nevertheless toned down its language. In the meantime, Haywood had been acquitted and Münsterberg feared the possibilities of legal action if he maintained too forcefully his judgment that the union leader was guilty.[35] He dropped his provocative comparison of Western socialism with Russian anarchism and introduced the question of "subjective truthfulness." His association tests, he wrote, had revealed that Orchard genuinely believed that he was telling the truth, but they could not determine the actual facts of the matter. In both versions, however, he claimed for the psychological expert the powers of a real-life Svengali. He could "pierce into the mind" and bring to light its deepest secrets. "Even the best bluffer," he asserted, "will . . . be trapped in his effort to conceal anything." As he wrote elsewhere, "the hidden feeling betrays itself often against the will of the best comedian in life."[36]

Far from violating human rights, Münsterberg argued, such scientific methods of interrogation, using word-association tests and physiological measurements, would humanize police procedures. The psychological expert could arrive at the truth without brutalizing the victim. The antiquated and vicious methods of the "third degree" often led to false testimony and untrue confessions; the new scientific methods were "swifter and cleaner, more scientific, more humane, and more reliable in bringing out the truth which justice demands." Münsterberg readily conceded that the accused could not, in fairness, be compelled to take the tests. He should submit to them voluntarily. But such a restriction on the investigators was irrelevant:

> An innocent man will not object to our proposing a series of one hundred associations to demonstrate his innocence. A guilty man, of course, will not object, either, as a declination would indicate a fear of betraying himself; he cannot refuse, and yet affirm his innocence.[37]

Lost in the scheme was the idea that the individual had inviolable rights of privacy, or that he deserved any protection against self-incrimination.

Such an interest in the scientific detection of lies and self-deceit was suggestive in a man whom a colleague, Edwin Holt, once called "one of the most unconscionable liars who ever existed."[38] Holt's charge was extreme, but it contained an element of truth. Münsterberg once proclaimed, "The word lie is not in my lexicon,"[39] but he deceived himself with alarming frequency, and his distortions in certain cases bordered on outright falsification. Even as he was experimenting on the physiological symptoms of deceit, for example, he was misrepresenting to himself and to others the scientific disinterestedness of his writings on alcohol.

In a 1908 essay in *McClure's,* Münsterberg threw his weight as a psychologist against the campaign to prohibit alcohol. If any issue united German-Americans in the years before World War I, it was the threat of prohibition, and among the most alarmed were the leaders of the German-dominated beer industry. When, early in the year, Münsterberg indicated his support of alcohol to Hugo Reisinger, a wealthy German-American philanthropist and the brother-in-law of the beer magnate Adolphus Busch, he received an enthusiastic response: "I am very pleased that you now have also entered the fight against prohibition, and I believe Busch will be eternally thankful to you." After receiving what was apparently a prepublication copy of the *McClure's* article, Reisinger repeated the message, suggesting that a copy be sent to Busch.[40]

Whether Münsterberg sent Busch the article or not, he did solicit money from him, presumably to support a German-American institute in Berlin. And Busch clearly expressed his appreciation of the article after it appeared publicly: "I earnestly and sincerely hope," he wrote Münsterberg,

> that in due course of time you will make a great many more of *your good expressions* and assist the good beer industry of the United States in better understanding their case against the fanatics, cold water cranks and general hypocritical and hysterical foe.

He went on to promise one thousand dollars to further Münsterberg's plans. Shortly thereafter, he donated fifty thousand dollars to the Germanic Museum at Harvard. Reisinger, too, was a regular contributor to several of Münsterberg's projects, including the museum, which is now named the Busch-Reisinger. A few years later a second brewer, Gustave Pabst, joined the ranks.[41]

From the first, rumors circulated of a payoff to Münsterberg by the beer industry. His denials were at best misleading. In a letter to Lowell shortly after the *McClure's* article appeared, he claimed that he had taken up the problem of alcohol solely as a result of his personal interest in social psychology. On Reisinger he wrote, "while I have kept intimate relations with him, we have hardly spoken about prohibition in our lives." He did admit "some overenthusiastic letters" from Busch, but he still considered "it as merely an unfortunate accident that he made the first promise of fifty thousand dollars for the museum a few weeks after the appearance of my paper."[42]

It would have been interesting to submit Münsterberg to the sort of tests that he outlined in the same year in "The Traces of Emotions and the Criminal." Taking up hints from Mosso especially, he argued in that essay that, since all mental states had their physical counterparts, sophisticated psychological and physiological instruments could theoretically measure feelings of guilt. ("The problem of privacy," B. F. Skinner wrote in a similar vein decades later, "may, therefore, eventually be solved by technical advances.")[43] In particular, Münsterberg suggested that changes in respiration, skin resistance to electrical currents, and blood pressure—the three factors upon which polygraphy today is based—would indicate falsification. Münsterberg to be sure softened the position that he had taken in the Haywood essay: "Experiment," he warned, "gives us so far not sufficient hold for the discrimination of the guilty conscience and the emotional excitement of the innocent." But he argued that, when carefully applied, his techniques offered real assistance in detective work and held great promise for the future.[44] At his encouragement, several investigators in his laboratory worked in the 1910s on various physiological indices of deception. One, William M. Marston, did important studies of systolic blood pressure. Twenty years later, Marston created the comic strip character Wonder Woman, whose Amazon strength so admirably complemented the technological efficiency of the lie detector in the fight against crime.[45]

By taking recourse to superhuman powers, whether those of the polygraph or those of Wonder Woman, the psychologist presumed that ordinary human capacities were not adequate for securing justice. One year after the appearance of *On the Witness Stand,* John H. Wigmore, the nation's leading legal expert on evidence, attacked Münsterberg's work on just these grounds in the *Illinois Law Review.* Wigmore subtitled his scathing review, "Being a Report of the Case of Cokestone *v.* Münsterberg," and he set the trial in the Superior Court of Wundt.[46] He perceived Münsterberg's work accurately: The patron saints of common law, Edward Coke and William Blackstone, at least as Americans understood them, had just cause to sue. American criminal law, like American popular thought in the nineteenth century, rested on notions of individual responsibility, and it assumed a universe of reasonable men, able to judge both themselves and the world around them reasonably accurately. Built into the jury system was a distrust of "expert" judgment that might fly in the face of common sense and the assumption that ordinary men were fit to rule on complicated matters of fact. Furthermore, in its concerns for the rights of the accused, especially in protecting them against self-incrimination, it hinted that the integrity of the individual might rival in importance the claims of society, and even of the "truth."

Münsterberg took a very different attitude toward society and the place of the psychological expert within it. The central premise of his legal psychology, and of his view of testing, was that the individual could not accurately judge the real world that existed outside him, or for that matter the nature and processes of his own mind. This, after all, had been the lesson of psychology. Efficient police investigations and courtroom procedures, whose purpose in Münsterberg's view was to determine matters of fact, therefore, required assistance from the psychologist. Münsterberg soon came to insist that a psychology capable of measuring the mind could contribute in a more fundamental fashion to law and order. Crime, he argued, was caused by misfits—men and women who had failed to find their proper niches in society. By measuring their capacities, the psychologist could direct them toward those niches. This assumption led Münsterberg to the problem of vocational guidance.

Psychology and the Social Organism: Vocational Guidance

Concern for vocational guidance had a lengthy pedigree. Throughout the nineteenth century, educators, entrepreneurs, and philanthropists had sporadically attempted to organize guidance by establishing counseling services, and they occasionally called phrenology and anthropometry into service in order to provide scientific measurements of the capacities of young men. By the turn of the century, however, the problem of selecting a vocation had—it seemed—become critical. A whole generation of social thinkers fantasized that, in the pastoral utopia of the preindustrial world, children had grown happily and freely into their chosen vocations. The natural order of society fortuitously reinforced God's calling. But that order, critics believed, was breaking down in a nation beset by rapid industrialization, a proliferation of urban masses, and an uncontrolled influx of foreign immigrants. In the modern world, science had to do for vocation what natural arrangements had done in the past.[47]

In America it was the Boston jack-of-all-reforms, Frank Parsons, who first attacked the problem systematically. "Men work best," Parsons wrote in 1894, "when they are doing what Nature has especially fitted them for." "A sensible industrial system," he continued, "will therefore seek . . . to put men, as well as timber, stone, and iron in the places for which their natures fit them." Like Münsterberg, he perceived society as organic. He suggested that, if all the cells of the social organism were perfect, "they will group themselves in perfect forms, assume true relations, and the whole will be perfect." Yet to Parsons that sensible system did not exist; many individuals in society were unable to express the perfection of their form.[48]

To aid the individual in that expression, Parsons, who was to become a professor of law and economics at the Boston University Law School, took up the rationalization of guidance. In 1908 he persuaded the philanthropist Mrs. Quincy Adams Shaw to establish under his direction a Boston Vocation Bureau—the first such organization in the country—which would "aid young people in choosing an occupation, preparing themselves for it, finding an opening in it, and building up a career of efficiency and success."[49] The effort was typical of the Progressive years. Parsons himself had had a long career of educational and reform activity. He was director of the Breadwinner's Institute in Boston, a night school for working men; he had edited the series *Burt's Library of the World's Best Books* (from which he excluded *Gulliver's Travels* as immoral); he advocated at one time or another cooperative socialism, eugenics, simplified spelling, and direct election of senators. The executive committee of the Bureau contained such members as Paul H. Hanus, professor of education at Harvard and chairman of the Massachusetts State Commission on Industrial Education, and Lincoln Filene of Filene's Department Store in Boston, known for its progressive employment practices. The committee also included an assortment of labor leaders, philanthropists, and social workers. Filene, as well as serving on the executive committee, was by 1910 providing substantial financial support for the new organization. The bureau was a classic alliance of responsible business and labor for the sake of social reform and social efficiency.[50]

Parsons offered two services to his clients: He supplied general information on careers and he provided individual guidance based on an assessment of interests and capacities. His method of determining these capacities was eclectic. He regularly depended, for example, on self-analysis by the candidate himself, shrewd intuition on the part of the counselor, and even physiognomatic observations. Good progressive that he was, he also enlisted science as a supplement to common sense. He hoped to find in the new field of psychological testing an accurate way of measuring mental capacities.

Parsons was not the first to call for such a use of mental tests. Cattell, among others, had repeatedly suggested that tests, already so successful in diagnosing misfits and predicting the performance of high school and college students, could serve vocational purposes. Münsterberg had hinted at this possibility as early as 1891, when he published a description of a set of mental tests for school children. From these tests, which for the most part measured various reaction times, he hoped to derive information of vocational value. They might be useful, he suggested, in answering the question "whether the mental make-up of the worker, the doctor, the judge, the teacher, the officer, and so forth, points to recognizable differences in their elements." Seventeen years later, in a *McClure's* article entitled "Psychology and the Market," he explicitly called for the extensive use of testing in the transportation industries—a question that the French psychophysiologist J. M. Lahy was exploring at the time in Paris.[51]

Münsterberg therefore found the assignment congenial when Parsons called on him as the local expert to test Bureau candidates, and his initial contact with Parsons left him impressed by his work. Münsterberg popularized the Bureau early in 1910 in another *McClure's* article, "Finding a Life's Work," and in subsequent years he continued the discussion of guidance in *Psychology and Industrial Efficiency* and his two texts for correspondence courses, *Business Psychology* and *Vocation and Learning.*[52]

Münsterberg's general rhetoric on vocation was close to that of Parsons and the multitude of counselors who soon emerged. The current haphazard system of vocational guidance, he argued, was inadequate, both in its waste of human resources and its toll in personal maladjustment. Apparently forgetting his own difficulties in selecting a vocation, Münsterberg argued that there were no problems for the exceptionally talented: Such youths knew where they belonged. The remaining four-fifths of mankind, however, required exact knowledge of the demands of the various vocations and of their own individual capacities, as well as an efficient organization to bring the two together.[53]

But Münsterberg went far beyond Parsons and most of his successors in vocational guidance in his reliance on mental testing. By stressing the place of the expert and downgrading self-analysis and common sense, he hoped to forge an objective science of vocational guidance. "Scientific exactitude," he insisted, had to be "brought into the calculation of the life development."[54] He charged Parsons with naiveté because he accepted the candidate's own estimate of himself. It was worse than useless for a counselor to ask, as Parsons did, such questions as, "Is your will weak, yielding, vacillating, or firm, strong, stubborn?" "The ordinary individual," Münsterberg contended in 1913, "knows very little of his own mental functions: on the whole, he knows them as little as he knows the muscles which he uses when he talks or walks." Furthermore, subjective observations by amateur counselors, and even by friends, were of little value. "Half an hour's experimenting in the laboratory," he wrote, "may tell us more about a man's attention than half a year's living with him."[55]

This position was exactly the one that Münsterberg had taken in *On the Witness Stand*, where he had argued that the psychological expert was better able to rule on the reliability of confessions and testimony than the judge and the jury. By the second decade of the century, a growing body of psychological work supported this argument. Cattell and his student H. L. Hollingworth, for example, conducted experiments that proved, in their own minds, a low correlation between self-analysis, the judgment of associates, and scores on objective tests. Walter Dill Scott demonstrated that the employers of salesmen were generally bad at estimating the objective success of their employees. Shortly before his death, Münsterberg himself performed a set of experiments on students at Harvard modeled on the work of Cattell and Hollingworth. He reported "grave unreliability" and "many sources of error" among his subjects when they assessed the qualities of their acquaintances, "but the most discouraging figures are after all those of the self-estimate."[56]

Not only was the individual unreliable in judging his own capacities; according to Münsterberg, he was also incapable of significantly improving what he had. "We can learn to keep house with our resources," he observed in his correspondence course on business psychology. But such scientific management of capacities "cannot deceive us as to the fundamental fact that the decisive tendencies of our mind are inherited and cannot be fundamentally changed." The unmusical might learn to play the piano a little, but they remained unmusical. The man with no memory for faces might employ mnemonic devices to remember the name of an acquaintance, but "neither good-will nor training will furnish him with that memory which he lacks."[57] A positive attitude and a dedicated will were essential attributes for a successful worker, but they could not make a man a success in a vocation for which he was not suited.

By the twentieth century, Münsterberg therefore tended to minimize the role of ambition in vocational success. In taking this position, he was close to many in the vocation movement. Compared to Parsons and the psychologists H. L. Hollingworth and Edward K. Thorndike, Münsterberg adopted an extreme position, but they, as much as he, rejected the Horatio Alger myth that every boy (not to mention every girl) could be president. Parsons, for instance, to judge from his own accounts of his work, spent a good deal of time convincing young women that homemaking was a worthy profession and young men who aspired to be lawyers that their talents fitted them to be stenographers. Stratton Brooks, public school superintendent in Boston, recognized this tendency in vocational guidance when he lamented in 1911 that its chief motto was no longer, "Aim at the highest."[58] He was right, for its goal had become to reconcile the individual to his or her fate.

In Münsterberg's view of society, the individual's fate properly followed his mental and physical capacities, and the psychological expert, who could measure these capacities, could guide the individual into his proper slot in the social hierarchy. Münsterberg could hold out hope for all members of society because he assumed a preordained harmony between the variety of human capacities and the requirements of social progress. A perfect fit between personality and function, therefore, was possible. "There is no mental type," he wrote in 1916, "for which society has not a place where he can do useful work which makes him happy and which serves the world. Nothing is necessary but to discover the capacities and dispositions with which an individual has to make his struggle for existence." The untalented and the eccentric had their vocational niches as well as the talented and the normal. Misfits did not exist, only the misfitted. Even the so-called "born criminal," endowed with a mind that "by its special stupidity or carelessness or vehemence gives to crime an easier foothold," had a place in the social organism. "The central issue for the entire problem [of social organization]," Münsterberg stated in *Grundzüge der Psychotechnik*, "lies in the fact that men are unequal and that social organization in our complicated times demands inequality of social functions."[59] He might have added social rewards.

Psychologies of
Commitment

Münsterberg's commitment to a systematic applied psychology—and his attraction to the public spotlight—led him to the questions of psychopathology and psychotherapy as early as 1906. In that year Morton Prince and James Jackson Putnam, the leaders of the "Boston School" of psychotherapy, enlisted him for the editorial board of their newly founded *Journal of Abnormal Psychology.* The following year he contributed to a symposium on the subconscious in its pages with Joseph Jastrow and two French psychologists, Alfred Binet and Pierre Janet, among others, and for the next decade he dabbled in therapy with patients at Harvard.[1] In March 1909, several months before Sigmund Freud's celebrated visit to America, he published a description of his own work under the title *Psychotherapy.*

In important ways, Münsterberg's therapeutic practice epitomized his social psychology of the 1910s. The treatment that he offered was symptomatic and cosmetic. He relied on behavioristic and suggestive remedies that often ignored the conscious processes of the patient. He assumed that mental disorder was generally a problem of maladjustment, and that its roots lay neither in the basic structure of the patient's mind nor in the society that formed it. In years when Christian Science and mental healing were flourishing, his therapies, whether for the individual or for society as a whole, called more often for doses of positive thinking, self-renunciation, and aesthetic uplift than for meaningful self-analysis.

Psychotherapy, in Münsterberg's hands, addressed itself to individual problems, but he, like so many of his contemporaries, considered America's failure of will to be national in scope. In the past, so a standard argument of the Progressive years went, settling the frontier and forging a nation had almost accidentally given Americans a purpose, and patterns of localism had provided a sense of community (and the possibility of communication). In the "big marketplace of civilization,"[2] however, where immediate ties were weakened and distractions compelling, what would hold society together and individuals to their purpose? By the 1910s Münsterberg had come to recommend a conscious social program of symbol-building and communal reintegration. For help in forging a therapy of commitment, to use Philip Rieff's phrase,[3] he enlisted several of the very organs of mass culture, including the press and the film, that he had held partly responsible for the disorder.

Individual Therapy

Abnormal psychology and mind cures were in fashion in the first decade of the century. Popular journals reveled in tales of hypnotic cures, multiple personalities, and the divination of dreams. Lay organizations such as the Christian Science church and the Emmanuel movement—both Boston-based—broadcast the doctrine that faith and science were reconcilable and that the mind could cure the body. At the same time, an increasing number of medical men and psychiatrists in America, France, and Austria adopted psychogenic theories of insanity and explored the possibilities of psychotherapy. Prince and Putnam, for example, replaced the old prescriptions of rest and water treatment with "talking cures," which they justified by theories of the subconscious, submerged personalities, and even sexual repression (in Putnam's case). From time to time, accounts of their successes, scarcely less spectacular than those of Mary Baker Eddy and the Emmanuel movement's Reverend Elwood Worcester, appeared in the popular press.[4]

Münsterberg deplored this situation, but as always he discovered a way to exploit it. In 1909 he published his *Psychotherapy* as an advertisement for the curative powers of modern psychology and a warning against lay intrusion into the field. "Scientific medicine," he wrote, "should take hold of psychotherapeutics now or a most deplorable disorganization will set in, the symptoms of which no one ought to overlook to-day." In particular, he attacked two schools of psychotherapists: those who worked "with and through and in the subconscious" and those who made "psychotherapy a kind of triumph of the mind over the body." The former, apparently including such men as Janet, Putnam, and Freud (whom he misunderstood in this respect), confined themselves to "suggestions to the subconscious." The latter relied solely on "persuasions and encouragements to the conscious will." Both, however, were wrong in theory and misleading in practice, even if they occasionally succeeded. "There is no subconscious," Münsterberg asserted, "and . . . there is no psychological fact which is not at the same time a physiological one." Any therapy that assumed the existence of an unconscious or a disembodied consciousness, therefore, was unscientific.[5]

Münsterberg instead based his psychotherapy on the Action Theory. Psychology, he wrote, recognized "no mental fact which does not start an action," and it taught "that every change in the system of actions involves a change in the central experience." Whenever that system of actions (or pattern of behavior) was poorly adjusted to the environment, "some therapy of the physician has to set in." The psychotherapist might attack the mind directly through such suggestive techniques as hypnosis or indirectly by manipulating the patient's behavior. For disorders like neurasthenia and hysteria, these procedures could offer relief. Münsterberg, however, tempered the claims of the mind-healers. In cases of genuine insanity, paranoia, and melancholia, not to mention physical disease, psychotherapy had no adequate answers.[6]

Münsterberg defined sanity entirely in functional terms. "The only real test of health," he wrote, "is the serviceableness to the needs of life." The sound mind, as he described it, was well organized and well adjusted to its surroundings. It could concentrate and it possessed a well-formed will, secure in its purpose and able to resist temptations. The pathological mind, on the other hand, was out of balance, distorted into a caricature of itself through a failure of inhibition and undisciplined habits of association. The task of the psychotherapist was to retrain the will of the patient and to replace bad mental habits with good. In doing so, he restored the mind to its "harmony of health" and eliminated those distortions that diminished its "chances of existence."[7]

The psychotherapist might achieve this end, Münsterberg wrote, by removing the source of the disturbance, altering the patient's environment, or curing the diseased organ by medical means. Where these remedies were not possible, he might

> work directly on the psychophysical state, inhibiting the pain, suppressing the emotion, substituting pleasant ideas, distracting the whole mind, filling it with agreeable feelings, until the normal equilibrium is restored.

Münsterberg used an impressive array of techniques in the process—hypnosis, cathartic treatment, drugs, behavioristic training, and messages of inspiration. Behind them all, however, were the principles of suggestion and conditioning. The patient surrendered his volitional controls to the will of the therapist and sacrificed intelligent self-direction and self-knowledge. Münsterberg warned against "short-cut treatment by making believe," but he also contended that the patient sometimes profited "from suggestion the more, the less he understands about its nature."[8]

Münsterberg illustrated his psychotherapy with a series of cases taken from his own practice. In most he employed methods reminiscent of the rote learning he recommended for school children. He had one sufferer read "ten times a day a letter of mine which contained appropriate suggestions." Another patient was a morphine addict, "a picture of the lowest type of hopeless manhood" and a veteran of three sanatoriums. Over the course of four months, Münsterberg hypnotized him, first daily and finally weekly, inducing him to cut back his dosage slowly from forty grams to none. "It meant a terrible struggle," Münsterberg reported, but in the end the patient achieved a complete cure. In a third case, he treated a rich and spoiled, but "feeble-minded," boy of twelve who talked only nonsense. Münsterberg saw to it that the boy's "whole life was brought under strict discipline and no parental indulgence was permitted." The child of course would remain feeble-minded for life, but as a result of "the training of inhibition" and the rebuking of "every haphazard reaction," he could expect to lead "externally a harmonious life."[9] In each case the treatment was similar: Attack the symptoms, repattern behavior to conform to social expectations, and the patient was cured.

The meaning of the therapist's words in the treatment was irrelevant, as long as they succeeded. Münsterberg wrote that the "spoken word" (the behaviorists would call it verbal behavior) was to be seen "as the physical air-waves which stimulate certain brain centers." At least as far as psychotherapy was concerned, only the ability of the words to restore the patient to appropriate behavior was important. Münsterberg insisted, for example, that "the faith in God is not more valuable than the faith in the physician and the moral appeal of no higher order than the influence through the galvanic current." Even guilt and fear might in some cases serve the purpose:

> The one who is instinctively overmuch afraid of being found out in wrong-doing will live a faultless life from the standpoint of law; just as truly as his neighbour who obeys the laws from a moral conviction.[10]

This functionalist approach to therapy anticipated the twentieth-century concern for adjustment, but it sacrificed in the process any hope for self-understanding. In this respect, Münsterberg's therapeutic model differed radically from Freud's, despite the autocratic structure of both.

Freud's expressed purpose, from which, to be sure, he occasionally deviated, was "to make everything conscious that is pathologically unconscious." The therapist was to fill "all the gaps in the patient's memory, to remove his amnesia." Only in this way could the patient exert some kind of rational control over his emotional life.[11] Münsterberg's therapy operated on principles that were exactly opposite: His formula was to force the disturbing ideas out of the mind and to suppress the undesirable behavior. He hoped to create amnesia—to induce his patients to forget their disturbances—as often as he attempted to eliminate it. If psychoanalytic techniques served this purpose, so much the better. Münsterberg specifically borrowed from Jung the use of word associations as a diagnostic tool, and he acknowledged the successes of Freudian methods, but he had no interest in the theory that lay behind them.

Münsterberg was aware of Freud's work and he soon established himself as one of Freud's leading opponents. Like most of his German colleagues, he considered psychoanalytic theories mystical and their emphasis on sexuality one-sided. When Freud lectured at the Clark Conference in 1909, Münsterberg was in Canada and, consequently, was one of the few leading American psychologists who were absent. It is likely, therefore, that the two never met, but in any case they had little use for each other. Shortly before the American trip, Jung—who had already charged Münsterberg with plagiarizing his association tests—warned Freud that, among American psychologists, "I expect double dealing only from Münsterberg." On another occasion, Jung remarked that the preference of the Leipzig psychologist Wilhelm Specht for Münsterberg over Freud was "a scandal."[12]

Despite his opposition to depth psychology, Münsterberg did acknowledge the importance of sexual factors in certain neuroses. He never doubted that the biological demands of sex were real, and he spoke of "the explosive sexual system of the youth," which apparently lurked beneath the adolescent mind, ready to seize hold of the entire personality if allowed the chance. Society's responsibility was to see that the instinct never reached a mental level, that the individual never fell prey to "secret sexual thoughts."[13]

For Freud the situation was different. He assumed that sexuality inevitably received mental expression, whether consciously or in symbolic form, and that the denial or unconscious repression of sexual drives was a source of mental disorder. When a modern " 'civilized' sexual morality"— what we today would call Victorian standards—straightjacketed these urges, it extorted a high psychic price. "Experience teaches us," he wrote in 1908, "that for most people there is a limit beyond which their constitution cannot comply with the demands of civilization." Psychoanalysts

attempted to persuade their patients to adopt a more realistic set of expectations. Freud did not go as far as some of his followers, who wished
to open the gates to the free expression of all sexual urges, but he did
hope to put reason and self-understanding in the place of guilt, with its
disastrous side effects, as a source of self-control.[14]

Freud's demand for increased frankness in sexual matters was paralleled in America by what the historian Nathan Hale has called a "repeal
of reticence." Few Americans accepted Freud's criticism of "civilized"
morality, but during the early decades of the century they increasingly
discussed sexual questions. A Progressive crusade to wipe out prostitu-
tion, beginning in the 1890s, fixed public attention on sexual questions,
and widespread concern over sexual hygiene and venereal diseases kept it
there. In these years, too, a movement for the introduction of sexual education into the schools gathered momentum.[15] To Münsterberg such developments were disastrous, and he demanded in their place a "policy of
silence." Even the thought of sex, he argued, stimulated a "psychophysio-
logical reverberation in the whole youthful organism with strong reactions on its blood vessels and on its nerves." Any sexual information,
therefore, "however slowly and tactfully imparted," he wrote in an essay
on sex education, "must mean a breaking down of inhibitions which held
sexual feelings and sexual curiosity in check." He insisted instead that inhibitions be strengthened by encouraging "those feelings of shame and
decency which belong to the steady learning of a clean child from the
days of the nursery."[16] The object was not to discuss immorality but to
make any thought of it repugnant. (For all Münsterberg's inability to recognize the possible effects of such a policy, it must be admitted that he
had a better understanding of the potential destructiveness of sexuality
than did many of his critics. He suffered from none of the illusions of liberal reformers, who believed that it could be exorcised through reasonable
discussion in sex education classes.)

In *Psychotherapy* Münsterberg dealt explicitly with several cases of
functional disorder whose origin he considered psychosexual. In one case
he treated a woman who experienced occasional attacks of anxiety at
work, where she sold men's gloves and ties. After analyzing the woman
through hypnosis and word associations, he concluded that her problems
stemmed from a broken engagement eight years before. That engagement
had excited "sexual emotions"; their later suppression caused an underly-
ing neurosis, which triggered the anxiety attacks when she fitted her customers. In this case Münsterberg believed psychotherapy was not
necessary. Instead, he insisted that his patient change her place of work to
"a house where she would have to do only with women, and . . . sell articles which did not bring her into personal contact with customers."

Within six months the symptoms disappeared. As Münsterberg diagnosed it, the woman's problem did not stem from suppressed sexual urges, in a Freudian sense, but rather from the suppression of the sexual ideas excited by her engagement. If she had not been engaged, presumably, the sexual anticipation would not have arisen and therefore the fits of anxiety would not have occurred. The prevention and cure of such disorders, therefore, was obvious: Remove the temptations and eliminate the sources of excitement.[17]

In another case Münsterberg treated a school teacher of twenty-five whose only complaint was "a persistent idea that she may at any time get a child." The woman was a perfect example of the results of the morality that Freud deplored. According to Münsterberg:

> She never had any intimate acquaintance with any man, she was never engaged, she hated bitterly every thought of immorality, she knows and has assured herself by much reading that it is entirely impossible that she might get a child without sexual contact.

The disturbing thought, nevertheless, constantly recurred. Its persistence embarrassed and depressed her, interfered with her work, and kept her away from company.

Münsterberg traced the woman's obsession to an event that had occurred when she was about thirteen. A young friend whom she admired for her beauty had given birth to a child, who died within a few days. The patient claimed that at the time she was "completely naive" (an assertion Freud would have disputed) and felt only sadness at the death. In Münsterberg's opinion, "this strong emotional experience early in life had become the starting point for that secondary absurd thought" of pregnancy. Exaggerated by the emotion of sadness, the experience had caused "a deep physiological brain excitement which had irradiated toward the ideas of her personality" and had stirred up undesirable associations. These associations remained with her as an adult, although their sources were long forgotten.

To cure his patient, Münsterberg "sidetracked" the physiological after-effects of the trauma. In other words, he retrained her powers of inhibition and redirected her emotions toward "appropriate" associations. He hypnotized the woman and asked her to think herself back into the original experience. She was to see her friend on the street and

> to tell the girl how indignant she feels over her behavior; she is to tell her that she understands now all which she did not understand in her childhood, that she knows now that she must have lived an immoral life; that she must have had a friend and that a pure girl like herself could never under any circumstances come into such a situation, that no pure girl could suddenly have a child.

She followed his directions and, after four such treatments, was cured. The obsession disappeared, and "the subcortical complex . . . evidently found its normal channels of discharge."[18]

Although he did not make his point entirely clear, Münsterberg was arguing that the woman felt impure (and therefore pregnant) because as a child she had had the poor judgment to have an impure friend. She compounded her sense of guilt by not having confronted her friend about the impurity. Münsterberg offered an extraordinary therapy. He hoped to allow the guilt-ridden woman to escape the consequences of her misdeed by presenting her, under hypnosis, with a second chance, an opportunity to perform her duty where she had failed before. In this way, he claimed to have relieved the woman's burden by allowing the normal expression of her feelings (albeit in an imaginary situation), which had been blocked for years.

On the surface, the therapy seemed Freudian, but in fact it was the reverse. "Few factors," Münsterberg had written, "are more disturbing for the mental balance than feeling and emotions which do not come to a normal expression."[19] When he used the word "normal," however, he evidently had in mind behavior that accorded with the norms of one's society but not with natural inclinations. Münsterberg traced the woman's disturbance to her repression, at least retrospectively, of social standards of morality that had been thoroughly internalized. In effect, he "cured" her by suppressing the "natural" emotions of sympathy for the friend and sadness at the death of the baby and by securing a "normal" expression of the civilized sexual morality. His therapy, as a result, could apparently apply only to those who were fundamentally moral; for the truly immoral he suggested confinement. Freud, on the other hand, might have ascribed the woman's problems to the distortion of a natural and innate instinct through unconscious repression and would have based any therapy on a recognition of (although not an acquiescence to) the demands of that instinct.

The comparison between Münsterberg's and Freud's psychology is instructive because Münsterberg's, despite its German origins, anticipated America's domestication of psychoanalysis. Freud, especially in his American lectures, traced psychoneurosis to a conflict between modern civilization and the nature of man. "What we call a normal man," he told his Clark audience, was "the bearer, and in part the victim, of the civilization that has been so painfully acquired." Psychoanalysis could offer no "cure" in the classical sense. The therapist, he wrote, did not seek to bring the patient relief "by receiving him into the catholic, protestant, or socialist community." He could only communicate an analytic attitude that transformed "hysterical misery into everyday unhappiness." Analysis sought aggressively to destroy all illusions, and Freud assumed that the sane individual was at least in some sense alienated from his community, if to be sure he was still a law-abiding and functioning citizen.[20]

Münsterberg identified therapy with resocialization and health with "self-fulfillment" through recommitment to the social community, as he defined it. In effect, he hoped to build up illusions, not only through psychotherapy but, in the long run, through a thoroughgoing social and metaphysical idealism. In this respect he was close to those Americans of his generation who welcomed the Freudian concept of sublimation. Men such as Putnam believed that this process could inspire a reconstruction program and that the minds of individuals could be elevated to higher realms through art and religion. For Münsterberg, absolute values, especially those of beauty, served much the same purpose. The individual finally found meaning in life when he lost his individuality and merged into the *Uber-Ich*. Coincidentally, Freud too spoke of an *Uber-Ich*, translated into English as the "superego," but he traced its origins to wholly terrestrial sources. Far from being derived from an internal logic, it was an agency that civilization had set up within each individual to restrain his or her aggressive desires. It was, as Freud described it in a famous passage, a garrison of authority stationed in the conquered city of the mind.[21]

Münsterberg's denial of the unconscious mind and his oversimplified views of natural inclinations were predictable in a man so weak in self-perception and so unwilling to come to terms with his own emotions. By his own account, he was a model of rationality; he had rarely been the victim of uncontrolled motives or acted in an ill-considered fashion. On several occasions he made the claim that he never dreamed. When he discussed dreams in his university courses, he could only speak of them, he reported, "just as a blind man might speak of colours." Yet, unlike most blind people, he considered his narrowed vision an advantage. "The remainder of mankind," he asserted good-naturedly, "is, indeed, rather to be pitied for its dreams, which may bring a confusion of themselves with the real past."[22] Münsterberg also remarked on at least two occasions that, as a psychologist, he could speak with personal authority on the full range of human emotions, with the sole exception of anger. He could only speculate, however, on the subjective content of that emotion, never having experienced it himself.[23] Few of his friends would have seconded this judgment by a man whose career was best known for its storminess.

One long-term friend and colleague, Edwin Holt, suggested in a not-so-veiled case study that Münsterberg suffered from a "partially suppressed ego." Another friend, Max Dessoir, made much the same judgment when he claimed to have found a "hazy romanticism" lying deep within him. That romanticism was evident in Münsterberg's youthful poetry, through which ran themes of self-discipline and self-renunciation. One striking poem, considering that it was written by a man who claimed never to have dreamed, described a revery that disrupted an evening's lonely scholarship. In the dream the author, hard at work in a garret room, began inexplicably to grow, until he burst from the house as a giant. Still growing, he soon dwarfed the city, smashing beneath him houses, a church (whose steeple he used as a walking stick), and the surrounding forests. He crossed the ocean in a single stride, finally challenging the stars themselves. But the giant's will to power proved no match for the infinite spaces. Recognizing his megalomania as futile, he shrank back to the scholar in his room, and the night slipped by in faithful work.[24] The poem was a stylized piece, with all the fatuousness of youth, and it developed a standard romantic conceit of the lonely scholar with dreams of grandeur. But, despite its obviously autobiographical nature, Münsterberg clearly did not intend its ludicrous suggestiveness: a young Jew using a church steeple as a walking stick and the son of a lumber merchant smashing forests. More interesting, however, than Münsterberg's partial recognition of grandiose and destructive urges was the ease with which they were exorcised. The giant was not sublimated in any Freudian sense, nor was he even repressed. He simply disappeared without a trace. In real life, Münsterberg found his destructive urges less cooperative.

As his poem hinted, Münsterberg's duty-bound compulsion for work and meaningful activity amounted to a form of self-control and a defense against his inner world. Ralph Barton Perry suggested that James's praise of vigor and strenuousness reflected a fear of "morbid self-preoccupation." The frenetic pace at which Münsterberg conducted his life served the same function. One need only scan a list of his publications, even recognizing his capacity for work. He dictated the entire 400-page *Psychotherapy,* for example, between the second of January and the twelfth of February 1908. The following month he wrote three separate articles for popular and academic journals, and, as if this were not enough, dictated the 430-page *Eternal Values.*[25] "His brain never tires," James had written years before.[26]

James, however, was wrong. Like others of his generation, Münsterberg suffered from nervous problems for most of his career. His personal correspondence, particularly with James, included one complaint after another. "My heart becomes abnormal, clearly nervous origin," he wrote the neurasthenic James in 1901. "I think it was a second edition of your troubles." Only a year after this letter, he experienced a nervous breakdown, apparently from overwork, complicated by a bout of diptheria. His colleague George Herbert Palmer offered him a sound piece of advice. "You must learn how to shirk, as the rest of us do," Palmer wrote. "I wonder if you ever sit with folded hands?" But Münsterberg rarely allowed himself this luxury.[27]

Münsterberg's nervous problems were commonplace; more significant was his refusal to probe for their source and to come to terms with them. The same physical symptoms could be found in James and in G. Stanley Hall. Both James and Hall, however, attempted in a more direct way to face their mental underworlds, whether in the former's interest in abnormal and religious psychology or in the latter's frank recognition of sexual needs in adolescence. Their educational and psychological theories grew in part from such attempts. Münsterberg's theorizing, on the other hand, complemented his attempt to deny the destructiveness of his compulsions; his cosmetic approach to psychotherapy minimized the depth of mental disorders. At least by the twentieth century, Freud warned against the sort of treatment that failed to address itself to deeper causes. Münsterberg, however, exhibited very little concern over possible side effects or relapses. In one striking case, he claimed the successful cure of an alcoholic, although the sufferer fell back into his habit a year later. By restoring the addict to normal behavior, the therapist had done his duty, Münsterberg argued.[28] With a little more insight into the complexities of his own behavior, Münsterberg might better have recognized the shallowness of the cure.

Social Sanity: Propaganda and Art

Münsterberg's patients often exhibited a condition of nervousness that for decades had been a subject of debate in popular literature. More than thirty years before, the New York physician George Beard had popularized the syndrome of neurasthenia, a vague nervous condition that left its victims incapable of work and inflicted upon them an array of symptoms, including headaches, the fear of responsibility, graying hair, and insomnia. To read certain accounts, it had reached epidemic proportions by the early twentieth century. "Two-thirds of our acquaintances have neurasthenia," Münsterberg wrote in 1909, "and nervous prostration is the fashion for men and women alike." For some it was a badge of gentility, but for the champions of civilization, work, and order, the contagion meant disaster; it overturned the nineteenth-century verities of consciousness and will and threatened the nation's virility.[29]

Beard explained the malady as an organic disease of the nerves and the brain, and he traced it to the conditions of modern life. The nervous system, he wrote, resembled a dynamo that could produce only a certain

amount of force. Under the stimulating circumstances of modern civilization, however, the dynamo was overloaded. Individuals with weak consti-
tutions could not generate enough energy, and they fell victim to nervous
exhaustion. "Modern nervousness," Beard suggested, "is the cry of the
system struggling with the environment."[30]

A later generation of medical men and social commentators rejected
the crude materialism and sometimes the somatic bias of Beard's model,
but they generally accepted his identification of neurasthenia with modern civilization. The German psychologist Richard von Kraft-Ebing expressed the orthodox position clearly in 1895:

> In the course of the last decades changes have taken place in the political
> and social—and especially in the mercantile, industrial and agricultural—
> conditions of civilized nations which have brought about great changes in
> people's occupations, social position and property, and this at the cost of the
> nervous system.

That system, as a result, was forced "to meet the increased social and economic demands by a greater expenditure of energy, often with quite inadequate opportunity for recuperation."[31] The argument further held that,
since the pace of civilization was most hectic and the decay of traditional
institutions most advanced in the New World, neurasthenia was a particularly American condition. Some called it "Americanitis."

Münsterberg acknowledged the American style of nervousness. A popular culture that featured yellow press, cheap drama and literature, sensational advertising, and soon motion pictures stimulated hyperactivity in
Americans and encouraged patterns of motor restlessness, "manifested in
the use of rocking-chairs and chewing-gum." At a more serious level,
Münsterberg cited "the rapid growth of divorce, the silly chase for luxury,
the rivalry in ostentation and in gratification of personal desires in a hundred forms"—in short, the effemination of culture. These symptoms, however, indicated a mental rather than a somatic disorder: America's "so-
called nervousness" did not reflect an actual depletion of nervous force
but, instead, an inability to focus and direct it. It expressed "the victory
of involuntary attention and the defeat of voluntary attention." Americans, in other words, exhibited a "bad habit of the nerves" and "a weakness of will and attention;" they suffered from a "wrong of mind," not a
mental disease.[32] In this way Münsterberg reversed Beard, transferring
the blame from the debilitated physical condition of the victims to their
weak moral fiber.

By asserting that bad mental habits led to the nation's restlessness,
Münsterberg absolved technology and civilization of all responsibility.
He had no sympathy with those—like Beard and Kraft-Ebing—who ar-

gued that "the nervousness of our time comes with the necessity of a natural effect." "It is an illusion," he wrote, "that the material and social conditions under which we live are favorable to nervous diseases." Technology in particular did not oppress the mind; it liberated it. Such improvements as telephones, eyeglasses, railroads, and paved roads conserved effort and allowed the mind to concentrate on higher things. In fact, he assured his readers, the modern era was no more "nervous," in an organic sense, than its predecessors; Americans, instead, had succumbed to a mass hypochondria and a national "fear of nerves." Their cure, therefore, did not depend upon coddling, as for example Beard suggested when he recommended replacing the gospel of work by one of rest. Münsterberg demanded instead a rededication to purpose and an end to self-indulgence. "What we need," he proclaimed at one point, "is a stream from a hose to wake us up and a clout on the back to arouse us to a sense of duty."[33]

Like most conservatives, Münsterberg had sought in his earlier writings a solution to America's nervousness in the family and traditional schooling. Moral education could reinforce individual will and purpose in an emerging mass society; to borrow David Riesman's terms, it might restore to the twentieth-century's "outer-directed" man his inner gyroscope —his internalized code of conduct and inner-directed standards of behavior.[34] Inner-direction for Münsterberg, however, meant little more than the will to do what one ought to do, even without external compulsion. Neither the family nor the school, as he conceived them, played a mediating role between the individual and the total community, nor did they protect a sphere of privacy from the whole. In the 1910s, therefore, he found it easy to transfer his attention from institutions whose expressed goal was to build up strong-willed, duty-bound personalities to ones that, in the interests of the whole, broke down the inner-direction of those personalities and bound them more securely to external authority.

Münsterberg abandoned neither his traditional appeals to ideals nor his concern for the proper training of wills, but he increasingly sought to recapture a lost sense of communal purpose through the techniques of modern psychology. In a series of essays, many of which were collected in *American Patriotism* (1913) and *Psychology and Social Sanity* (1914), he engaged in what might be described as therapeutic first aid. He looked for short cuts, ways in which weak-willed Americans could be bound to their tasks in a differentiated civilization. Several years earlier he had attempted this on an individual basis through psychotherapy. By the teens he noted the need for a systematic rehabilitation of society's symbols. "The historic spirit of human progress," he wrote in an essay on sex education, demanded "its symbols, its conventions, and its beliefs." In recent years, however, he suggested, "the flood of truth-talk" (what Weber called "disenchantment") had swept them aside. Society's responsibility was to build the dam back up, and the psychologist's was to provide guidelines for its reconstruction.[35]

One conventional but revealing dam against truth-talk that Münsterberg recommended was alcohol. First in his 1908 *McClure's* article and later in *Psychology and Industrial Efficiency,* he attacked the prohibition movement on the grounds that the drug consumed in moderation yielded social benefits. He readily conceded the dangers of intemperance, and he admitted that drinking at work reduced efficiency. But, he argued, alcohol had the power to alleviate some of the ills of civilization. For industrial workers, he suggested in 1913, "it may produce that narrowing and dulling of consciousness which extinguishes the cares and sorrows of the day and secures the night's sleep, and through it increased efficiency the next morning." The truly aesthetic and creative (who presumably were not wage earners) might not require it, but for the masses of mankind it offered "some kind of help to open their minds to the message of the unpractical and unselfish." In a curious but revealing way, therefore, Münsterberg identified the "narrowing and dulling of consciousness" with the expansion of what he called "ideal values." "Better America inspired than America sober," he had proclaimed earlier in *McClure's,* "if soberness is to mean absolute abstaining."[36]

Münsterberg's prescription of alcohol in moderation was psychologically crude, but it illustrated his reliance on manipulative procedures that overrode natural inclinations and indeed "consciousness." In this respect, it paralleled his advocacy of "suggestion," the process that he had found so useful in his psychotherapy. The term was a vague one, much in fashion among popular writers early in the century, and Münsterberg's work did little to clarify it. Even as he affirmed its everyday nature, he described it in terms that must have conjured up images of telepathic mind control. Under its influence, he wrote in his textbook, "the individual submits to propositions for motor settings or actions which he would not perform, if he were only following his own impulses or his reason." It had, in other words, the power to break down the resistance of those upon whom it operated. Münsterberg warned that it could be exaggerated and lead to abnormal and even harmful states, as in the case of the Chicago murderer Ivens. Nervous exhaustion, emotion, fatigue, and of course alcohol heightened suggestibility to dangerous levels. But the process as a whole was benign and even necessary, for it could raise the individual to social purposes beyond himself. We see it operating all around us, Münsterberg wrote: "The voter who is imposed on by the big parade, or the customer who is carried away by the bargain prices of the great removal sale" was under its influence. Education, art, politics, and religion depended upon it, and without it "life would be dreary and commonplace, without enthusiasm and without convictions."[37]

The most obvious example of suggestion in early-twentieth-century America was advertising, yet in its popular form this medium struck Münsterberg as the epitome of the nation's nervous style. Its overblown claims appealed to the cheapest instincts and gave the popular press a hectic tone. By encouraging unrestrained competition between indistinguishable brands, it expressed the disorganized, laissez-faire past whose demise Münsterberg celebrated. Yet, like so much that was sensational in America, it caught his eye. As early as 1908, he was collecting typical examples of the art, and in subsequent years he sought to bring order to advertising's chaos.

Münsterberg's work in advertising followed nearly a decade of investigations by others. Suggestion was already a popular concept among psychologically-minded advertisers, although just what process—beyond a play upon the much-discussed human "instincts"—they were describing when they declared a picture "suggestive" was not always clear. By the turn of the century, a number of psychologists, the most prominent of whom was Walter Dill Scott, a former student of Wundt teaching at Northwestern, offered the services of experimental psychology to the rationalization of advertising. They hoped that their science might indicate what appeals were likely to impress a product's name and merits on the reader's mind. Scott first promoted psychology's potential in this field in his *Theory of Advertising* (1903) and *The Psychology of Advertising* (1908); Daniel Starch, H. L. Hollingworth, Münsterberg, and others soon joined in. No modern businessman, the psychologists argued, could ignore experimental science's answers to such questions as: What size magazine advertisement had the greatest memory-value? What were the advantages of a large advertisement compared to those of repeated small ones? What was the success of colors and pictures in drawing the attention and exciting the interest of the reader?[38]

For Münsterberg the rationalization of advertising meant more than increased sales for individual businessmen—this, after all, had been the goal of nineteenth-century hucksterism. Advertising, instead, could supply the crucial link between supply and demand that was missing in the modern economy. When pursued on a broad scale, it "binds men together and tightly knits the members of society into one compact mass." As "the industry which overcomes the isolation of man with his wishes and with his wares," it laid "the real foundation of the social structure."[39] Münsterberg expressed himself poorly, and he conveniently bypassed the question of whether advertising allowed existing "wishes" to be met or whether it manufactured new ones. But his observation was striking. He argued, in effect, that psychologically sophisticated advertising, broadcast by organs of mass culture, might hold individuals to their social duty—in this case consumption—and provide a framework for social organization. Münsterberg's explication of this principle, which he had already sketched in his *Philosophie der Werte*, was early, but the message it conveyed anticipated what was to become a litany among advertisers and psychologists in the next two decades: Advertising had to transcend mere profit-seeking and help build a new social order of mass production and mass consumption.[40]

Advertising thus became, in Münsterberg's universe, a vehicle of social propaganda—a part, it sometimes seemed, of an orchestrated program of symbol-building. Nothing was extraordinary about such a program: Münsterberg had grown up in a culture that invested a great deal of energy in the cultivation of national symbols. Its novelty, however, lay in its application of the techniques of modern psychology to the design of the symbols. Men for centuries, for example, had attempted to inspire religious sentiments through church architecture, but according to Münsterberg they did not understand the psychological effects of their work. This ignorance, he wrote in 1914, took its revenge, "just as if the principles of mechanics has been sinned against." Neither the common-sense judgment of untrained men nor the intuition of the artist sufficed for building symbols; only the "careful investigations of systematic science" could deduce the proper guidelines.[41] Whether such an approach in fact tied society together effectively was beside the point. What was significant was that symbols of community had become works of propaganda.

Münsterberg extended this principle, at least in theory, to the whole cultural environment, every aspect of which came to express a transcendent moral purpose. In his classic study *Homo Ludens,* the Dutch historian Johan Huizinga has argued that the "play-element" of Western civilization has been on the decline since the early nineteenth century; "utilitarianism, prosaic efficiency and the bourgeois ideal of social welfare" were successfully rooting out all disinterested and nonpurposeful elements from culture. It is not necessary to accept Huizinga's scheme completely to observe that Münsterberg, whose intellectual origins lay more in German Idealism than utilitarianism, contributed his "psychotechnology" to just this process. In his textbook *Psychology,* for example, he suggested the restructuring of leisure activities normally thought to be diversions. Play educated children and athletics disciplined young men, he argued, echoing a truism popular then as well as now. Psychology could help these activities achieve their goals and increase their effectiveness: "The ball games and the card games," he wrote, "can be steadily improved by an insight into the mental demands."[42]

In *American Traits* Münsterberg had argued that the artist had no need for an understanding of aesthetic theory, but by the 1910s he had, without acknowledging it, reversed that position. In his later writings he outlined a psychotechnology of art, an activity traditionally reserved in German Idealist thought for the creative free play of the mind. For Kant, to follow Max Horkheimer and Theodor Adorno, the judgment of beauty depended upon a "secret mechanism in the soul" that forged a world of harmony according to laws of its own. By mid-century G. F. Herbart, and especially Gustav Fechner, attempted to expose that mechanism, not by logical deduction, as was customary, but "from below" through psychological investigations of the aesthetic sense.[43] Münsterberg, who himself played the cello, found this work of particular interest, and, throughout the decade before World War I, his laboratory, alone in the world, maintained uninterrupted studies in the psychology of aesthetics. He suggested in 1914 that these, more than any other laboratory studies, could be "immediately transformed into advice for the outside world," and that they seemed "predestined to be applied in practical life." Their results suggested to the artist how he might achieve specific effects, for example, that he could create the "glittering effect of a sunlit summer landscape" by painting small color spots side by side. Münsterberg also claimed that the psychologist could measure the aesthetic satisfaction derived from one or another combination of shapes, colors, tones, or rhymes. On a dark background, "the order of pleasantness" of colors was red, yellow, green, and blue; or, if a short vertical line were placed just left of the center of a picture, a long one near the right-hand frame would create "the most satisfactory aesthetic impression."[44]

The crudeness of Münsterberg's prescriptions is not important, nor is his confusion of learned standards of harmony with an innate mental mechanism. Their significance lies instead in the extent to which they dispossessed the artist of his creative role and transformed him into a draftsman. Münsterberg to be sure denied that this was his intention. "It would be an absurd misunderstanding," he wrote, "if the psychologist's advice were looked on as a substitute for true artistic inspiration."[45] The psychologist merely provided a set of "psychotechnical rules," not fundamentally different from those employed in the mixing of colors or the carving of stone. But the analogy was a false one. It equated the artist's audience with the passive media out of which he forged his art, and it therefore reduced communication to techniques of manipulation. At the same time it shifted the source of the conventions according to which the artist practiced his craft. These conventions, Münsterberg implied, ought not remain the property of the artist, any more than the lawyer (or legal traditions) ought to determine courtroom procedure or the laborer the organization of the workplace. All of these were problems of human management, which Münsterberg considered to be the sphere of the applied psychologist.

In a more fundamental way, Münsterberg eliminated "free play" from aesthetics, because, following a number of post-Kantian Idealists, he justified it functionally. Kant had argued that the sense of beauty reflected a disinterested pleasure that was grounded in the rational demand for unity, order, and harmony. It expressed "purposefulness without purpose." The form of a work of art exhibited internal purpose and offered a glimpse "into the hidden harmony of things," but as an object it had no practical function.[46] For Münsterberg, although he never made the comparison explicit, art played a function very close to the one to which he assigned alcohol. It offset the dreariness of life; it allowed recuperation from the demands of the workplace; and it provided a generalized social inspiration. Münsterberg had long lamented the absence of a strong aesthetic tradition in America, which might have alleviated the nation's fear of nerves and its social distress. He remarked in 1905, for example, on the need to cultivate "a love for beauty in the masses"; such a sensibility would allow "rest in the things of our world," and it might grant a vision of harmony, where all was in balance and everything in its appointed place—just as in the organic society toward which civilization was evolving.[47]

Once again, Münsterberg's position was not new. Many before him had perceived the function of an antifunctional art. In fact, he was merely importing to the New World a truism of German thought: that art was the unifying element in society and that it dissolved the burdens of everyday life. As George Mosse has written of nineteenth-century Germany, "the sense of beauty was supposed to make men feel at home in this world by providing them with a reality other than that of daily life in an industrializing society."[48] Toward this end, the cultivation of aesthetic sentiments through a national propaganda of art and ceremony had reached a high level.

Art was effective because it allowed an escape (or the illusion of escape) from the physical world into a higher spiritual reality. True to the aesthetic principles of the Idealists, Münsterberg found in it a freedom from worldly passion and individuality. "The fundamental condition of art . . . ," he wrote in 1916, "is that we shall be distinctly conscious of the unreality of the artistic production, and that means that it must be absolutely separated from the real things and men, that it must be isolated and kept in its own sphere." Art did not imitate life; it overcame reality by rejecting its constraints. Physical reality consisted of an unending chain of cause and effect, but the transformative power of art could break that chain. It showed "us the things and events perfectly complete in themselves, freed from all connections which lead beyond their own limits, that is, in perfect isolation."[49] This meant, in particular, isolation from the desires and interests of the individual: "The relation of the work [of art] to us as persons," Münsterberg wrote, "must not enter into our awareness of it at all." Instead it had to satisfy "by itself every demand which it awakens"; in it "nothing must remain unexplained and nothing unfinished." Art, therefore, was unlike propaganda and advertising, which impelled their audiences to action by exciting new and unfulfilled demands. It provided instead complete rest in a world of continuous striving.[50]

Early in 1915 Münsterberg discovered a new aesthetic medium with unique potential in the modern world: the film. For most of the 1910s he had considered motion pictures to be just another trivial and distracting aspect of American life, below the dignity of a Harvard professor. He purposefully avoided them, and he occasionally warned against them as a threat to social discipline. "The unhealthy influence of the motion pictures," he wrote in *Psychology: General and Applied,* "... too often make[s] crime and vice seductive and create[s] a hysteric attitude by their thrills and horrors." He searched instead for "wholesome appeals to the desire for amusement" by which the masses might be diverted.[51] During the war, however, he reversed his position.

A chance viewing of *Neptune's Daughter,* whose depiction of mermaid antics may have reminded him of the epic that he had written in childhood, convinced Münsterberg of the aesthetic possibilities of the film. "Surely I am now under the spell of the 'movies,' " he wrote a few months later," and, while my case may be worse than the average, all the world is somewhat under this spell." At the time of the *Lusitania* crisis and a disastrous break with his old friend Josiah Royce, movies offered him an escape from his wartime troubles. By the summer of 1915 he had turned to a wholehearted study of the psychology of the new medium: "I went with the crowd to Anita Stewart and Mary Pickford and Charles Chaplin," he wrote, and he spent many vacation hours viewing films.[52] He also struck up relations with the moguls of the young industry, who were happy to receive scholarly recognition. He visited the studios of Paramount, Pathé, Vitagraph, and Universal, among others. He put together for Paramount a filmed series of mental tests, which were widely shown under the title, "Testing the Mind," and he wrote several scenarios for the "Paramount History of Mankind," which never appeared.[53] In the fall of 1915 he wrote a preliminary article on motion pictures in *Cosmopolitan,* entitled "Why We Go to the Movies," and the following year he published his brief volume, *The Photoplay: A Psychological Study*—for which, rumors had it, he received payment from the cinema industry.[54]

Whether commissioned or not, *Photoplay* presented a flattering view of the film in years when most intellectuals scorned it as cheap. Münsterberg described motion pictures as an ideal source of the social and aesthetic inspiration so lacking in modern America. Their increasing popularity, he implied, testified to their potential as a surrogate religion, which could unify the nation and offer a glimpse of a higher harmony. The film possessed "an incomparable power for the remolding and upbuilding of the national soul"; to live up to its potential, however, it had to communicate "an enthusiasm for the noble and uplifting, a belief in duty and discipline of the mind, a faith in ideals and eternal values." Above all, the potential of the film was as an aesthetic medium. It was not, as so many critics contended, a poor imitation of the theater, but rather an authentic art in its own right, and it offered

> a new form of true beauty in the turmoil of a technical age, created by its very technique and yet more than any other art destined to overcome outer nature by the free and joyful play of the mind.

It was no wonder, therefore, he wrote, "that temples for the new goddess are built in every little hamlet."[55]

Film, according to Münsterberg, was particularly effective as art not only because it reached a wide audience, but also because it could reproduce the mind's own "freedom from the bondage of the material world." In his philosophy of values, Münsterberg had argued, like Kant and Fichte, that the mental world of will was free, unconstrained by the laws of cause and effect that operated in the world of appearances. Because the film, unlike the theater, did not depend on the manipulation of physical objects and real people to tell its story, it enjoyed a similar freedom. Münsterberg therefore opposed any technical innovations that might have reduced its "far-reaching disregard of reality." Sound, color, and three-dimensional photography, he argued, only imitated nature and as a result negated film's special potential. Motion pictures were instead to create a neverland of the mind. For the moviegoer, he wrote,

> the massive outer world has lost its weight, it has been freed from space, time, and causality, and it has been clothed in the forms of our own consciousness. The mind has triumphed over matter and the pictures roll on with the ease of musical tones.[56]

Münsterberg emphasized that it was the mind of the viewer that created this neverland, and therein lay its freedom from the physical world. When we watch a motion picture, he wrote, "we do not see the objective reality, but a product of our own mind which binds the pictures together." Movement, for instance, was "not really seen from without, but is superadded, by the action of the mind, to motionless pictures." At the same time, the film could reproduce or "objectify" the acts of mind in all their freedom on the screen. In the closeup, for example, "everything which our mind wants to disregard has been suddenly banished from our sight and has disappeared," just as it did subjectively when we fixed our attention on an object. The film in this way "objectified in our world of perception our mental act of attention." In the same fashion, the flash-back represented "an objectification of our memory function." "In both cases," Münsterberg wrote,

> the act which in the ordinary theater would go on in our mind alone is here in the photoplay projected into the pictures themselves. It is as if reality has lost its own continuous connection and become shaped by the demands of our soul.[57]

Münsterberg's language in these passages consistently testified to the active role of the viewer, but it should be stressed that "the free and active play" of the moviegoer's mind was in fact thoroughly constrained. In Münsterberg's Action Theory, the mind participated in the creation of its perceptions, but it did not do so spontaneously. It was simply a reactive mechanism more sophisticated than that of the associationists. Münsterberg valued film not because it allowed more creativity on the part of the audience, but because it permitted more control by the artist over the aesthetic experience. In stage drama, he wrote, "if we really enter into the spirit of the play, our attention is constantly drawn in accordance with the intentions of the producers." The careful use of shading, background scenery, and so forth "all play on the keyboard of our mind and secure the desired effect on our involuntary attention."[58] But, with its ability to "objectify" the viewer's mental processes, the film was far more effective in enforcing the viewer's participation and eliminating the influence of his individual peculiarities. The film, therefore, did just the opposite of allowing the mind free rein; it prescribed absolutely what the mind was to attend to and how it was to do so. The mental act was taken out of the mind of each viewer and placed upon the screen, where all recorded its passage in an identical fashion.

What message ought the filmmaker impress upon his audience? Like any artist's, his duty, according to Münsterberg, was to communicate "a unity which does not lead beyond itself but is in itself perfectly harmonious," thereby securing for the viewers "that restful happiness which the beautiful landscape or the harmonious life relation can furnish us in blessed instants of our struggling life." For a more critical tradition, represented by Friedrich Nietzsche among others, this aesthetics of isolation offered a "promise of happiness" against which to measure the deficiencies of the world.[59] For Münsterberg, however, the happiness was not merely promised but actually granted; instead of fixing attention on the ailments of the real world, it made them irrelevant.

In his psychotherapy and much of his social psychology, Münsterberg argued that social distress reflected a failure of adjustment; real conflict did not exist. "Our social difficulties," he wrote in 1914, "are ultimately dependent upon mental conditions which ought to be cleared up with the methods of modern psychology." In *Photoplay* and his metaphysical work, however, he went beyond this position: Conflict, struggle, and suffering, as well as joy, were built into the eternal dialectic of progress. But art meant freedom from that dialectic and from self-interested obsession with pleasure and pain. At times Münsterberg in fact denied any material basis to happiness. "Only in contact with an isolated experience," he wrote, "can we feel perfectly happy," and for him "isolation" meant the renunciation of transitory physical and even emotional gratification. "The people," he insisted, "still has [sic] to learn the great difference between true enjoyment and fleeting pleasure, between real beauty and the mere tickling of the senses."[60] The photoplay, therefore, did not derive its value from its purely diversionary qualities. National in scope and popular in appeal, it provided a new and unifying source of inspiration and self-discipline. It offered the possibility—it seemed—of extending for a while to ordinary people the peace and passivity that art had always instilled in the cultivated. That this peace allowed its viewers to recuperate before they returned, renewed, to the strenuous performance of duty made it all the more valuable.

10

Industrial Efficiency

Münsterberg's concern for the recuperative value of art suggested his interest in the problem of work in modern society. No questions in applied psychology, in fact, attracted him more than those of industrial organization and efficiency. For more than half a decade, beginning with his article in 1909 on "Psychology and the Market," he extended his view to the entire range of economic psychology: vocational guidance, advertising, personnel management, mental testing, fatigue and monotony, motivation, and the "mind" of labor. Shortly after his return from Berlin in 1911, he completed *Psychologie und Wirtschaftsleben* (Psychology and Economic Life), and in 1913 he issued a modified English version of the work under the title *Psychology and Industrial Efficiency*, which appeared briefly on the nonfiction best-seller lists.[1] Together these two books confirmed Münsterberg as the leading systematizer of the new field.

Münsterberg took up the psychology of work at a time when industrial efficiency preoccupied important segments of the business community, especially those that faced the new problems of mass transportation or relied on the new sciences of electrical and chemical engineering. Profits for the industrialist increasingly depended on the rationalization of his enterprise, which meant more than the application of recent technology to production. Beginning in the 1880s, a movement for systematic management introduced to the factory modern accounting procedures, the centralized purchasing and standardizing of materials, and more direct ways to regulate labor itself, including time cards and job clocks. One aspect of this development was the increasing separation of the planning from the labor, making the latter a commodity on the same level as other raw materials in the production process. Management of the work force became, in its own way, as important as management of the machinery.[2]

Labor proved to be a far more recalcitrant resource than did other commodities. Industrial spokesman, armed with freshly gathered statistics, charged that the available labor pool was unsuitable, especially when compared with the wonderful machines that technology could produce. By the 1910s, high rates of labor turnover and industrial accidents, as well as widespread truancy and malingering, offered very tangible evidence of inferior "human material." One manager wrote that "the frailty of human nature" caused 80 percent of the accidents on the railroads, which were killing over ten thousand people a year by 1911. Another claimed that one out of every three of the sixteen thousand operators for the Bell Telephone Company left work or was dismissed within the first half year. A number of corporate leaders and managers, many of them engineers themselves, turned to systems of human engineering in the hope that they might duplicate the successes of engineering in physics and chemistry.[3]

More perceptive managers recognized the extent to which the sciences of physiology, psychology, and social psychology could contribute to efficiency at work. The industrial and corporation schools that emerged in the United States at the turn of the century, for example, often borrowed from the latest psychological work on teaching skills. Investigations of fatigue and monotony by Kraepelin at Munich and Mosso at Turin in the 1890s justified, and in some cases encouraged, industrial experiments on the effect of shorter working hours, rest pauses, and similar improvements in working conditions. In 1908 the German Verein für Socialpolitik, reform-minded association of social scientists, launched a series of extensive studies on the sociology and "psychophysics" of the workplace in specific industries; American progressives used these and other investigations to support their arguments for efficiency and reform.[4]

The best-known attack on the "labor problem," if not the most sophisticated psychologically, was Frederick Taylor's program of scientific management. Taylor's system achieved national prominence in 1910 when, in the famous Eastern Rate Case, Louis Brandeis linked the principles of scientific management with efficiency and economic reform. In the previous decades Taylor, a former shop foreman and an engineer by training, had experienced remarkable success in reorganizing plants for increased production. His approach was to step up the rate of work by standardizing it. He and his colleagues in the efficiency movement advocated careful, scientific analysis of industrial tasks through stopwatch-regulated time-and-motion studies. From these the scientific manager could determine "the one best method" of performing each task, and he could define a fair day's work. Wage-incentive programs, administered through either a piece-rate system or bonuses, could spur the individual worker to achieve and even surpass the daily production quota. Such rewards, Taylor argued, would overcome any initial resistance that workers might have to the system. "Workmen ... are in time reconciled to time study," he wrote an associate, "when they appreciate that the ultimate outcome of it means higher wages for themselves." But the system was authoritarian and coercive. Experts, rather than the process of collective bargaining, determined wages, working conditions, and the rules of shop management. Labor (and management) conformed. As Taylor recommended, "If a man won't do what is right, *make* him."[5]

Such a system inevitably ran into difficulties in its application. By avoiding industries that had strong unions, Taylorites lent plausibility to their assertion that "there has never been a strike under scientific management." The illusion burst in 1911 when molders in an army-run arsenal in Watertown, Massachusetts, walked off the job rather than submit to a time-and-motion study. The strike was short-lived, but it led to a four-month congressional investigation that raised serious questions about the effectiveness of scientific management. Above all, critics concentrated on Taylor's tendency to regard labor as simply another machine and his failure to understand the "human factor."[6]

Among the more vocal of the critics of Taylor's "technicist" bias were members of a small but growing group of industrial psychologists who by the 1920s had secured for themselves an important place in both psychology and industry. The British psychologist C. S. Myers summed up the attitude of his colleagues in 1920 when he charged that Taylorism ran "counter to known psychological principles." It led to a system of "so-called 'scientific' management, mechanically formulated by the engineer, in which the mental factors of personality, sentiment, and sympathy are sacrificed to purely physical considerations."[7] Almost a decade before, Münsterberg was making these same points.

In his work on industrial efficiency, Münsterberg admitted considerable respect for Taylorism, despite what he considered its psychological naiveté. He acknowledged that scientific management represented an advance in the rationalization of the workplace. And he seconded Taylor's basic principle that the science of work belonged in the hands of independent experts, whatever the short-term interests of the laborers (or their employees) might be. He observed with approval that scientific management had, on the basis of its experiments, replaced "everything which usually is left to tradition, to caprice, and to an economy which looks out only for the most immediate saving" with "entirely new means and tools, where nothing was left to arbitrariness." In other words, control of the work had been taken out of the workplace and away from those who performed it, supervised it, and even paid for it. According to Münsterberg, an experimental industrial psychology that considered the mental structure of the worker as well as the mechanics of work was essential to this rationalization. Through experimentation by the psychologist, he suggested,

> a certain acknowledged system of rules and prescriptions may be worked out which may be used as patterns, and which will not presuppose any scientific knowledge, any more than an understanding of the principles of electricity is necessary for one who uses the telephone.

The meaning of this passage was clear, even if Münsterberg did not develop it explicitly: The organization of work in the interests of efficiency meant the decline of skill. Industrial progress, in his view, depended on the transformation of work habits and crafts—skilled and unskilled alike—into direction-following.[8]

Like Taylor, Münsterberg also argued that any science of work should be neutral. It served economic progress and social order as a whole rather than "a reckless capitalism on the one side" or "a feeble sentimentality on the other side." The industrial psychologist impartially asked

> what psychological facts ought to be considered if the aim is to make the commercial actions as efficient as possible in the interests of both employee and employer.

Münsterberg readily admitted that psychological techniques could be, and in fact were, misused, just as the anarchist (but not, apparently, the state) might pervert the chemist's science by appropriating it for the manufacture of bombs. He sympathized, no doubt, with the complaints of his former student O. V. Fry, who was employed as a psychologist by the Pennsylvania Railroad. The railroad, Fry wrote him in 1915, attempted to distort his work "in such a way that it would be an effective instrument in handling refractory employees, especially Union men."[9] To avoid just this sort of abuse, Münsterberg had recommended unsuccessfully to both Kaiser Wilhelm II and Woodrow Wilson that independent government research bureaus be established in applied and industrial psychology.[10]

Even in the most "neutral" of arrangements, however, it was clear who bore the burden of any inconveniences that industrial reforms might entail. In language reminiscent of Taylor's, Münsterberg cautioned in *Psychology and Industrial Efficiency* that "some irritation" could be expected to "accompany the introduction of psychological improvements in the methods of work," just as it had the introduction of the factory system in earlier generations. "Not a few wage-earners may at first have to lose their places because a small number of men will under the improved conditions be sufficient for the performance of tasks which needed many before." As a consolation, Münsterberg offered his assurances that "from the point of view of the whole community such an apparent disturbance has always been only temporary."[11]

Münsterberg, on the other hand, judged many of Taylor's actual methods to be misguided. Taylor's reliance on bribery and coercion, he argued, assumed a worker motivated by conscious reason rather than a host of irrational personality factors, and his mechanical approach to the workplace, which concentrated on the nature of the task, ignored the facts of human psychology and individual variation. A truly efficient industrial organism required the adjustment of working conditions and technology to the mental demands of the worker and, at the same time, the worker's mind to the conditions of his labor. The satisfaction that would follow this dual adjustment, Münsterberg suggested, would have results that extended far beyond the workplace. "The economic experimental psychology," Münsterberg wrote in his conclusion to *Psychology and Industrial Efficiency*,

> offers no more inspiring idea than this adjustment of work and psyche by which mental dissatisfaction in the work, mental depression and discouragement, may be replaced in our social community by overflowing joy and perfect inner harmony.[12]

Extending his earlier vocational rhetoric, Münsterberg argued that the first step toward ensuring inner harmony at work was to place workers in positions that fitted their mental types. According to recent studies, he asserted, monotony and fatigue were subjective states of mind, linked to individual psychological dispositions. Even those jobs that on the surface seemed most boring, therefore, might be fascinating to the right people. To illustrate the point, Münsterberg cited an interview that he conducted with a woman in an electric lamp factory who packed light bulbs in tissue paper. She had worked at the same job continuously for twelve years, packing thirteen thousand bulbs a day at the rate of twenty-five every forty-two seconds. Yet she reported her work "really interesting," and, far from being bored, she felt "an inner tension" as she anticipated how many boxes she would be able to fill before the next rest pause. Münsterberg speculated that the woman's satisfaction at work reflected a finer than normal ability to discriminate minute differences, which allowed her to discover variety in tasks that most people would have found monotonous.[13]

Münsterberg claimed that such a joy in repetitive tasks was measureable. The employer had only to test applicants for assembly-line positions in order to ensure a happy labor force. He could thereby exploit for society's benefit a trait later characterized by the industrial psychologist Morris Viteles as "the boon of stupidity."[14] But it never occurred to Münsterberg to ask whether there were enough men and women with a sense of "inner manifoldness" to fill all the boring jobs. Nor did he ask whether the mental state that allowed the woman to find her job interesting was inherent or whether it developed as a result of twelve years of wrapping. And it never occurred to the man who only a few years before had developed a lie detector that she might have been lying. Instead, he elevated to the level of science a self-serving and unexamined myth—that menial laborers, because of their special traits of mind, were at least as happy at their worldly duties as the highly pressured professionals were at theirs.

The idea that the industrial organism worked more smoothly if people were in the right places was widespread by the second decade of the twentieth century. One constant, although secondary, element of Taylor's work had been to fit the appropriate worker to the task; for example, in his famous pig iron test at Bethlehem Steel in 1899, he institutionalized the "scientific" selection of specially competent workers. For years specific industries also had used physiological tests, such as for color blindness in prospective railroad engineers, to screen applicants, and some corporations, including General Electric, had developed extensive testing procedures for trainees. Other businesses employed various pseudoscientific schemes based on assumed racial characteristics, physiognomy, and even graphology. "A very common notion among industrial and employment managers," the psychologist Henry Link wrote in 1919, "is that all their problems will be solved when a scheme has been devised which will make it possible to select *the right man for the right place.*" Or, as one railway manager put it after reading *Psychology and Industrial Efficiency,* a well-run factory required for the sake of production and worker satisfaction that "there is in each position a man who is in the best place in the world for him."[15]

Techniques of mental testing, already haltingly applied by guidance counselors, often seemed an improvement over other methods of selecting employees, and they proved a handy tool for personnel managers. A program that in the hands of Parsons had aimed at facilitating self-expression and personal fulfillment was soon transformed into a means of screening for industrial efficiency. H. L. Hollingworth described the process with approval in 1916:

> The first definite contribution of vocational psychology is thus not so much
> toward the guidance of the individual worker as for the guidance of the em-

ployer who may be required to select from a number of applicants those
whose general intellectual equipment is most adequate.[16]

In the process, the aim of testing ceased to be the assessment of general
"personality" traits, such as will power or interest; it became the measuring of specific mental skills required for efficient and profitable production in one position or another.

Münsterberg recognized early that mental tests could serve personnel
managers as well as vocationists. His *McClure's* essay on "Psychology
and the Market" broached the question of employee selection in 1909,
and two years later, immediately on return from his year in Germany, he
addressed himself enthusiastically to the problem. The initial task, as he
understood it, was to determine the exact requirement of various industrial positions—a goal that he set about to achieve through the very questionnaire method that he had attacked ten years before when it was used
by the child-study movement. He sent out circulars to one thousand man-
ufacturers asking what mental traits they considered essential in their various employees. Several hundred of the firms answered, and some, like
the Gillette Safety Razor Company, worked out detailed statements.
Münsterberg also believed that direct psychological investigation was a
necessary supplement to the questionnaires, and he personally visited the
plants of the General Electric Company in Lynn, the International Har-
vester Company in Chicago, the Waltham Watch Company, and others,
in order to assess the nature of the work.[17]

Together with his popular essays, these forays into the day-to-day operations of industry made Münsterberg's work known in industrial circles.
It was no surprise, then, that the New York director of the Hamburg-
American shipping line wrote Münsterberg in October 1911 asking him if
he could construct a test that would eliminate incompetent ship captains.
Münsterberg readily accepted. His goal, as he saw it, was to devise a way
to test for the act of decision. After a long series of experiments, he recommended a set of cards, upon each of which were printed twenty-eight
random vowels arranged in four columns. The candidate was to sort these
cards as fast as he could into four piles, depending on whether the vowel
A, E, O, or U predominated. Münsterberg claimed that by comparing the
speed and the accuracy of the candidates' work, he could pick out men
"of perfect reliability in making quick, correct decisions in complex life
situations."[18]

The following spring Münsterberg was approached again, this time by
the American Association for Labor Legislation, a progressive group
financed in part by John D. Rockefeller and Elbert Gary and best known
for its attempts to convince labor of the value of unemployment insur-

ance. Could he, the committee asked, investigate the mental traits that predisposed trolley drivers to accidents?[19]

Münsterberg once again accepted, and to assist his investigations he secured the cooperation of the Boston Elevated Railway Company. In this case he rejected the relevance of one-factor tests, such as the measurement of reaction-time to optical stimuli. Traits isolated in such a fashion, he argued, bore no relation to the experience of driving a trolley car. Nor would a scale model work, for there was no reason to assume that "a reduced copy of an external apparatus" would arouse a state of mind that would have anything to do "with the processes of actual life." Instead, he contended, the essential condition was "the inner similarity of the mental attitude"; the test had to reproduce what it felt like to drive a trolley. After abandoning several approaches that failed to differentiate accident-prone from accident-free drivers, he arrived at a complicated device that he considered satisfactory.

The machine resembled a conveyor belt. A black velvet band with widely spaced rectangular windows spanned two revolving drums. Under the belt was a stack of twelve cards, each divided into a checkerboard of squares, nine wide and twenty-six long. On the grids were randomly placed the digits 1, 2, and 3 in black and red. The prospective employee would slowly crank the drums, causing the window in the belt to scan down the top card, revealing one horizontal row at a time. On this horizontal row the center unit, which was lettered, represented the railway track; the figure 1 was a pedestrian who could move one block, the figure 2 a horse that could move two blocks, the figure 3 an automobile that could move three blocks; black figures moved parallel to the trolley, red figures moved at right angles. As the candidate scanned down the card, he was to record each time that a pedestrian, horse, or automobile endangered his car. Münsterberg then came up with a rank order of candidates by arbitrarily correlating the number of mistakes each man made with the speed with which he went through the twelve cards. He also ranked successful and unsuccessful operators already employed by the company on the same scale—a sophistication he had not incorporated into the ship-captain tests. A comparison of the scores of the successful drivers with those of the candidates, he claimed, would allow the weeding out of the accident-prone.[20]

These tests and similar ones on telephone operators and salesmen, all of which Münsterberg described in *Psychologie und Wirtschaftsleben* and *Psychology and Industrial Efficiency,* were among the first mental tests specifically designed for filling industrial positions, and they attracted the immediate attention of psychologists and businessmen. "The significant point of it all," wrote Walter Dill Scott, Northwestern's expert on the psychology of advertising,

> is that simple tests have been devised and applied in certain typical economic situations and that there is a positive correlation between the standing in the tests and the standing in the practical work.

On the whole, however, professional psychologists were skeptical. One of the strongest critics, G. M. Whipple, a leading expert on tests, rejected what he considered Münsterberg's "hypothetical" approach. Whipple cited an investigation in Cincinnati in which a psychologist had rerun Münsterberg's test on decision-making. This experiment found that a number of individuals who had displayed "unusual quickness" in real emergencies scored low on the test. But the crushing blow to Münsterberg's case was the discovery that "the person most fitted for sea-captaincy of all those tested [in the Cincinnati experiment] . . . turned out to be a 'co-ed.' " Whatever their technical faults, Whipple also claimed, Münsterberg's test had by 1916 made "little impression upon the hardheaded men of business."[21]

The criticism voiced by Whipple and others fixed on Münsterberg's methods and his popularizing style rather than on the concept of testing itself. But considerable resistance existed within the business community itself to testing at all. A Philadelphia railway man argued, "for the most part I believe that the traffic manager will be able to judge of his men a good deal better than Professor Münsterberg or any other of those people who give new names to familiar facts." "It is not probable," he suggested, "that anything will ever be discovered which will take the place of personal contact between human beings in the matter of inspiring the routine toiler to sturdy loyalty."[22] It was a defense of common sense and practical experience that Münsterberg had already encountered in his attempts to apply psychology to law.

On the other hand, Münsterberg's work, if not always his specific tests, received recognition among the corporate engineers who were forging management policies. Reviewing *Psychology and Industrial Efficiency,* the *Engineering Record* found in his testing "large possibilities of preventing waste" and of eliminating misfits. *Survey,* a progressive journal "with close corporate connections," perceived in his work the beginnings of a new science that would systematically place the psychological experiment "at the service of education and industry" and might some day "prevent the tragic waste of misfit starts in life and go far toward solving the problem of vocational guidance for schools."[23]

Münsterberg's work also inspired a rash of studies on psychological testing in industry, as well as a series of attempts to apply the science of mental testing to the selection of employees. Several of his tests were adopted by industry. The American Tobacco Company used his salesman tests until 1915, when it turned to Scott to devise a new set. The Dallas Consolidated Electric Street Railway Company put a modified version of his tests for motormen and ship captains into practice in examining prospective trolley drivers. These tests, the Superintendent of Transportation claimed, eliminated the slow, the careless, and the indecisive applicants. By 1915, Hollingworth reported, tests for twenty types of work had already been proposed, recommended, and, to one extent or another, tried out.[24]

Testing, however, attacked only half of the problem of industrial efficiency. How could psychology, Münsterberg asked, contribute to the productivity of the worker on the job, and how could it increase "inner harmony" at work?

At the simplest level, Münsterberg suggested a psychologically sophisticated Taylorism, substituting more behavioristic techniques of manipulation for overt coercion, but maintaining the emphasis on work speedup. Psychological experiments, he wrote, had proved that any talking during labor led to distraction and a lessening of efficiency. He contended, however, that "a tyrannical demand for silence would, of course, be felt as cruelty, and no suggestion of a jail-like discipline would be wise in the case of industrial labor, for evident psychological reasons." (Most would have considered the reasons political rather than psychological, but then the tendency of Münsterberg's scientism was, in Mannheim's terms, to transform political questions into technical ones.) Instead, Münsterberg praised those factories that "in rearranging their establishments according to the principles of scientific management have changed the positions of the workmen so that conversations become more difficult or impossible." Along these same lines, he offered another hint to industrial managers: Psychological experiments showed that a subject's maximum grip increased when he could see certain colors or hear particular tones. Expose the worker to these colors or tones and his or her rate of production might increase.[25]

Münsterberg insisted, however, that such techniques were in the end ineffective unless the conditions of work and the operation of machines were fitted to the rhythm and structure of the workers' minds. Münsterberg in effect asked, How can we induce in the laborer a state of mind that will contribute to care and efficiency at work? Although its subject matter lay outside the workplace, a memorandum on street lights prepared by Münsterberg in 1914 for the National Electric Light Association's Street Lighting Committee illustrated his approach to the question of adjustment. In the memorandum Münsterberg contended that simple tests of visual acuity could not by themselves determine the most effective and safest means of street illumination for drivers and pedestrians. "The mere possibility of visual discrimination does not ensure comfort and still less safety on the street." A street light company, instead, had to consider the effect of various intensities and spacings on attention and other mental functions: "Fair chances to see are of small use," he wrote, "if the pedestrian or the driver come into a benumbed state in which their attention is dulled and in which their reactions are slow."[26]

After receiving Münsterberg's report, the NELA hired his student Harold E. Burtt to conduct experiments for it, but in the end the Street Lighting Committee rejected his approach. This rejection indicated one difficulty faced by Münsterberg's brand of psychology when it came to actual application in industry. The committee preferred to ask how street light companies could achieve a satisfactory level of illumination most cheaply, and it relied on the testimony of competent observers and experiments on perception. One member of the committee, the electrical engineer Charles Steinmetz, suggested fatigue tests, but even here the question was one of physiology, rather than of mental attitudes such as alertness. The approach was essentially Taylorian: Determine the least expensive means of lighting the streets above a certain minimum level and make or teach the consumers to accept it.[27] Implicit within Burtt's experiments and Münsterberg's discussion of testing was the assumption that people possessed certain innate traits or ingrained habits of mind (not merely of body) that society ignored at its peril.

A more striking illustration of the limited success of Münsterberg's innatist approach was the fate of his concern for fitting the work to meet individual traits, for example in his discussions of typewriters. Recent experiments in Germany, he wrote, indicated that if speed, efficiency, and comfort were the goals, then the kind of machine (for instance, one with visible writing versus one whose writing was hidden, or one with a shift key versus one with two complete keyboard alphabets, one upper and one lower case) should harmonize with the mental type of the operator. Industry, of course, did not adopt such a course, and the failure of Münsterberg's quixotic and thoroughly impractical attempt to halt standardization reflected the reception of his organic "individualism" in an industrial world that valued interchangeable parts. When industrial psychology emerged as a full-fledged discipline in the 1920s, it found an environmentalist view of mind and a functionalist anthropology more congenial, for they both suggested a more tractable mental structure.[28]

It should remain clear, however, that Münsterberg's concern for "individual adjustment" in his discussions of typewriters, or for that matter of lamp-packing, did not mean a commitment to individual autonomy any more than it had in his vocational rhetoric. He disagreed with behaviorists like John Watson on the malleability of men and women, and therefore the efficacy of training, but, like later industrial psychologists, he found "inner harmony" at work absolutely consistent with an increasing subdivision of tasks within the social organism and a decreasing role for its members in defining the nature or purposes of those tasks. An individualizing psychology, according to him, was simply a more efficient means of holding individuals to their functions, especially when by inclination they balked. "Only when the mental mechanism, the individual dispositions, associations, and reactions are made clear," he wrote in *Grundzüge der Psychotechnik,* "can it be possible to overcome inner resistances and to avoid frictions, which are in most cases equally to the disadvantage of the employer and the employee."[29]

In 1913, after completing *Psychology and Industrial Efficiency,* Münsterberg undertook a project to map "the individual dispositions, associations, and reactions" of American laborers—and therefore presumably to overcome their "inner resistances." Following the example of Adolf Levenstein, who had shortly before surveyed a large group of German miners, textile workers, and metal workers, Münsterberg drew up a questionnaire that he hoped to distribute to fifteen thousand factory and mill workers. It "would form," he wrote Harvard's President Lowell, "a kind of sociological background for certain investigations on monotony and similar questions which are being examined at present in our psychological laboratory." The plan never came off because Lowell feared it might tarnish Harvard's name, but its questions indicated Münsterberg's concern with job satisfaction and motivation.[30] "Do you think it important," he asked, "for the factory to provide good health conditions, good light, fresh air, cleanliness and attractive grounds, or do you not care for that?" More broadly, "Do you feel any pride in or loyalty to the company for which you work, or is it indifferent to you for whom you work?" And, "Do you enjoy your work as something which helps the progress of the country, or do you not care for that?" (On the question, "If you had a million dollars, what would you do with it?" one reviewer—apparently the labor leader Samuel Gompers—to whom a copy of the questionnaire had been sent for comments recommended, "Beleive [*sic*] you should omit." In a revised version, the question did not appear.)[31]

In covering letters Münsterberg suggested that his questionnaire would yield information "truly helpful to the working man" and lead "toward better and happier conditions of work." And he assured his prospective informants that no employers would ever see their answers. Gompers had warned Münsterberg that "the experience of the workingman has made them distrusting of 'investigations' and intolerant of patronage," and

Münsterberg feared, no doubt, that his study would be confused with the efforts of such industrial groups as the Ford Motor Company's new Sociological Division, whose principle responsibility, according to the historian Daniel Nelson, was "to insure, through investigations of the workers' homes and family life, that they conformed to their employer's middle-class values and thus warranted the five-dollar day."[32] But the leading nature of Münsterberg's questions belied his claims to neutrality.

Although Münsterberg had criticized Levenstein's survey for its built-in assumptions, his own questionnaire bore the imprint of his vision of industrial order.[33] It implied that workers ought to feel loyal to their companies, at least if the companies treated them humanely, and that they ought to feel pride in their contributions to the progress of their country (although many industrial workers were unnaturalized immigrants who expected to return to their homeland in a few years).[34] The questionnaire did not allow its informants to consider just what was meant by progress, or whether their work did in fact contribute to it. And the questionnaire did not anywhere admit the possibility that "job satisfaction" might be related to a sense of craftsmanship or control over the conditions of work. It reaffirmed, instead, the compatibility between "inner harmony" and the increasing regimentation of wage earners. Loyalty and pride, evidently, could cover a multitude of social sins.

Laborers had another, more fundamental reason to suspect the intentions of Münsterberg's questionnaire, for, despite the crude level of much of his psychology, he assumed a connection between knowledge and the power to control. If a psychologist knew the "inner resistances" of his subjects, he was apparently in a much better position to overcome them. Speaking not of industry but of society as a whole, Münsterberg offered in *Grundzüge der Psychotechnik* a revealing description of the proper role in his science:

> The masses [he warned], when they group themselves together, may exercise a function legitimate for their own interests, and nevertheless it might be more valuable from the standpoint of the whole society to suppress this function, or at least to restrict it.

In such a case, society as a whole had to know "how, through psychological means, it could break the strength of such a crowd in its midst." Often, Münsterberg suggested, the psychotechnical rules of social organization were best hidden from the members of the group to be organized and reserved for "others, who from the point of view of the general social interest, wish to take care that the masses, in unconscious cooperation, reach their proper goals."[35]

It is clear that Münsterberg considered loyalty, pride, and a sense of duty to be the primary bonds that held workers at all levels to their social function. His industrial psychology, therefore, depended on the same sort of commitment therapy as his social psychology did. He filled his essays with testimonials to the transcendental value of work in the modern industrial setting. "There is under no factory roof a workman so forlorn," he wrote in an essay of 1913 on socialism, "that the work of his hands is not aiding the fulfillment of . . . [a] . . . great and . . . ideal purpose of civilized mankind, the development of economic civilization." Apparently unaware that in this passage he implicitly identified handwork with a forlorn state, Münsterberg went on a few pages later to assert that, as soon as the industrial community became

> inspired by the belief in the ideal value of the work as work and as a necessary contribution to the progress of mankind, the social question will be solved, as all the differences which socialism wants to eliminate then appear trivial and insignificant.[36]

Like so many industrial psychologists who succeeded him, Münsterberg had come to suggest that a mental revolution would blunt the threat of a socialist one—a threat that he conceded had become real even in the individualistic New World. He found it easy to assign the blame for this development. The "problem of suffering" at work, he wrote, not only led to inefficiency; it had become "the real fountainhead of the socialistic flood which threatens to inundate our present-day social structures." Yet suffering was not an inevitable by-product of those structures. The socialists, and for that matter the more conservative advocates of an ideal of craftsmanship, were wrong when they traced boredom to "the character of the work itself." Just as the alpinist who climbed with a goal in mind could overcome his "exhausting muscle strain" and pursue his avocation with a passion, the worker could, with the proper mental attitude, transform labor that had been strenuous, tedious, or dull into meaningful activity.[37]

Such exhortations sounded closer to the inspirational messages of the mind-curists and self-help faddists than to the programs of modern science, but they epitomized the rhetoric of personnel management and industrial psychology in their early years. Walter Dill Scott, for example, made a similar point on the "problem of suffering," although he expressed it less grandly:

> If I want my work to be interesting and to compel my undivided attention, I should then try and make my work appeal to me as of more importance than anything else in the world. . . . I must regard the work as a service to the house; and I must in every possible way try to "get into the game."[38]

Both Münsterberg and Scott were attempting to add meaning to the demeaning, one through an analogy to sport, the other through reference to the higher purposes of history. It is hard to imagine that their appeals impressed the bulk of American working men and women or significantly affected the rates of labor turnover, industrial accidents, and strikes or the growth of unions. But then, outside of an occasional captive audience in industry-sponsored schools and Americanization programs, its major consumers were neither the unskilled and semiskilled nor the masses of unassimilated immigrants who manned so many of America's industries. They were the new middle classes, that growing group of white-collar professionals who took correspondence courses with such titles as "Business Psychology" and "Vocation and Learning." For them the rhetoric offered a convenient and heartening rallying cry.

The positive thinking of a new middle class rationalizing its success was one thing; a quite different question was the actual organization and application of a psychology of testing and motivation. Münsterberg's appeals to Wilhelm II and Wilson for the establishment of government bureaus of applied psychology failed to convince either man, but throughout the second decade of the century the ideal of neutral and professional psychological expertise became increasingly institutionalized, with Münsterberg among its leading propagandists. In 1915 the Carnegie Institute of Technology set up a program of applied psychology that included the first psychological consulting service for industry, and soon established a Bureau of Salesmanship Research and a Research Bureau for Retail Training in order to aid businesses in selecting, training, and rating employees. The first director of the program, Walter V. Bingham, was apparently persuaded initially by Münsterberg of the need for applying psychology to industrial problems.[39] The following year the Economic Psychology Association appeared, listing Münsterberg, along with such specialists as Hollingworth and Thorndike, among its "Scientists and Special Investigators." Intending to provide a meeting ground for representatives of industry and academia, organizers of the association described their efforts as "the beginning of a greater manifestation of the Human Nature element as it affects business and economic life."[40]

Despite these developments, it was the war that converted both orthodox psychologists and the federal government. G. Stanley Hall noted the contributions of psychologists to the German and French war efforts at a joint meeting of the American Psychological Association and the American Association for the Advancement of Sciences. Favorable reception of this speech led directly to Hall's founding of the *Journal of Applied Psychology* in early 1917, nearly ten years after the appearance of a similarly titled journal in German.[41] More significant, psychologists came to play important roles in the war effort, especially after the organization of the

National Research Council's Committee for Psychology. Robert Yerkes, a student, assistant, and for a number of years colleague of Münsterberg, headed the committee, and he oversaw the development and implementation of the Army's famous Alpha and Beta tests. Another Münsterberg student who was active in the military testing program, Richard Elliott, later testified, "it was Münsterberg's influence which 'set' me for enthusiastic participation in the work of the Army's psychologists in World War I."[42] In the wake of the war, the government dismantled its psychological program, but professional psychologists maintained their interest in the practical application of their science. By 1920, four years after Münsterberg's death, more than half the psychologists in the United States, according to one estimate, were engaged in research in applied psychology.[43]

It was ironic that Münsterberg's campaign for an applied "psychotechnics" of society gained its major impetus in America from the war effort against Germany. But it was appropriate, for Münsterberg often compared the ideal social organization to an army or a warship, in which lines of command were rigidly hierarchical and all members worked selflessly for a higher goal, dictated by history (and divined by a few). Like so many Americans in the Progressives years, Münsterberg considered efficiency to be in the end a national concept; all efficiencies, whether social, industrial, or personal, contributed to national efficiency, and a reform was truly efficient only if it served the state. The aim of his psychologies of testing and motivation, therefore, was to bind the individual to his duty within the national organism—even when common sense or personal inclinations led elsewhere. World War I only temporarily shook Münsterberg's faith in the transcendental meaning of the nation, and as late as 1916 he could look optimistically ahead to the rationalized world of the future. But this faith was possible only because for him the reason of state had come to stand for reason.

Science and the State: World War I

World War I crystallized the logic of Münsterberg's social thought and his career in America, and it underlined the internal contradictions in both. For years he had worked for scientific internationalism and a mutual understanding between Germany and America. But the war made clear that he did so as a German, serving the ends of his Fatherland. For Münsterberg the nation, not some abstract principle of world community, propelled the evolution of society. Internationalism in science brought personal rewards and advanced the whole of human knowledge, but, above all, it provided a framework that allowed *Wissenschaft* to bring prestige to Germany abroad and the scholar at home. Like the *Psychotechniker,* the academic scientist properly served the state that nourished him.

The nation and its corporate embodiment, the state, comprised for Münsterberg a social organism. Progress meant efficiency and rationalization within the organism. But it should be remembered that efficiency for Münsterberg was an organic, not a mechanical, concept; the organism required a consciousness, a will to hold it together. Just as Münsterberg insisted that the loyalty of workers was necessary to industrial production, he recognized that patriotism was essential to national progress. Indeed, like many of his colleagues in Germany, he could rejoice in the first months of the war that a renewed surge of national feeling had wiped out internal dissension and swept away selfish materialism. The social and personal costs of the war forced Münsterberg's views to mellow as the years went by. But they never led him, as they might have, to question the fundamental assumptions of his social thought: that a progressive teleology, fueled in the end by a principle of will, guided mankind toward self-perfection and that, within that progress, no real conflicts could exist between individual, social, and national purposes. His distance from his homeland and his early death in 1916, before the United States had entered the war, saved him from the disillusionment of a Freud or a Weber.

Before discussing the wartime climax to Münsterberg's work in cultural diplomacy, the story of his international politicking should be picked up where it was left off in 1908. His activities in the half-decade before the outbreak of the war illustrate the continuity of his second career and highlight the ambiguity of his commitment to American academia—and its commitment to him. They also throw light upon the movement to internationalize science in the prewar years and the entanglement of this movement with national political interests.

When Charles Eliot chastised him late in 1908 for meddling in cultural politics, Münsterberg promised that he would desist from such activities in the future. But Münsterberg was unwilling to give up his life's task so easily. He was already deeply immersed in plans to create a trans-Atlantic institute in Berlin whose purpose, as he put it, was to organize "in the interests of German cultural world power" the whole of German-American cultural relations.[1] The strictures placed on Münsterberg's activities by Eliot, whose retirement was near, may have increased his sense of estrangement from Harvard, but they could not override his excitement about the Berlin institute.

By the early twentieth century Germany had lost her academic preeminence in the United States. Not only was the number of American students in Germany decreasing, but, Münsterberg reported in 1910, the prestige of the German Ph.D. in America was low, "and the influence of German intellectual work upon the American universities, which are developing with incomparable speed, is in frightening decline."[2] American academics, if they looked abroad at all, turned to France and England. For Friedrich Althoff, this development spelled the failure of Germany's cultural offensive and it spurred his attempts to attract American students once more to the German centers of higher learning. Among his favorite projects was the creation of a central bureau in Berlin under the Prussian ministry in order to facilitate study by Americans in Germany. By the summer of 1908 he had drawn Münsterberg, his unofficial ambassador to American academia, into the planning.[3]

At about the same time, a conversation with the American ambassador to Germany, David Jayne Hill, suggested to Münsterberg how Althoff's project might be expanded. The Smithsonian Institution in Washington financed an exchange of printed matter with an agency in Leipzig, but it found the program costly and one-sided. In one year, for instance, sixty thousand packages were sent from the United States to Germany, while only eight thousand came back in return. To avoid a collapse of the exchange, the American government asked the German Foreign Office to establish a bureau to carry on its end. As Münsterberg wrote Friedrich Schmidt two years later, "an important source of understanding and interest in German character and manners is running dry." At the same time, he noted somewhat scornfully, "American enthusiasm for Paris derives its principle nourishment from French fictional literature."[4] Münsterberg recognized that a single organization, acting as a central clearing house for cultural affairs, could meet both Hill's and Althoff's needs. In a memorandum of September 1908, he outlined plans for an institute designed to "overcome the chaotic conditions of cultural relations." Specifically, it would conduct the book-exchange program, assess the relative value of the various American degrees, and support scholars in work related to America.[5]

Althoff died in October, but his replacement, Schmidt, secured approval for the institute from his superiors, including the Kaiser. Gifts from the German-Americans James Speyer and Jacob Schiff and a contribution from the Koppelstiftung, a German fund established to promote the international exchange of scholars, provided the finances. In the spring of 1910 Schmidt asked Harvard to name Münsterberg its exchange professor for the coming academic year and to grant him a full year's leave, rather than the customary half, so that he could head the new Amerika-Institut in its first year of existence. Lowell wrote later that Schmidt's choice had surprised him, and he hinted darkly—and incorrectly—that Münsterberg's appointment had been dictated from "higher up." But, whatever Lowell's reaction at the time, Harvard acceded to the request of the Prussian ministry, and Münsterberg set sail for Berlin in June.[6]

The Amerika-Institut took shape as a modest enterprise, staffed at first by seven full-time employees and its honorary director. An early circular described its scope:

> The Institut is to be devoted to the furthering of the cultural relations between Germany and the United States. Everything political and commercial lies outside of its realm. Its chief emphasis will lie on the interests of scholarship and research, of education and vocational life, of literature and art, of travel and social connections.[7]

Operating directly under the Prussian Ministry of Education, it took over the German end of the Smithsonian exchange. It also published occasional reports on such subjects as the relative status of American universities and the occupational distribution of German-Americans. It assumed responsibility for copyrighting German books in the United States, protecting 2,500 volumes by 1920. Most important perhaps, a sizeable donation by Schiff allowed the purchase of an extensive library. By 1941, according to one authority, the Amerika-Institut owned the most extensive European collection of literature from America. World War II, however, doomed the Institut, and in 1945 Allied bombs delivered the final blow.[8]

Despite its tangible successes, the institute never fulfilled Münsterberg's hopes. "There has always been systematic organization of internal politics, law and commerce," he wrote in 1910 to Karl Breul, a German teaching in England, "but in the cultural relations everything has been left to haphazard influences." He anticipated that the Institut would become "the beginning of a new great movement" for international organization, serving as a prototype for similar establishments in other countries. And he expected it to expand in Berlin into a general *Auslandsinstitut,* directing the export of German culture to all corners of the world. The institute, he wrote later, "works for the necessary modernization of international intercourse, a kind of efficiency management in the world of ideals."[9]

Münsterberg repeatedly, although privately, made clear that the institute was an arm of German cultural diplomacy. As he wrote to a colleague in 1912, he promoted understanding between Germany and the United States "first of all naturally—because I am a citizen of the Reich—in the interest of Germany and German *Kultur.*" Kant, Fichte, and Helmholtz, he assumed, offered America more than technical contributions to philosophy and science; they testified to the purity and vigor of German life. "The world power of the German soul," Münsterberg proclaimed in his inaugural address as exchange professor to the University of Berlin, "extends as far as does the love of German art and the belief in the German Idea." This cultural imperialism shaded easily into more political and economic concerns. The transmission of *Kultur,* the argument went, created not just friends of German culture, but friends of Germany, German policies, and finally the Kaiser. In September 1910 in a lengthy letter to Schmidt, Münsterberg explicitly outlined the linkage of culture and politics:

> It hardly needs mentioning that this work, although it excludes the political and the commercial, must indirectly be of service to the political and economic interests of Germany. Sympathy overseas for Germany grows along with reciprocal understanding, and—precisely in those countries with a pub-

lic opinion as pronounced as America's—a willingness for political and economic cooperation grows along with a sympathetic disposition.[10]

The Amerika-Institut, however, failed as an organ for transmitting *Kultur* to the New World. Two simultaneous and related feuds erupted during Münsterberg's tenure—one between him and the American press
corps in Berlin and the other between him and Columbia's exchange professor, C. Alphonso Smith of the University of Virginia. In neither case
was the fault entirely Münsterberg's, but the scandal that resulted tar-
nished him in the public's eye. *Kultur,* as reflected in the events of the
winter, seemed to mean not the Kantian ideals of self-discipline, service,
and selflessness, but rather self-righteousness, pettiness, and a fetish for
titles and ceremony.

The details of the feuds, which had their origins in the long-standing
rivalry between Harvard and Columbia for a position of preeminence in
German-American academic relations, are not important. None of the
major participants—Münsterberg, Smith, President Lowell of Harvard,
President Butler of Columbia, and John W. Burgess, Columbia's leading
Germanophile—conducted themselves well, and the American press blew
a petty squabble over court prerogatives into major proportions. The affair climaxed in March, when Smith publicly charged that Münsterberg
had, for reasons of jealousy, sabotaged his and his wife's presentation to
the Kaiser at a court ball. The *New York Times* gave the accusation front-
page treatment, and other newspapers followed suit.[11] Münsterberg's
well-publicized defense only compounded his difficulties.

Lowell, who had initially encouraged Münsterberg in his machinations
for Harvard in Berlin, attempted to restrain him when the incident first
hit the press:

> To us the question of the length of time the Emperor talks to different
> professors, the invitations to court balls, and the precedent among profes-
> sors, do not seem very important. They appear trivial beside anything that
> tends to lower the dignity of the University or of its representative. That a
> professor should care so much about such things as the talk in the newspa-
> pers would seem to imply, strikes the public as showing a lack of sense of
> proportion inconsistent with the temperament of a scholar.

But the warning came too late. Playing up Münsterberg's German citizenship, the *Times* editorialized that Smith (whose behavior was as
questionable as Münsterberg's) "will not miss the sympathy of his fellow-
citizens." Other papers were even more critical. "I think, on the whole,"
Ambassador Hill understated in a letter to Lowell, "that Professor Münsterberg has not been kindly treated in the newspaper representations."[12]

The Smith affair was significant because it epitomized Münsterberg's
difficulties with his colleagues and the public, and it underscored the fail-

ure of German cultural diplomacy as a whole. For all his claims to a canny understanding of the human mind, Münsterberg had, as Lowell indicated, completely failed to gauge the temper of his audience. The same miscomprehension doomed efforts as different as Prince Henry's visit to America and the propaganda of World War I. More immediately, Smith's charges led to the banishment of Münsterberg from the American community in Berlin and damaged his academic reputation in America. He found himself once again, as in 1908, in disfavor with the Harvard administration. By May he was actively seeking a position in Germany, where his work had earned him the Kaiser's Order of the Red Eagle, second class. But the medal, a high honor for an academic, could not secure for him the *Ordinarius* at a major university that he desired, and he returned to Harvard in the fall of 1911.[13]

In the years that followed his return, one of Münsterberg's favorite—and most controversial—themes was the historical purpose of national rivalry and its corollary, the absolute value of patriotism. As early as *Der Ursprung der Sittlichkeit* in 1889, he had hailed the decline of the eighteenth-century principles of cosmopolitanism and their replacement by the transcendental ideal of the nation. From a humanistic point of view, Münsterberg readily admitted, the cosmopolitan approach was legitimate. But there were historical eras, he proclaimed in his Freiburg lectures,

> in which only a vigorous self-conscious emphasis upon nationality can serve overall progress and in which this nationalism, with its strength-building competition between nations, serves progress more effectively than flabby and unpatriotic ethical sentiments.

The present was such an era, and, in a fit of youthful patriotism, he exulted:

> How the proud words of our Kaiser have recently delighted the nation when he proclaimed, rather forty-two million Germans be left on the battlefield than a single stone of German territory be lost.[14]

More than two decades later, Münsterberg's position was more moderate, but it had not changed significantly. In the title essay of *American Patriotism,* written in 1913, he welcomed the recent surge of nationalism in the United States, Germany, Italy, China, and Russia, as well the continued national pride in England and France. "Everywhere," he wrote on the eve of World War I, "this belief in the world task of compatriots became the yeast in the nations. It gave rise to every memorable achievement."[15]

Münsterberg based his defense of nationalism on a symphonic view of international relations, which was common among Germans of his generation and received its classic formulation in Friedrich Meinecke's *Weltbürgertum und Nationalstaat* (Cosmopolitanism and the National State). Each national grouping, according to this view, had a particular character to contribute to historical progress. In Münsterberg's version, Germany expressed the principles of efficiency and social idealism and America those of self-reliance and self-direction. Or, in metaphysical terms, as Münsterberg put it in 1915, "The Anglo-Saxon system is controlled by the belief in the individual as such and the Teutonic ideals are bound by the belief in the overindividual soul."[16]

In this international order, a nation might borrow from others, but every people had a duty to remain true to their individuality, and in an ideal international order, Münsterberg wrote, "all the different national instruments play together in the harmony of the orchestra."[17] It was an exact replica of Münsterberg's social organism on a supernational level; a historical dialectic reconciled all apparent competitions—whether between two species for an ecological niche, two men for a single woman, or two nations for a colonial prize. The only problem lay in nations that failed to live up to their historical ideals.

Despite his outlandish glorifications of the Teutonic soul, Münsterberg's pronouncements found an echo in American as well as German social and political thought. He could have been, and occasionally was, quoting Theodore Roosevelt on patriotism's invigorating effect on the individual and the historic duty of the great world powers. And, like Roosevelt, he assailed what he considered artificial schemes for international harmony. Münsterberg considered himself an advocate of peace and international understanding, and he had little sympathy with the pan-German and imperialist wing of German politics. But, he argued, the attempt to legislate peace through Hague conferences and arbitration treaties was doomed to failure; these efforts could never "abolish the fundamental law of five thousand years of history that ultimately the life needs of a healthy nation are decisive." Instead, national preparedness and vigilance were the surest guarantees of peace. Yet, even they could not and ought not eliminate a war that resulted "when the wholesome growth of two rivals has reached a point at which there is no longer any room for the expansion of both." The Russo-Japanese War, Münsterberg wrote in 1913, offered an example of such a conflict; in it the abstract issues of justice did not apply. "The question of right and wrong," he asserted, "was not involved when two giants were wrestling for supremacy in the East."[18]

For almost a decade before World War I, Münsterberg had proselytized for this view of international relations. He understood it as a specifically German one, and his criticisms of pacifism and cosmopolitanism often verged on special pleading for German interests and culture. In a well-publicized speech before Andrew Carnegie's National Arbitration and Peace Congress in 1907, he defended conscription in Germany as "a national school time" of discipline and asserted that it was impossible for a German, raised on the writings of Schiller and Fichte, "to say that war is the worst evil under all circumstances." The speech earned Münsterberg praise from a conservative deputy on the floor of the Reichstag, but it appalled an audience convinced that the German army was a major threat to world peace. And it elicited public criticism from Nicholas Murray Butler and Carnegie.[19]

More circumspect, perhaps, but undaunted, Münsterberg continued his criticisms of the superficiality of "a colorless cosmopolitanism," and in the years that followed he promoted the vigor and idealism of *Kultur*. By 1916 he had become, in the words of his admirer George Sylvester Viereck, "unquestionably the leader of all those who fought the battle of German culture in the United States."[20] The outbreak of the war in Europe raised that battle to an urgent level and launched Münsterberg into the most controversial period of his life.

War galvanized academic opinion in Germany and, true to their mission as the embodiment of the nation's soul, German academics of all political stripes rallied to a twofold duty: the encouragement of morale at home and the defense of *Kultur* abroad. In scores of books, pamphlets, petitions, and letters, university professors carried the prestige of *Wissenschaft* and German Idealism into battle for the Fatherland. They painted a picture of a united and regenerated German people, defending the Kantian principles of duty and transcendent values against the half-civilized Russians and the shopkeeper English. The Amerika-Institut entered the fray when its director, R. W. Drechsler, coauthored the semiofficial pamphlet, "The Truth about Germany," but the most controversial of the manifestoes was a broadside, "To the Civilized World!" signed by ninety-three prominent intellectuals, including Wilhelm Wundt, Wilhelm Windelband, Max Planck, and Münsterberg's old friend from Freiburg, Alois Riehl. For many American academics, the justification by these *Wissenschaftler* of such German acts as the invasion of Belgium and the destruction of the University of Louvain seemed to outrank the acts themselves as a war crime.[21]

From the first, Münsterberg considered himself a soldier of the Reich in the New World and he immediately took up its defense. Soon after hostilities began, the *Boston Herald* solicited from him a brief essay, which appeared under the title "Fair Play" in approximately fifty American newspapers. The slogan was taken up by Viereck in his new organ of German propaganda, *The Fatherland,* and it became a rallying cry for pro-German sentiment in America.[22] In the following months Münsterberg produced a number of additional essays and two books, *The War and America* (September 1914) and *The Peace and America* (April 1915). Throughout the early period of the war, at least, he received encouragement in his efforts from the German embassy in Washington, from Schmidt in the Prussian Ministry of Education, and from the German Foreign Office. At the same time, he maintained contact with the German Information Bureau, a government-run propaganda agency in New York, which promoted his writings and for whom he confidentially solicited money from German-Americans.[23]

Münsterberg's early arguments mirrored in most respects the "ideas of 1914" that had captivated German academia. In "Fair Play" he charged that the reportage of the war was unneutral in America, that the struggle involved a "historic world conflict" in which German *Kultur* stood alone against "the onrushing Slavic world," and that the French and English had attacked Germany "from behind" for the immoral ends of commerce, personal glory, national aggrandizement, and revenge. In *War and America,* published a month and a half later, and other essays, he offered answers to specific charges—for instance that Germany violated Belgium's neutrality—and he added another theme common in Germany (and among American cultural nationalists): War regenerated effete civilizations and served as "a positive creator of better and higher forms of the life of mankind"; it tested the moral worth of the combatants, if only they were allowed to fight on an equal footing. "No reasonable man," Münsterberg wrote, giving American reason more credit, perhaps, than it was due, "would judge a university by the victories or defeats of its football teams.... The truly valuable energies of a college are not expressed in such a sport appendage. But it is different with the war team of a nation."[24]

The Boston intellectual community provided a hostile environment for Münsterberg's defense of *Kultur.* His attempt to explain the war as a historic world conflict between the Teutonic ideal of thought and the Slavic ideal of feeling impressed few. Germany's cultural diplomacy of almost fifteen years had, as Schmidt conceded, failed to effect "a better understanding of our people and our land and our conditions and our endeavors." Only two of the exchange professors—Münsterberg and Burgess—publicly defended the central powers,[25] and American academics as a group sympathized strongly with the Allies. In 1915 Harvard's librarian, Archibald Coolidge, expressed doubt to a friend "that Harvard, or pretty much any American university would be a pleasant place for a German professor to teach or reside in, as long as the war lasts." As early as August, the *Boston Transcript* called for Münsterberg and his German-born colleague, Kuno Francke, to resign. Throughout the war similar demands cropped up, and Münsterberg gradually severed his academic and social connections. By the time of his death he had become, in the words of a Cambridge clergyman, "the most unpopular person of the community."[26]

Inevitably, old suspicions about Münsterberg's relations with the German government resurfaced. It was commonly assumed (by Wilson's Secretary of State Robert Lansing, among others) that he was a German "agent," and occasionally these assumptions reached print. In September 1914, the *Times* of London published an inaccurate front-page article, "The Kaiser's American Agents," which called Münsterberg a member of the "General Staff" of the German press campaign in America and described Harvard, of all places, as "the seat . . . of inveterate pro-German agitation in the United States." Later in the war Allied publicists issued an English version of Emil Witte's book of 1907, which had charged that Münsterberg was a paid German propagandist. In some circles the rumors were more outlandish: Münsterberg was suspected of belonging to the German Secret Service and, his Cambridge neighbors surmised, the pigeons fed by his daughter in his back yard carried secret messages to spies.[27]

Münsterberg's alleged activities and his published articles presented Harvard with its first wartime issue. After reading the *London Times* article, Clarence Wiener, a former Harvard student then living in England, wrote the university rescinding a bequest of ten million dollars that he claimed to have willed to it. He would reinstate it, he asserted, only if Harvard fired Münsterberg.[28] The letter, which he had sent to the *Boston Globe* to ensure publicity, was obviously a crank. Fifteen years before, Harvard had dismissed Wiener, whom Lowell called a "weakling," for what it considered immoral behavior, and acquaintances regarded him as mentally unbalanced. Furthermore, by all accounts Wiener had nowhere near the money he claimed. The Harvard administration regarded his threat as a joke and tried to ignore it, but it did precipitate enough anti-Münsterberg agitation among Harvard alumni to force Lowell to compose a standard letter on the inadvisability of muzzling professors.[29]

Münsterberg escalated the incident into a crisis when at a faculty meeting he offered his resignation if Wiener would immediately give Harvard half the bequest. At the time his friend Viereck called the move "a masterstroke," but Münsterberg later pleaded, in a rare admission, that it had been an ill-considered attempt to bring such accusations to an end.[30] In any case, Lowell was furious. He regarded Münsterberg's action as an attempt to maneuver Harvard into refusing his resignation and thereby vindicating him. The Harvard Overseers did not seriously consider accepting it, and Lowell neatly turned the affair into a demonstration of Harvard's integrity rather than its support of Münsterberg's activity. But, if the episode made Harvard a champion of academic freedom, it also increased Münsterberg's estrangement from the university community. Lowell and many of Münsterberg's colleagues no longer regarded his extracurricular behavior as merely an annoyance; they actively hoped for his departure. Münsterberg for his part never again attended a faculty meeting, and he increasingly withdrew from academic affairs.[31]

Münsterberg's own bravado generated much of his difficulty in the Wiener episode, and not simply because he resigned unnecessarily. The London article, for example, had been the direct result of vague boasts by Münsterberg to several editors of the *New York Times,* a newspaper well known for its sympathies with the Allies.[32] Yet, incredibly, although he toned down his propaganda in the wake of the affair, Münsterberg increasingly dabbled in covert activities. Until the German ambassador in Washington, Johann von Bernstorff, called the operation off late in December, Münsterberg solicited money confidentially from prominent German-Americans, apparently to finance an attempt by William F. McCombs, the controversial chairman of the Democratic Party, to swing the administration and the American public to the German side.[33] He also sounded out the views of Roosevelt on war issues and personally presented the German case to him at the explicit request of Berlin. With the enthusiastic support of the German Foreign Office, at least after the fact, he wrote Wilson a lengthy letter outlining the unneutrality of American policies and threatening a revolt against the Democrats by German, Irish, Swedish, and Jewish voters.[34] Finally, he joined with a small group of German and German-American planners—including Bernhard Dernburg, head of the German propaganda apparatus in New York, Harry Rubens, a prominent German-American lawyer from Chicago, and Richard Barthold, a German-born congressman from Missouri—to organize the millions of German-Americans in the United States into an effective political force. Specifically, these men hoped to swing the electoral weight of ethnic votes behind such "neutral" policies as an arms embargo directed at all belligerents.[35]

Within a few months, however, the German propaganda effort suffered a crippling blow. The sinking of the *Lusitania* in early May delivered, as Kuno Francke described it, "the most serious defeat that Germany up to that point had suffered on any front." For most Americans it constituted a crime against humanity and many old allies of Germany fell away. The event turned one major contributor to the Amerika-Institut, Jacob Schiff, against Germany and ended Bernstorff's friendship with another, James Speyer. German-American partisans like Hermann Ridder of the *New Yorker Staatszeitung* and Viereck attempted to place the blame upon the *loses friendship*

victims, who had taken transit on a ship carrying war materials, but saner minds, including Münsterberg, recognized the need for silence. "We might as well admit openly," Bernstorff wrote his home office, "that our propaganda here has *collapsed completely* under the impact of the Lusitania incident."[36]

Shortly after the sinking, Münsterberg wrote for a German audience: "Only those who stand in the middle of American life can know how much good will has sunk with the Lusitania." In fact, the incident led directly to one of the most serious personal blows of his life—the ending of his twenty-year friendship with Josiah Royce. Two days after the news of the disaster reached America, Royce returned several volumes to Münsterberg that he had borrowed three years before. To them he attached the note: "I hope for the health of your family, for your prosperity, and for that of all who are dear to you who travel by land or by sea." In a subsequent letter Royce vented his anger more explicitly:

> The destruction of my countrymen on the Lusitania was a wanton and a willful assault upon all that humanity holds dearest, and upon all that makes mutual understanding, either of nations, or of colleagues, or of brethren possible.

It was, he wrote, "a horror which civilized mankind ought never to forget." In still another letter, he addressed Münsterberg as "my formerly dear friend."[37]

Royce could have been speaking for any number of members of the Harvard community, including Eliot or the former chairman of the Philosophy Division, Ralph Barton Perry. But Royce's reaction was particularly painful to Münsterberg. Especially after his estrangement from James, Münsterberg had considered Royce an ally in the unphilosophical New World. It had been he, more than anyone else, who had persuaded Münsterberg more than ten years before to remain at Harvard and continue the struggle for Idealism in America. And Royce, alone among Americans, understood the absoluteness of values. For years he had preached a world community of civilized nations united in fulfilling the purposes of the absolute. Yet, as Münsterberg saw it, in Royce's heated reaction to the war—which, like any war, brought with it individual acts of inhumanity—he had written Germany and all Germans who did not renounce their Fatherland out of the community of civilized nations and identified them with disloyalty, barbarism, and in the end evil.[38]

Royce's defection crushed Münsterberg, but even before the *Lusitania* crisis he had begun to cut down on his public visibility and to seek a broader and more philosophical perspective. "Six months have made us all sympathizers and sufferers and mourners," he wrote in February in

Peace and America; "we pray for delivery, we long for peace." Occasionally in that volume, which appeared in April, he launched into bitter attacks on both England and Belgium, but on the whole he struck an Olympian pose, anticipating the resolution of the partisan issues of the day in a future peace without victory. At about the same time, Münsterberg had turned to motion pictures for his own personal delivery from the war, and he devoted much of the summer to his book *Photoplay.*[39] In this case, art served its recuperative function: He returned to Harvard renewed for battle.

Münsterberg began the campaign early in the fall with a controversial article, "The Impeachment of German-Americans," published in the *New York Times* and the *Boston Herald.* In it he applauded the "Teutonic masses" in America for insisting "on a forceful influence upon the national life of the country." (And he fabricated: "I have never participated in a political action of the German-Americans, I have never signed a petition.") In December he startled the German-American community with an essay, published in the *Fatherland* but explicitly denied editorial support, that praised Theodore Roosevelt as pro-German at heart. German-Americans, Münsterberg advised, should not automatically rule the former president out as a candidate in 1916, despite his bitter attacks on "professional German-Americans" and his outspoken advocacy of war with Germany. Rather, they should remain uncommitted, holding their votes in ransom for American neutrality. Münsterberg asserted later that he had intended the article as a warning to Wilson, whom he claimed secretly to support, lest the president count too confidently on German-American votes.[40] In fact, he was currying favor from both Wilson and Roosevelt, playing each against the other. His efforts inevitably failed at a time when both men considered strong German-American support a liability. His politicking also disturbed German officials in Washington.

Relations between Germany and America were at a critical level for much of the winter of 1915–16. While delicate negotiations over Germany's submarine warfare repeatedly neared breakdown, a stream of revelations of secret German operations in the United States—including the forging of passports, successful and unsuccessful attempts to purchase newspapers, and the fomenting of strikes and isolated acts of sabotage in war industries[41]—raised legitimate doubts about Germany's good faith and jeopardized the position of German-Americans.

Ambassador Bernstorff consistently recommended moderation to Berlin, and, recognizing the strength of anti-German sentiment in America, he sought to restrain the excesses of German and German-American publicists. He therefore advised Münsterberg against involvement in German-American affairs and American politics. In the spring he killed a

prospective Münsterberg article in *Fatherland* because it attacked the
Wilson administration. "You ought not forget," Bernstorff warned, "that
people here often consider you to be a secret agent of the German government. Although this is not the case, a danger nevertheless exists if you . . .
intercede as a political opponent of the president."[42]

Even more volatile were Münsterberg's private communications with
the German chancellor, Theobald von Bethmann-Holweg, apparently beginning as early as a September 1915 telegram recommending that Germany yield in the *Arabic* crisis.[43] Bernstorff asked Münsterberg several
times to refrain from writing directly to Berlin—through mails that were
screened by the British—and instead to go through him. His fears were
reasonable, and, as he wrote Münsterberg in February 1916, "the man
who, as I, will have to bear heavy responsibility before world history if
the United States enters the war against us has also the unconditional
right to hold all the threads completely in his hand." But Münsterberg
apparently did not comply. In May 1916 he addressed a lengthy letter to
Bethmann, which lamented a recent "slump" in German-American ethnic
consciousness and confided, "I am doing all in my power to aid pacifism," including work on several articles, "which, however, will appear
unsigned."[44] The following fall, publication of this letter, which the British had intercepted, precipitated Münsterberg's final confrontation at
Harvard.

The articles to which Münsterberg referred appeared late that summer
under his own name in the *Illinois Staatszeitung* and were subsequently
collected in English under the title *Tomorrow: Letters to a Friend in Germany.* Together with "Allies of the Future," published in July in the *New
York Times,* they represented an attempt by Münsterberg to construct a
basis for postwar internationalism. In part, of course, these essays were,
as Münsterberg indicated to Bethmann, propaganda documents aimed at
American academics.[45] But they offered a vision of international harmony
consistent with Münsterberg's prewar views and reflected, in fact, a soft-
ening of his wartime attitudes.

Münsterberg's mellowing paralleled the "demobilization" of a West-
ern-minded minority of German academics, including Max Weber, Friedrich Meinecke, and Hans Delbrück. Like them, he had come to attack
modern war as "appalling and horrible," and he repeated his assertion
that, in this as in almost every struggle of nations, the question of war
guilt was irrelevant. He renounced all territorial ambitions for Germany
in Europe, demanding for it only a reasonable share of the world's colo-
nies. He stressed the theme of international understanding, without which
any peace was impossible, and he argued "that political harmony can be
developed best from a mutual cultural understanding." Above all, with

Weber, Meinecke, and Delbrück, he reasserted the cultural and political unity of the West and particularly of the "Teutonic" nations. As the basis of future peace, Münsterberg promoted an alliance of Germany, Britain, and the United States, "the three Teutonic master-nations in which the aristocratic will toward highest civilization [is] blended with the democratic spirit of individual responsibility." These "three really progressive peoples," he wrote, "ought to work in growing friendship for the glorious advance of the world."[46]

The motive power behind this new internationalism was nationalism, and the state emerged as the ultimate unit of world order. It was here that Münsterberg's vision of internationalism revealed its fundamental direction—and its internal contradictions. Just as his idealist metaphysics had failed, finally, to construct any meaningful absolutes in a world of flux, so his internationalism could not supply any values that transcended the national. Münsterberg's applied psychology had assumed the progressive transformation of political questions into administrative ones, but this was only possible because the politics in the end were assumed. The historic purposes of Germany, America, and perhaps even Russia, he argued, might be rationalized, or streamlined for efficiency, but science could never transcend those purposes or arbitrate between them. It was the will of nations, not the reason of men, that finally guided the evolution of civilization.

Since the nation was the ultimate unit and the final source of value, science itself became national. "The present knows," Münsterberg had said in 1910, "that even *Wissenschaft* is and should be thoroughly national." In taking this position, he challenged the official rhetoric in the West, according to which science sought a "truth" that transcended national politics and provided a perspective above partisan considerations. The function of the scholar, Arthur Lovejoy wrote in a critique of one of the many manifestoes by German intellectuals, was one "of detached criticism, of cool consideration, of insisting that facts, and all the relevant facts, be known and faced." Scholars were the bearers of what Ernst Troeltsch described as the Western "ideal of fundamentally equal human beings in a rationally organized community of all mankind." In its place, Troeltsch and Münsterberg would have contrasted the German "ideal of a wealth of national minds, all struggling together and all developing thereby their highest spiritual powers."[47]

In *Peace and America* Münsterberg challenged the position represented by Lovejoy. Recalling a lesson from his legal psychology, he argued that the perception of so-called facts depended upon the prejudices and the expectations of the perceiver. In *Tomorrow: Letters to a Friend in Germany* he went much further. Those in America, he wrote, who "cannot harmonize the harsh one-sidedness of French and German, English, Austrian and Russian scholars with their lifework, which ought to be devoted to the truth," took "a low view of scholarly truth and a lower view of patriotism." He argued instead that "the scholar who, uplifted by a healthy patriotism, proclaims historic and political facts as they appear from the angle of his hopes and as he sees them shaped by his nationalism is not disloyal to the spirit of scholarship." Philosophers like the Frenchman Bergson and the German Eucken, who took very different views of the war, were "loyal to the ideas of the truthseeker just because they affirm the values and ideals in which they believe." "Truth," Münsterberg asserted, "is ultimately belief."[48]

Münsterberg, it should be emphasized, did not use this position to undermine a belief in the universality of science. To do so would have denied any value to *Kulturpolitik,* for its successes depended upon a respect for German scholarship abroad. He insisted that science in all its national varieties contributed "to the world system of knowledge, which cannot be split into a pro-Ally and an anti-Ally scholarship." The ultimate test of the value of any national science, and therefore of the nation that produced it, would "remain its influence on the thought of the world." Münsterberg expected Germany, with its unique gift for blending theory and practice, to come out ahead in the competition, and he opposed all plans, already broached in Germany and elsewhere, to build a Chinese Wall to protect the purity (and the secrets) of national science. "The German attitude toward life and the world, the German spirit," he wrote in *Peace and America,* "may sometime become the yeast for the world's noblest civilization."[49] German *Kultur* would assure Germany great power status, and the German scholar would resume his position of front rank at home and abroad.

In his own terms, therefore, Münsterberg's defense of Germany, and indeed his own propaganda as well as that of his colleagues, did not represent a "treason of the intellectuals." His first duty as a scholar was to guard the national, not the international, cultural heritage. And the national heritage of Germany meant its historic reality, Kaiser and all. Münsterberg simply could not accept the possibility that this loyalty might at some fundamental level contradict a *Wissenschaft* whose espoused goals were critical thought and the dismantling of superstitions: His status as an academic depended on his ignoring any potential conflict between his dual role of bearing *Kultur* and seeking the truth. He turned instead, like so many of his colleagues, to what amounted to a crude sociology of knowledge. He escaped a complete relativism not through a special exemption for the classless class of intellectuals, as Karl Mannheim was later to do, but through the simple faith, presented as a logical necessity, that science and the nation went hand in hand in the evolution of society. The belief was unfounded, but it had at least a certain integrity that was lacking in those Allied scientists who upheld the objectivity of science with one hand and churned out propaganda with the other.

Münsterberg's essays on the postwar future failed to convert the intellectuals to whom they were directed, although some took them seriously as trial balloons floated from Berlin. An editor of the *New York Times,* for example, asked Münsterberg whether the views expressed in "Allies of the Future" were personal or reflected those of "leading men of German official circles." At the same time, however, the essays brought Münsterberg under attack by Germans and German-Americans. Bernstorff, who, like Münsterberg, had always espoused a German *Westpolitik,* pronounced the "Allies" article useful, but even he advised Münsterberg "not to allow the German territorial demands to appear too unimportant" in his forthcoming book. Alexander Fuehr of the press bureau in New York reported that the article had received mixed reactions in his circles. Viereck, editor of the *Fatherland,* put the same point more strongly: The German-Americans, he wrote Münsterberg, were not yet ready for his proposals. "Having taught the Germans the Hymn of Hate it is not so easy to make them forget it."[50]

While Münsterberg's relations with many German-Americans were strained by the fall of 1916, his position at Harvard was rapidly becoming untenable. The previous spring his feud with Lowell had broken into open warfare as a result of a dispute with Edwin Holt, a long-time friend and colleague and the translator of *Die Amerikaner.* Holt, who was in the midst of personal difficulties, had been circulating stories that Münsterberg frequently falsified his experimental results, and in his book, *The Freudian Wish and Its Place in Ethics,* he referred to Münsterberg in veiled but recognizable form as an "unconscionable liar" with "a partially suppressed ego."[51] The correspondence between the two men that resulted was bitter. Münsterberg returned Holt's psychologisms with enthusiasm: "Your downfall is the result of a Freudian wish of yours," he wrote in one letter. And later, appropriating Freud to his own purposes, he added: "Your whole book is a thinly veiled expression of the repressed wish for the death of your mother." Münsterberg claimed later that he intended the letter as a therapeutic shock. Holt was in fact near a nervous breakdown, in part evidently because he was saddled with an invalid mother whose condition prevented any normal social life. And *The Freudian Wish* did contain a strong passage warning against the consequences of overprotectiveness in mothers. But Münsterberg's letter failed in its aim. It also provided Holt with ammunition in an attempt to oust Münsterberg from his post.[52]

In the middle of the dispute, Holt turned over a copy of the exchanges to Lowell. The Harvard president, it seems, was interested in finding a "concrete issue" over which to discipline and perhaps even dismiss Münsterberg, and he took the opportunity to reprimand him in person. Lowell's criticisms, which Münsterberg summarized in a subsequent letter, reflected a number of old grievances. He ordered Münsterberg never again to write a colleague in the tone that he had assumed with Holt; he charged that Münsterberg neglected his experimental work and indulged "in popular writing and speechmaking for self-advertisement"; he suggested that Münsterberg had slighted the laboratory and the training of advanced students, yet "strangled" one colleague (Leonard Troland) in his work; and he termed Münsterberg's resignation in the Wiener incident a stab in the back. Münsterberg considered the charges unjust; to him they were one more indication of Harvard's prejudice against him as a foreigner and a German.[53]

By the fall Münsterberg's position had deteriorated. In August the British released a translation of his May 12 letter to Bethmann, which they had intercepted. After it failed to elicit much reaction, they released it again in a slightly different translation shortly after the academic semester had begun. Perhaps the most curious fact about the letter was that Münsterberg had written it at all, for he knew full well that the British censors were likely to publish anything they found to be in their interest. Münsterberg privately hinted that he had hoped for the letter's publication, believing that it would ease pressure on the German-Americans and establish himself as an advocate of conciliation and a supporter of Wilson. Such devious reasoning was consistent with his style of politicking, but, if these had been his intentions, his action completely backfired. The letter confirmed to many that he was indeed a German agent and it led his fellow Harvard philosopher, William Hocking, to demand in a widely publicized open letter that he clarify to what extent he was "an official representative" of Germany and that he state publicly the activities that he carried on in that nation's behalf.[54]

The Bethmann letter and the Hocking-Münsterberg exchange that followed Hocking's initial sally set off another flurry of demands for Münsterberg's resignation. The Boston branch of the American Rights League, a pro-Ally group that included numerous Harvard alumni and several members of the Harvard faculty, charged that he was "engaged in undermining American citizenship, and in promoting the interests of a foreign power." It found his views inconsistent with his role as a teacher and faculty member "in an American university or institution for the training of American youth." A month later Reginald Robbins, chairman of a Harvard overseers' review committee for the Division of Philosophy,

Psychology, and Social Ethics, informed Münsterberg of the difficulty
that his position was creating. "I hardly think even you realize," Robbins
wrote,

> how very general is the feeling among Harvard graduates . . . that a German,
> however gifted, who engages in public utterance or writing which favors
> German culture in America, would be far more wisely and appropriately
> placed if educating Germans in Germany than Americans in America.[55]

Lowell and the Harvard faculty once again resisted the pressure, but
the complaints of Robbins and others suggested that the position of the
American university professor was just as ambiguous as that of the German. Lovejoy may have considered "detached criticism" to be the proper
function of the scholar. But for perhaps the bulk of Harvard alumni and
the American public the scholar trained young Americans in personal
and national virtues. The college professor, as the *Chicago Post* put it in
an editorial demanding Münsterberg's resignation, fills a "public position
as an educator of American youth."[56] This argument was close to the ideological rationale of the Wilhelmian academic, who tied *Wissenschaft* inextricably to *Bildung* and equated ideal service to science with ideal
service to the nation. Scholars might not always have recognized the potential tension between the detachment of science and the demands of the
nation, but Münsterberg's career as a loyal German at an American university illustrated it graphically.

That career was drawing to a close. Münsterberg was fully aware of the
tenuousness of his position as war between the United States and Germany approached. In the spring of 1916 he wrote the State Department
asking what his status would be if war broke out; he hoped to be treated
as a semiofficial ambassador. By the fall, as prospects for peace seemed
more favorable, he faced a more serious concern. His health was failing,
he wrote Lowell, and he feared the possibility of sudden death or disable-
ment through a stroke. Three months later—barely four months before
the entry of the United States into the war on the side of the Allies—Münsterberg's fears were realized. On December 16, while lecturing on introductory psychology at Radcliffe, he fell dead at the age of fifty-three of a
cerebral hemorrhage.[57]

Münsterberg did not fare much better in death than he had in life.
Harvard canceled classes in his honor and Hocking praised him as a pa-
triot, but, more tangibly, Lowell turned down Robert Yerkes's request
that the university continue his salary through the year to alleviate his
family's distress. If Germany was more grateful for Münsterberg's services, it was not willing to show it. The German Foreign Office refused a
petition from his sole surviving brother, Oscar, for assistance to Münster-

berg's widow.[58] At the same time, rumors continued to pursue him: He had poisoned himself, some hinted, to prevent exposure by his former German-American friends, who were furious at what they considered his betrayal.[59] Perhaps worst of all, Münsterberg was adopted by his most despised of foes. Shortly after his death, a Boston medium reported a startling message from an "excarnate being" identifying himself as Münsterberg. "Spirit return is a truth," recanted the recently departed professor after a lifetime of debunking reports of psychic phenomena.[60] There was an ironic appropriateness to this last interview, which Münsterberg for once could not disown. As he had been so often in life, the selfless defender of absolute values and the dignity of *Wissenschaft* was appropriated posthumously by the public to meet its own needs.

In the meantime, Harvard and the American academic community worked hard to erase Münsterberg's traces—quite literally, according to a widely believed rumor. Münsterberg, so the story goes, once occupied the empty chair in a group portrait, hanging in Emerson Hall, of three of Harvard's leading philosophers—James, Royce, and Palmer—during the department's "golden age," but his figure was painted over during World War I. In fact, Münsterberg had never been in the portrait; he had been left out because he found unsuitable the place to which he had been assigned. For aesthetic reasons, the artist recalled, "he claimed his position should be center front."[61] If the artist can be believed, the empty chair testified only to Münsterberg's self-importance, but the point of the story is not its literal meaning. Rather, its lengthy career and its wide acceptance suggest that, in a more figurative way, Münsterberg was indeed painted out.

Conclusion

Edwin Boring, in his standard history of experimental psychology, reduced Münsterberg's contributions to "some little experiments" from his
Freiburg years and suggested, somewhat uneasily, that the mind of his
predecessor at Harvard was too original to be confined to the laboratory.
Five years after Münsterberg's death, the psychologist Frank Angell expressed the same sentiments more strongly. "Despite much sound advice
and scholarly admonition," Angell wrote, Münsterberg's writings and
public career opened "the gate for the flood of pseudo-psychologizing and
commercialized psychologues now inundating the country."[1] Yet Angell
was writing as if, by the 1920s, such luminaries of the profession as John
Watson and James McKeen Cattell (not to mention the maverick Walter
Dill Scott) had not dedicated themselves enthusiastically to commerciali-
zation, and as if Münsterberg, with his remarkable instinct for the sensational, had precipitated the flood rather than merely ridden its crest.

The founder of American behaviorism, John Watson, offered a different assessment of Münsterberg's career. Münsterberg was "really a great
psychologist," Watson was quoted as saying in 1921, and his *Grundzüge*
(*der Psychotechnik,* most likely) was a "magnificent and masterful performance"; his work helped initiate the modern science of vocational psychology, and it paved the way for psychology's application in World War
I.[2] Such an estimate of Münsterberg's psychotechnics was understandable
from a man who, in 1913, stated that the final goal of his scientific research was the uncovering of "general and particular methods by which I

may control behavior."[3] For, of all the psychologists in the years before World War I, Münsterberg developed the most sweeping program for the control of human behavior.

Münsterberg's significance, however, goes beyond his contribution to applied psychology: His career, even in its eccentricities—and perhaps especially in them—mirrored stresses that were characteristic of his age. The psychologist Kenneth Keniston has referred to "a long tradition of studying the extreme to understand the typical."[4] Münsterberg offers a case in point. Moving as he did from nineteenth-century Germany to twentieth-century America, his confrontation with modernity was extreme, and so was his reaction to it. But in many respects that extreme reaction helps us understand the typical. The evolution of Münsterberg's social prescriptions from character-building to behavior modification reflected one of the paths taken by turn-of-the-century thinkers as they confronted an emerging mass society, an unassimilated immigrant population, and the political challenges of Populism, feminism, and a growing labor movement.

Münsterberg's call for a psychotechnics, administered by experts and bypassing the consciousness, coincided with a general questioning among American political thinkers of such traditional principles as natural rights, common sense, and human equality. "The idea that men possess inherent and inalienable rights of a political or quasi-political character which are independent of the state," the political scientist Charles Merriam wrote in 1903, "has generally been given up." In the theory of John W. Burgess, the state came to replace the individual as the basis of society; for Woodrow Wilson the key to "self-development" was "mutual aid" rather than individual competition.[5] Münsterberg himself was only repeating a cliché among his colleagues when he told the Cosmopolitan Club of Detroit in 1905 that the Declaration of Independence was "a piece of state philosophy of the eighteenth century which is not any more in harmony with the responsibilities and duties of our age."[6]

Merriam also suggested that political liberty was linked to political capacity, reflecting both post-Darwinian social science and the realities of the imperial world into which the United States had just entered. (Significantly, when women, and to a lesser extent blacks, demanded full political participation early in the century, they did so not so much on the grounds of human equality but because of the contribution that their special sexual or racial traits would make to the nation.)[7] Münsterberg's and Parsons's work in vocation, which assumed an organic fit between the needs of society and human capacities, offered an analogous vision: Social function was linked to biological and mental structure. Münsterberg, at least, argued that the "laws of nature" prescribed the political arrangements of men and that scientists skilled in reading those laws were in a position to draw the blueprint for an efficient society. That this blueprint would reflect a traditional social hierarchy he left no doubt. "Whoever," he wrote in *Grundzüge der Psychotechnik,*

> wants to draw the lower races, or children of a certain age, or women in general, or for that matter men, into social tasks for whose fulfillment they lack the psychological preconditions must have his sociopolitical efforts corrected by the psychologist.

One of the contributions of the Army's psychological tests during World War I, Münsterberg's colleague Robert Yerkes suggested, was that they confirmed the validity of just such social and biological distinctions.[8]

It was no coincidence that, at a time when many social commentators were expressing their doubts about natural rights and human equality, psychologists of all schools were assaulting the notion, in Freud's words, that the ego was master in its own house.[9] Sober experimentalists like Jastrow and Stern testified to the vagaries of perception and memory; less careful members of the profession, including Walter Dill Scott and at times Münsterberg, occasionally went so far as to proclaim suggestion as the fundamental process of mind. Gustave LeBon's studies of crowd psychology proved especially popular in the United States, and reformers like Edmund A. Ross warned of the "herd" effect, in which "there is an unchaining in each man of the evil and secret lusts of his heart."[10] Although most behaviorists—but not Münsterberg—minimized such lusts, they undermined the concept of psychological autonomy in an equally effective manner, reducing will to a complex but fully determined reaction. The self-evident truths of common sense became determined by environment and habit, not by some internal logic, and the inner and private recesses of mind became objectified into behavior to be manipulated.

In the behavioristic aspects of his psychology, Münsterberg was an apostate from the German Idealist tradition—while attempting to preserve its ideological function. "Self-fulfillment" and "self-determination" had always been central to the Idealist definition of individualism. Enough has been written about the "German idea of freedom" to make it unnecessary to dwell on the limits to this self-determination: It meant the freedom to be what one ought to be and to do what one ought to do.[11] (A notion, it should be added, that was hardly unique to the Germans, as John Winthrop or Jonathan Edwards would have attested.) But Kant rooted self-determination in what amounted to a secularized "inner light"; in one sense or another, every rational being had the potential for an unmediated understanding of his own being and his proper role in the world. It was this aspect of Idealist thought that Emerson found so congenial and adapted to his own discussions of "self-reliance." The Kantian inner light or Emersonian self-reliance often amounted in practice to little more than the internalized demands of society, but they nevertheless incorporated what have been described as the "socially subversive impulses of the will";[12] as long as the will was considered free from, or at least independent of, the day-to-day constraints of one's environment, family, community, or nation, it could potentially sit in judgment on those constraints. For this reason, the autonomous will was an "inefficient" means to social organization, and an efficiency expert like Münsterberg worked hard to extirpate it.

Münsterberg's psychotechnics represented a positive intervention into the mind's traditional sphere of autonomy. Even as his applied psychology promoted a heterogeneous world of sharply differentiated function—and in its own terms promoted "individualism"—it tightened the external bonds of control and reduced for individuals the possibility of variety and spontaneity. It offered order and efficiency in the place of Emerson's "whim"[13] or James's "delicious mess of insanities and realities," and it did so at the most opportune of moments. If American social thinkers in the nineteenth century had generally valued common sense, equality, and self-reliance, they had with few exceptions restricted the application of those principles and tied them not only to sex, race, and age, but to a stake in society. By the late nineteenth century, however, Americans' perception of the society in which they lived had changed. Rights of personal autonomy and self-definition meant one thing in a relatively homogeneous community where social ties were strong and quite another in mass, urban society, especially when they were extended to women, children, racial or ethnic minorities, and large bodies of wage-earners. It is no wonder that so many social scientists were willing to sacrifice the values of spontaneity and self-definition in the interests of order and efficiency.

The attempts by Münsterberg and others to rationalize society with the help of applied psychology in fact blurred the traditional distinction between a nineteenth-century mode of "organicism," which took the "laws of nature" as fixed and used them to justify a hierarchical view of society, and a Deweyian "instrumentalism," a faith in the ability of human intelligence to shape the world according to its own needs and desires. It was the contribution of the Progressive movement, so a number of historians have argued, to replace the former "conservative" view with the latter "progressive" one.[14] But the contrast, however apt it may sometimes appear, is too neat, as Münsterberg's career illustrates. For he was a man who easily spanned the gap between nineteenth-century German organicism and twentieth-century social engineering. Münsterberg happily united an instrumental science, which by definition required an active human intelligence, with a deterministic, even biologically based, psychology that stressed human limitations. In the name of planning and reason, he restricted the sphere in which individuals could apply intelligence to their own lives. This, above all, was the meaning of the work of the "founder" of applied psychology.

Notes

Abbreviations in Notes

EP   Charles W. Eliot Papers, Harvard University Archives
HM   Hugo Münsterberg
JP   William James Papers, Houghton Library, Harvard University
LP   A. Lawrence Lowell Papers, Harvard University Archives
MM Margaret Münsterberg
MP   Hugo Münsterberg Papers, Department of Rare Books and Mss., Boston Public Library

Short Titles

American Patriotism	Hugo Münsterberg, *American Patriotism and Other Studies* (New York: Moffat, Yard & Co., 1913)
American Problems	Hugo Münsterberg, *American Problems from the Point of View of a Psychologist* (New York: Moffat, Yard & Co., 1910)
American Traits	Hugo Münsterberg, *American Traits from the Point of View of a German* (New York: Houghton Mifflin Co., 1901)
Beiträge	Hugo Münsterberg, *Beiträge zur experimentellen Psychologie*, 4 vols. (Freiburg i. Br.: J. C. B. Mohr [Paul Siebeck], 1889–92)

Grundzüge der Psychologie	Hugo Münsterberg, *Grundzüge der Psychologie.* Vol. 1: *Allgemeiner Teil: Die Prinzipen der Psychologie* (Leipzig: Johann Ambrosius Barth, 1900)
Hugo Münsterberg	Margaret Münsterberg, *Hugo Münsterberg: His Life and Work* (New York: D. Appleton & Co., 1922)
Natürlichen Anpassung	Hugo Münsterberg, *Die Lehre von der natürlichen Anpassung in ihrer Entwicklung, Anwendung und Bedeutung* (Leipzig: Metzger & Wittig, 1885)
On the Witness Stand	Hugo Münsterberg, *On the Witness Stand: Essays on Psychology and Crime* (New York: McClure Co., 1908)
Photoplay	Hugo Münsterberg, *The Photoplay: A Psychological Study* (New York: D. Appleton & Co., 1916)
Psychologie und Wirtschaftsleben	Hugo Münsterberg, *Psychologie und Wirtschaftsleben: Ein Beitrag zur angewandten Experimental-Psychologie* (Leipzig: Johann Ambrosius Barth, 1912)
"Studentenpflicht"	Hugo Münsterberg, "Studentenpflicht und Studentenrecht: Ein Wort an die deutsche Studentenschaft." 2d ed. (Leipzig: Guillermo Levien, 1890). First appeared in 1883
Tomorrow	Hugo Münsterberg, *Tomorrow: Letters to a Friend in Germany* (New York: D. Appleton & Co., 1916)
"Twenty-Five Years"	Hugo Münsterberg, "Twenty-Five Years in America: The First Chapter of an Unfinished Autobiography." *Century Illustrated Magazine* 94 (May 1917): 34–38
Ueber Aufgaben und Methoden	Hugo Münsterberg, *Ueber Aufgaben und Methoden der Psychologie.* Schriften der Gesellschaft für psychologische Forschung, no. 2 (Leipzig: A. Abel, 1891)
Die Willenshandlung	Hugo Münsterberg, *Die Willenshandlung: Ein Beitrag zur physiologischen Psychologie* (Freiburg i. Br.: J. C. B. Mohr, 1888)

Chapter 1

1. This was the judgment of several obituaries and similar testimonials. See for example Frank R. Angell, review of *Hugo Münsterberg: His Life and Work,* by Margaret Münsterberg, in *Psychological Bulletin* 19 (August 1922): 124; George Sylvester Viereck [G. S. V.], "Hugo Münsterberg," June 1913, in the Hugo Münsterberg Papers (hereafter MP), Boston Public Library; "Muensterberg Dies Addressing Class," *New York Times,* 17 December 1916, p. 19. The standard published source on Münsterberg is his daughter's adulatory and sometimes misleading biography: Margaret Münsterberg (hereafter MM), *Hugo Münsterberg:*

His Life and Work (New York: D. Appleton & Co., 1922). An excellent recent discussion of Münsterberg is given in Bruce Kuklick, *The Rise of American Philosophy: Cambridge, Massachusetts, 1860–1930* (New Haven: Yale University Press, 1977), chaps. 11 and 23.

2. See Edwin G. Boring, *A History of Experimental Psychology,* 2d ed. (New York: Appleton-Century-Crofts, 1950), p. 421.

3. William Stern, "Hugo Münsterberg: In Memoriam," *Journal of Applied Psychology* 1 (June 1917): 188. This obituary first appeared in the *Zeitschrift für pädogogische Psychologie und experimentelle Pädogogik.*

4. *Photoplay* has recently been reprinted in paperback, with an introduction by Richard Griffith, under the title *The Film: A Psychological Study* (New York: Dover Publications, 1970). Garth Jowett, in *Film: The Democratic Art* (Boston: Little, Brown & Co., 1976), called it "the earliest, and still one of the most important psychological studies of the motion picture" (p. 84). The passage from *The Americans* is in Henry Steele Commager, ed., *American in Perspective: The United States through Foreign Eyes* (New York: Random House, 1947). Commager described *The Americans,* not inaccurately, as "the fairest and most sympathetic analysis of the American character by any German" (p. 261).

5. Knight Dunlap, in *A History of Psychology in Autobiography,* ed. Carl Murchison and Edwin G. Boring, 6 vols. (Worcester, Mass.: Clark University Press, 1930–61), 2:42; Boring in ibid., 4:36; Titchener to Münsterberg (hereafter HM), 2 October 1912, MP.

6. James to HM, 28 June 1906, and HM to James, 1 July 1906, James Papers, Houghton Library, Harvard University (hereafter JP).

7. William James, "The Dilemmas of Determinism," in *The Will to Believe and Other Essays in Popular Philosophy* (New York: Dover Publications, 1956), p. 168. This essay first appeared in September 1884 in the *Unitarian Review.*

8. Robert Wiebe, *The Search for Order, 1877–1920* (New York: Hill & Wang, 1967). For "efficiency" as a guiding theme of the Progressive years, see also Samuel Hays, *Conservation and the Gospel of Efficiency: The Progressive Conservation Movement, 1890–1920* (Cambridge, Mass.: Harvard University Press, 1959); Samuel Haber, *Efficiency and Uplift: Scientific Management in the Progressive Era, 1890–1920* (Chicago: University of Chicago Press, 1964); Louis Galambos, "The Emerging Organizational Synthesis in Modern American History," *Business History Review* 44 (Autumn 1970): 279–90. See also the important recent studies of "professionalization": Burton J. Bledstein, *The Culture of Professionalism: The Middle Class and the Development of Higher Education in America* (New York: W. W. Norton & Co., 1976), and Thomas S. Haskell, *The Emergence of Professional Social Science: The American Social Science Association and the Nineteenth-Century Crisis of Authority* (Urbana, Ill.: University of Illinois Press, 1977).

9. Max Weber, "Science as a Vocation," in *From Max Weber: Essays in Sociology,* ed. and trans. H. H. Gerth and C. Wright Mills (New York: Oxford University Press, 1958), p. 155. The literature on Tönnies, Simmel, Weber, and other turn-of-the century social thinkers is vast. See especially Robert A. Nisbet, *The Sociological Tradition* (New York: Basic Books, 1966). The phrase "regimentation of the mind" is applied to Simmel by Nisbet (p. 309).

10. Karl Mannheim, *Ideology and Utopia: An Introduction to the Sociology of Knowledge,* trans. Louis Wirth and Edward Shils (New York: Harcourt, Brace & World, 1936), p. 118.

Chapter 2

1. Erich Keyser, *Westpreussen: aus der deutschen Geschichte des Weichseländes* (Würzburg: Holzner Verlag, 1962), pp. 47–49 and *passim*. See also Keyser, *Danzigs Geschichte*, 2d ed. (Danzig: A. W. Kafemann, 1928), on the history of Danzig. In 1850 Danzig had a population of 65,000, which made it the sixth largest city in Prussia. In comparison, Berlin had a population of 446,000 and Hamburg 193,000. Tertius Chandler and Gerald Fox, *3000 Years of Urban Growth* (New York: Academic Press, 1974), p. 20.

2. Keyser, *Westpreussen*, pp. 10–16; Keyser, *Danzigs Geschichte*, p. 232ff.; Detlef Krannhals, "Die Rolle der Weichsel in der Wirtschaftsgeschichte des Ostens," in *Die Weichsel: Ihre Bedeutung als Strom und Schiffahrtstrasse und ihre Kulturaufgaben*, ed. Richard Winkel (Leipzig: S. Hirzel, 1939), pp. 145–46.

3. Arthur Lindner, *Danzig* (Leipzig: E. O. Seeman, 1903), p. 2. See also comments of MM, *Hugo Münsterberg*, pp. 1–4.

4. Samuel Echt, *Die Geschichte der Juden in Danzig* (Leer/Ostfriesland: Gerhard Rautenberg, 1972), p. 58; Otto Münsterberg, *Vor vierzig Jahren: Streifzüge in die Entwicklung des Danziger Handels unter Benutzung von Errinerungen aus der Lehr- und Jugendzeit* (Danzig: A. M. Kafemann, 1911), p. 7; Keyser, *Danzigs Geschichte*, pp. 138, 248ff.; Keyser, *Westpreussen*, p. 40. My information on the Münsterberg family comes from photographs of family portraits that were destroyed in World War II. The photographs are in the possession of Dr. Hugo Munsterberg, Professor of Art History at the State University of New York at New Paltz and nephew of Hugo Münsterberg. Dr. Munsterberg's father, Oscar, wrote brief biographical notes on the backs of the photographs.

5. Otto Münsterberg, *Vor vierzig Jahren*, pp. 20–21.

6. Moritz Münsterberg, "Reise-Tagebuch von 1854–1879," p. 10. A typescript copy of this journal, transcribed by Oscar Münsterberg in January 1917, is in the possession of his son Hugo Munsterberg.

7. Jacob Katz, *Out of the Ghetto: The Social Background of Jewish Emancipation, 1770–1870* (Cambridge, Mass.: Harvard University Press, 1973), p. 169ff. and *passim*. On the status of Jews in Danzig, see Echt, *Die Geschichte der Juden*, and Max Aschkewitz, *Zur Geschichte der Juden in Westpreussen* (Marburg: Johann Gottfried Herder-Institut, 1967). For a view of a later period, which notes the modernism of the city's Jews, see Erwin Lichtenstein, *Die Juden der freien Stadt Danzig unter der Herrschaft des Nationalsozialismus* (Tübingen: J. C. B. Mohr [Paul Siebeck], 1973).

8. Echt, *Die Geschichte der Juden*, pp. 52, 60.

9. Moritz Münsterberg, "Reise-Tagebuch," *passim;* MM, *Hugo Münsterberg,* chap. 1.

10. Moritz Münsterberg, "Reise-Tagebuch," *passim*.

11. MM, *Hugo Münsterberg*, p. 4; HM, *The Peace and America* (New York: D. Appleton & Co., 1915), p. 87. Abraham Aaron Roback, a student of Münsterberg, has suggested that Münsterberg's excessive German nationalism was an overcompensation for his Jewish origins. Perhaps, but his position was not very different from that of many non-Jewish colleagues. See Roback, *History of American Psychology* (New York: Library Publishers, 1952), p. 206.

12. MM, *Hugo Münsterberg*, p. 3 and *passim;* HM, *American Traits: From the Point of View of a German* (Boston: Houghton Mifflin Co., 1901), p. 208; Moritz Münsterberg, "Reise-Tagebuch," p. 42.

13. Moritz Münsterberg, "Reise-Tagebuch," pp. 9, 12.

14. Ibid., p. 40; Otto Münsterberg to Oscar Münsterberg, 21 July 1881, quoted in Oscar Münsterberg, "Abschrift für meinen Sohn Hugo," an appendix to Moritz Münsterberg, "Reise-Tagebuch," p. 9.

15. "Auszug aus der Chronik der Familienstiftung Münsterberg begonnen zu Danzig am 29. Mai 1880," in Moritz Münsterberg, "Reise-Tagebuch," *passim.* See also *Wer Ist's,* 1909 and 1914, for entries on all the Münsterberg sons, as well as the brief biography of Otto in Ernest Hamburger, *Juden im öffentlichen Leben Deutschlands: Regierungsmitglieder, Beamte, und Parlamentarier in der monarchischen Zeit, 1848–1918* (Tübingen: J. C. B. Mohr [Paul Siebeck], 1968), p. 375.

16. Moritz Münsterberg, "Reise-Tagebuch," pp. 35–36.

17. HM, *American Traits,* pp. 45–46; MM, *Hugo Münsterberg,* chap. 2; Fritz K. Ringer, *The Decline of the German Mandarins: The German Academic Community, 1890–1933* (Cambridge, Mass.: Harvard University Press, 1969), p. 39. Wilhelm Lexis, in *Das Unterrichtswesen im Deutschen Reich,* 4 vols. (Berlin: A. Asher & Co., 1904), 2:177, 187, writes that in 1880 there were fewer than 12,000 students in the third year of the Prussian *Gymnasium.* Five years later, in 1885, there were fewer than 4,000 students in the ninth and final year. In the same year approximately 4,000 Prussian students passed the *Abitur* examination; most of these were recent graduates of the *Gymnasium.*

18. Friedrich Paulsen, as quoted in Ringer, *Decline of the German Mandarins,* p. 35. The volume of literature on *Bildung* and the German academic elite is enormous, but Ringer is the standard English source.

19. Ringer, *Decline of the German Mandarins,* pp. 44–45, 258–59, and *passim;* Walter Struve, *Elites against Democracy: Leadership in Bourgeois Political Thought in Germany, 1890–1933* (Princeton, N. J.: Princeton University Press, 1973), pp. 13–14; Fritz Stern, *The Politics of Cultural Despair: A Study in the Rise of the Germanic Ideology* (Berkeley, Calif.: University of California Press, 1961), esp. pt. 2.

20. Moritz Münsterberg, "Reise-Tagebuch," p. 16 and *passim.* On Jewish cultural aspirations, see especially Katz, *Out of the Ghetto,* esp. chaps. 4 and 7; Michael A. Meyer, *The Origin of the Modern Jew: Jewish Identity and European Culture in Germany, 1749–1824* (Detroit: Wayne State University Press, 1967); Peter Gay, "Encounter with Modernism: German Jews in German Culture, 1884–1914," *Midstream* 21 (February 1975): 23–65; David L. Preston, "The German Jews in Secular Education, University Teaching and Science: A Preliminary Survey," *Jewish Social Studies* 38 (Spring 1976): 99–116.

21. Peter J. Pulzer, *The Rise of Political Anti-Semitism in Germany and Austria* (New York: John Wiley & Sons, 1964), chap. 1. Jews in fact were over-represented in the *Gymnasium.* In 1880 over 10 percent of *Gymnasium* students in Prussia were Jewish, compared to only about 1 percent of the population. Lexis, *Unterrichtswesen,* 2:178. In Danzig slightly over 4 percent of the *Gymnasium* students were Jewish at mid-century. The percentage of Jews in the city was 1.3. Aschkewitz, *Zur Geschichte der Juden,* pp. 6, 127. See also Preston, "German Jews," p. 102.

22. Again, the literature on the *Gymnasium* is voluminous. See especially Lexis, *Unterrichtswesen,* vol. 2, secs. 1 and 2, and Frederick Bolton, *The Secondary School System of Germany* (New York: D. Appleton & Co., 1900).

23. Bolton, *Secondary School System,* pp. 42, 52.

24. HM, *American Traits,* pp. 48–49. See also MM, *Hugo Münsterberg,* chap. 2.

25. Münsterberg left a list of his early literary efforts in his "Lebenslauf," a di-

ary that he drew up near the end of his life, apparently in preparation for an auto-biography. This can be found in the Münsterberg Papers. Münsterberg's later correspondence includes an occasional reference to dramatic works. See, for ex-ample, HM to James McKeen Cattell, 2 October 1899, Cattell Papers, Library of Congress; and David Belasco to HM, 1 March 1913, MP. In the latter document, Belasco, a New York theater manager, turned down a play by Münsterberg. Ex-cept for the poetry that Münsterberg published as *Verse* (Grossenhaim: Baumert & Ronge, 1897) under the pseudonym Hugo Terberg, I have been unable to find any of his creative efforts.

26. HM, *American Traits,* pp. 49–51.

27. MM, *Hugo Münsterberg,* pp. 5–6. Oscar Münsterberg, "Abschrift für meinen Sohn Hugo," p. 7, writes that the crown prince had a house on the Mün-sterberg site in Langfuhr in around 1910.

28. HM, "Studentenpflicht and Studentenrecht: Ein Wort an die deutsche Studentenschaft," 2d ed. (Leipzig: Guillermo Levien, 1890), pp. 8–9 (a copy of this pamphlet can be found in one of the three bound volumes of Münsterberg pamphlets held by Widener Library at Harvard, which are hereafter cited as HM, *Pamphlets*).

29. HM, "Ein Traum," *Verse,* p. 104; Arthur Mitzman, *The Iron Cage: An His-torical Interpretation of Max Weber* (New York: Alfred A. Knopf, 1970), p. 20. Münsterberg did suffer from headaches as a youth. See Moritz Münsterberg, "Reise-Tagebuch," p. 39.

30. Quoted in French by MM, *Hugo Münsterberg,* p. 20.

31. Ismar Schorsch, *Jewish Reactions to German Anti-Semitism, 1870–1914* (New York: Columbia University Press, 1972), p. 68. In addition to the studies on German Jews already cited, see Uriel Tal, *Christians and Jews in Germany: Relig-ion, Politics, and Ideology in the Second Reich, 1870–1914,* trans. Noah Jonathan Jacobs (Ithaca, N.Y.: Cornell University Press, 1975); Jehuda Reinharz, *Father-land or Promised Land: The Dilemma of the German Jew, 1893–1914* (Ann Arbor, Mich.: University of Michigan Press, 1975); Michael A. Meyer, "Great Debate on Antisemitism: Jewish Reaction to New Hostility in Germany," *Publications of the Leo Baeck Institute, Year Book 9* (1966), esp. pp. 150–52, and Hannah Arendt, *The Origins of Totalitarianism* (New York: Harcourt, Brace & Co., 1951), pp. 64–65.

32. I have no direct evidence on the date of the Münsterbergs' conversion, but Hugo's nephew, Dr. Hugo Munsterberg, suggests that it occurred soon after Mo-ritz's death. Margaret Münsterberg does not mention her father's Jewish ancestry, and I have found no reference to it in Münsterberg's own writings and correspon-dence after 1897. On the other hand, his Jewish background was well known in America, at least in the academic community.

33. Schorsch, *Jewish Reactions,* p. 138. The source of Schorsch's statistics is Ar-thur Ruppin, who called his figures "careful" and "low." Ruppin, *Soziologie der Juden,* vol. 1: *Die soziale Struktur der Juden* (Berlin: Jüdischer Verlag, 1930), pp. 296, 299. According to N. Samter, who used church records, 132 Jews coverted in Prussia in the year 1880. Samter, *Judentaufen in neunzehnten Jahrhundert mit besonderer Berücksichtigung Preussens* (Berlin: M. Poppelauer, 1906), p. 146.

34. Schorsch, *Jewish Reactions,* pp. 138-39.

35. "Münsterberg's Ideals," *Boston Globe,* 17 December 1916, p. 17.

36. Quoted in Schorsch, *Jewish Reactions,* p. 139.

37. Katz, *Out of the Ghetto,* pp. 48–49; Preston, "German Jews," pp. 106–9;

Gay, "Encounter with Modernism," p. 33; Hamburger, *Juden im öffentlichen Leben,* pp. 95–96, 98, and *passim.*

38. Franz Eulenburg, *Die Entwicklung der Universität Leipzig in den letzten hundert Jahren* (Leipzig: S. Hirsel, 1909), pp. 19, 52, 70.

39. HM, "Studentenpflicht," p. 7. This sort of pronouncement was common in student speeches of the period. According to Ringer, student speeches in the Wilhelmian period demonstrated "how thoroughly the phrases and attitudes of the university professors were absorbed by the mass of cultivated Germans." *Decline of the German Mandarins,* p. 259. See also the manuscript of a Münsterberg speech in 1884 at a celebration in honor of the Grimm brothers (MP). Information on Münsterberg's student and early teaching years in this paragraph and the following comes from his "Lebenslauf" and MM, *Hugo Münsterberg,* chap. 3, unless otherwise noted.

40. Oscar Münsterberg, "Abschrift für meinen Sohn Hugo," p. 6, in Moritz Münsterberg, "Reise-Tagebuch." On Virchow, see Erwin H. Ackerknecht, *Rudolf Virchow: Doctor, Statesman, Anthropologist* (Madison, Wis.: University of Wisconsin Press, 1953). On the predilection of Jews for medicine, see Preston, "German Jews," p. 103.

41. On reductionism, see Chapter 3 of this study.

42. Joseph Ben-David and Randall Collins, "Social Factors in the Origin of a New Science: The Case of Psychology," *American Sociological Review* 31 (August 1966): 461–63. See also Ben-David and Awraham Zloczower, "Universities and Academic Systems in Modern Societies," *European Journal of Sociology* 3 (1962): 55–56. Münsterberg was aware of the surplus of medically trained men in the 1880s. In his speech "Studentenpflicht," given at about the time when he decided to take up psychology, he spoke of an unusual rush toward medicine (p. 8).

43. Accounts of Wundt and his laboratory can be found in any of the standard histories of psychology. See, for example, Edwin G. Boring, *A History of Experimental Psychology,* 2d ed. (New York: Appleton-Century-Crofts, 1950), and Richard Müller-Freienfels, *The Evolution of Modern Psychology,* trans. Walter Béran Wolfe (New Haven: Yale University Press, 1935). On Wundt as a voluntarist, see Antonio Aliotta, *The Idealistic Reaction against Science,* trans. Agnes McCaskill (London: Macmillan & Co., 1914), pp. 22–28, and John Theodore Merz, *A History of European Thought in the Nineteenth Century,* 4 vols. (London: William Blackwood & Sons, 1904–1912), esp. 4:254–56. See also notes to Chapter 3 of this study.

44. On Münsterberg's claim, see James Mark Baldwin, *Between Two Wars, 1861–1921: Being Memories, Opinions and Letters Received,* 2 vols. (Boston: Stratford Co., 1926), 1:86.

45. MM, *Hugo Münsterberg,* pp. 23–24.

46. On the position of the *Docenten,* see Alexander Busch, *Die Geschichte des Privatdozenten: Eine soziologische Studie zur grossbetrieblichen Entwicklung der deutschen Universitäten* (Stuttgart: Ferdinand Enke, 1959), and Friedrich Paulsen, *The German University and University Study,* trans. Edward Delavan Perry (New York: Charles Scribner's Sons, 1906), pp. 103–10.

47. Here and later, I am using "positivism" in a loose sense and do not have in mind the systems of Auguste Comte or Ernst Mach. By it I mean a system of science that regards all phenomena as regulated by deterministic and ultimately knowable laws, that stresses exact prediction, and that applies the experimental method to animate as well as inanimate phenomena.

48. William O. Krohn, "Facilities in Experimental Psychology at the Various German Universities," *American Journal of Psychology* 4 (August 1892): 585–94, and Krohn, "The Laboratory of the Psychological Institute at the University of Göttingen," *American Journal of Psychology* 5 (November 1892); 282–84.

49. Merz, *History of European Thought,* 2:518; Wundt to HM, 29 March 1896, MP. On the "anti-Wundtians," see especially James Ward, "Modern Psychology: A Reflexion," *Mind* n.s. 2 (January 1893): 54–82.

50. Wundt, "Zur Lehre von den Gemüthsbewegungen," *Philosophische Studien* 6 (1890): 384–93; Oswald Külpe, "Die Lehre vom Willen in der neueren Psychologie," *Philosophische Studien* 5 (1888): 233ff.; Edward B. Titchener, "Dr. Münsterberg and his Experimental Psychology," *Mind* 16 (October 1891): 594 and *passim.*

51. Georg E. Müller, review of *Beiträge zur experimentellen Psychologie,* vols. 1–3, by HM, in *Göttingsche gelehrte Anzeigen* 1 (1 June 1891): 394, 396, 428. See also Müller's review, "Berechtigung zu Prof. Münsterberg's Beiträgen zur experimentellen Psychologie, Heft 4," *Zeitschrift für Psychologie und Physiologie der Sinnesorgane* 4 (1893): 404–14.

52. Boring, *History of Experimental Psychology,* p. 342.

53. Titchener, "Dr. Münsterberg," p. 534; G. F. Stout, "Apperception and the Movement of Attention," *Mind* 16 (January 1891): 23–53; George Croom Robertson, "Dr. H. Münsterberg on Apperception," *Mind* 15 (April 1890): 234–45; William James, *The Principles of Psychology,* 2 vols. (New York: Henry Holt & Co., 1890), 2:505n.

54. Preston, "German Jews," pp. 106–8. Preston repeats the frequently cited statistics that in 1889–90 40 percent of converts holding a university position were full professors compared to 48 percent of Christians. But only 10 percent of Jews in faculty positions held full professorships.

55. Münsterberg was promoted to *Extraordinarius* on Feburary 11. See Ernst Theodore Nauck, *Die Privatdozenten der Universität Freiburg i. Br., 1818–1955,* Beiträge zur Freiburger Wissenschafts- und Universitätsgeschichte, no. 8 (Freiburg: Verlag Eberhard Albert Universitätsbuchhandlung, 1956). In philosophy, in the decade 1880–89, the proportion of men who reached full professorships to those who advanced to extraordinary professorships but went no farther was almost five to one. Ben-David and Collins, "Social Factors in the Origin of a New Science," p. 462. On the status of extraordinary professors, see Paulsen, *German Universities and University Study,* p. 79ff.

Chapter 3

1. Some of the more important works on the political and academic ideology of German professors are Fritz K. Ringer, *The Decline of the German Mandarins: The German Academic Community, 1890–1933* (Cambridge, Mass.: Harvard University Press, 1969); Frederick Lilge, *The Abuse of Learning: The Failure of the German University* (New York: Macmillan Co., 1948); Jurgen Herbst, *The German Historical School in American Scholarship: A Study in the Transfer of Culture* (Ithaca, N.Y.: Cornell University Press, 1965); Georg C. Iggers, *The German Conception of History: The National Tradition of Historical Thought from Herder to the Present* (Middletown, Conn.: Wesleyan University Press, 1968); Hajo Holborn, "Der deutsche Idealismus in sozialgeschichtlicher Bedeutung," *Historische Zeitschrift* 174 (October 1952): 359–84.

2. Karl Mannheim, *Ideology and Utopia: An Introduction to the Sociology of Knowledge,* trans. Louis Wirth and Edward Shils (New York: Harcourt, Brace & World, 1936).

3. The extent of the literature on *Naturphilosophie* and the biology that grew out of it is vast. Everett Mendelsohn, "The Biological Sciences in the Nineteenth Century: Some Problems and Sources," *History of Science* 3 (1964): 39–59, is a useful bibliographical essay for older sources. I found the following more recent articles of help: Everett Mendelsohn, "Physical Models and Physiological Concepts: Explanation in Nineteenth-Century Biology," *British Journal for the History of Science* 2 (June 1965): 201–19; Guenter B. Risse, "Kant, Schelling, and the Early Search for a Philosophical 'Science' of Medicine in Germany," *Journal of the History of Medicine* 27 (April 1972): 145–58; and L. Pearce Williams, "Kant, Naturphilosophie, and Scientific Method," in *Foundations of Scientific Method: The Nineteenth Century,* ed. Ronald N. Giere and Richard S. Westfall (Bloomington, Ind.: Indiana University Press, 1973), pp. 3–22. My understanding of the philosophical background for this section derives from: John Theodore Merz, *A History of European Thought in the Nineteenth Century,* 4 vols. (Edinburgh: William Blackwood & Sons, 1896–1914); Maurice Mandelbaum, *History, Man & Reason: A Study in Nineteenth-Century Thought* (Baltimore: Johns Hopkins Press, 1961). For the more specifically scientific issues: Erik Nordenskiöld, *The History of Biology,* trans. Leonard Bucknell Eyre (New York: Alfred A. Knopf, 1928); William R. Coleman, *Biology in the Nineteenth Century: Problems of Form, Function, and Transformation* (New York: John Wiley & Sons, 1971); and Karl E. Rothschuh, *History of Physiology,* trans. Guenter B. Risse (Huntington, N.Y.: Robert E. Krieger Publishing Co., 1973).

4. Mandelbaum, *History, Man & Reason,* p. 31.

5. The British biologist Richard Owen used this phrase to describe, approvingly, the work of the *Naturphilosoph* Lorenz Oken. Quoted in Mendelsohn, "Physical Models," p. 205.

6. Rudolph Virchow, "Standpoints in Scientific Method" (1877), in *Disease, Life, and Man: Selected Essays by Rudolf Virchow,* trans. and ed. Lelland J. Rather (Stanford, Calif.: Stanford University Press, 1958), p. 142. On the antivitalist campaign of the 1840s, see especially Oswei Temkin, "Materialism in French and German Physiology in the Early Nineteenth Century," *Bulletin of the History of Medicine* 20 (July 1946): 322–27; Paul F. Cranefield, "The Organic Physics of 1847 and the Biophysics of Today," *Journal of the History of Medicine* 12 (October 1957): 407–23; Thomas S. Hall, *Ideas of Life and Matter: Studies in the History of General Physiology, 600 B.C. to A.D. 1900,* 2 vols. (Chicago: University of Chicago Press, 1969), 2:258–85; and David Galaty, "The Philosophical Basis of Mid-Nineteenth Century German Reductionism," *Journal of the History of Medicine* 29 (July 1974): 295–316.

7. Emil DuBois-Reymond to Eduard Hallman, May 1842, in *Jugendbriefe von Emil DuBois-Reymond an Eduard Hallman,* ed. Estelle DuBois-Reymond (Berlin: Dietrich Reimer [Ernst Vohsen], 1918), p. 108; Mendelsohn, "Biological Sciences," p. 44.

8. This is the central point of Galaty, "Mid-Nineteenth Century Reductionism."

9. Helmholtz, quoted in ibid., p. 302.

10. On the reception of Darwin in Germany, see especially William M. Mont-

gomery, "Evolution and Darwinism in German Biology, 1800–1883" (Ph.D. dissertation, University of Texas at Austin, 1974).

11. Nordenskiöld, *History of Biology,* pp. 513–15, 519–20; Ernst Cassirer, *The Problem of Knowledge: Philosophy, Science and History since Hegel,* trans. William H. Woglom and Charles Hendel (New Haven: Yale University Press, 1950), pp. 162–64, 176–87.

12. G. Stanley Hall, *Aspects of German Culture* (Boston: James R. Osgood, 1891), pp. 149–50. On Haeckel's Volkism, see Daniel Gasman, *The Scientific Origin of National Socialism: Social Darwinism in Ernst Haeckel and the German Monist League* (New York: American Elsevier, 1971), pp. xxiv–xxvii, 8–9, and *passim.*

13. Wilhelm Wundt, *Grundzüge der physiologische Psychologie,* 3d ed., 2 vols. (Leipzig: W. Englemann, 1887), 2:547–49.

14. HM, *Der Ursprung der Sittlichkeit* (Freiburg i. Br.: Akademische Verlagsbuchhandlung von J. C. B. Mohr, 1889), p. 20; HM, *Die Lehre der natürlichen Anpassung in ihrer Entwicklung, Anwendung, und Bedeutung* (Leipzig: Metzger & Wittig, 1885), pp. 16ff., 38.

15. Leuckart as quoted by Jane Oppenheimer, *Essays in the History of Embryology and Biology* (Cambridge, Mass.: Massachusetts Institute of Technology Press, 1967), p. 155; Darwin as quoted by Merz, *History of European Thought,* 2:436.

16. Emanuel Rádl, *The History of Biological Theories,* trans. and ed. E. J. Hatfield (London: Oxford University Press, 1930), p. 253. See also Nordenskiöld, *History of Biology,* pp. 571–81. On Roux's significance in the history of biology, see Oppenheimer, *History of Embryology,* pp. 66–72; Frederick B. Churchill, "Chabry, Roux, and the Experimental Method in Nineteenth-Century Embryology," in *Foundations of Scientific Method,* ed. Giere and Westfall, *passim.*

17. HM, *Natürlichen Anpassung,* p. 43. Münsterberg derived this particular chain from Wilhelm Preyer, best known for his work on child psychology.

18. Ibid., pp. 51, 86–88, 44–48.

19. Ibid., 47–48, and *passim.*

20. Ibid., pp. 45, 70–71.

21. Ibid., p. 100.

22. Charles Coulton Gillispie, *The Edge of Objectivity: An Essay into the History of Scientific Ideas* (Princeton, N. J.: Princeton University Press, 1960), p. 304 and *passim;* HM, *Natürlichen Anpassung,* p. 18 and *passim.* The phrase, "nature red in tooth and claw," comes originally from Tennyson's poem "Memoriam."

23. HM, *Ursprung der Sittlichkeit,* p. 112. Compare the discussion of historicism in Iggers, *German Conception of History.*

24. Ranke, as quoted by Holborn, "Deutsche Idealismus," p. 367. On social organicism in German thought, see especially Ralph Bowen, *German Theories in the Corporate State, with Special Reference to the Period 1870–1919* (New York: McGraw Hill, 1947), and Francis William Coker, *Organismic Theories of the State as Organism or as Person* (New York: Longmans, Green & Co., 1910); Mannheim, *Ideology and Utopia,* esp. chap. 3.

25. HM, *Ursprung der Sittlichkeit,* p. 59.

26. Edward Titchener, "The Postulates of a Structural Psychology," *Philosophical Review* 8 (September 1898): 449–65, offers a good discussion of the aims of "structuralism," a general name for the Wundtian approach to psychology. Titchener repeated Ebbinghaus's reference to a "morphology" of mind. For this entire section, see the standard histories of psychology, especially Edwin G. Boring, *A*

History of Experimental Psychology, 2d ed. (New York: Appleton-Century-Crofts, 1950); Richard Müller-Freienfels, *The Evolution of Modern Psychology,* trans. Walter Béran Wolfe (New Haven: Yale University Press, 1935); and Gardner Murphy, *An Historical Introduction to Modern Psychology,* 4th ed. (New York: Harcourt, Brace & Co., 1938).

27. Max Dessoir, quoted by David Ballin Klein, *A History of Scientific Psychology: Its Origins and Philosophical Backgrounds* (New York: Basic Books, 1970), p. 487; Carl Stumpf, "Hermann von Helmholtz and the New Psychology," *Psychological Review* 2 (January 1895): 4.

28. Robert M. Young, *Mind, Brain, and Adaptation in the Nineteenth Century: Cerebral Localization and Its Biological Context from Gall to Ferrier* (Oxford: Clarendon Press, 1970), offers an excellent discussion of the development of knowledge of the brain, with an emphasis on English and French thought. I have used it in this and the following paragraphs. Müller's credo is cited in Stumpf, "Hermann Helmholtz," p. 2.

29. Boring, *History of Experimental Psychology,* pp. 71–74; Young, *Mind, Brain, and Adaptation,* p. 5 and *passim;* Hermann von Helmholtz, "The Relation of the Natural Sciences to Science in General," *Selected Writings,* ed. Russell Kahl (Middletown, Conn.: Wesleyan University Press, 1971), pp. 123–43.

30. Merz, *European Thought in the Nineteenth Century,* 3:285–93, and especially 4:707–35. For a discussion of the late-century revival of interest in the various forms of voluntarism and Idealism, see Aliotta, *Idealistic Reaction against Science.*

31. Theodore Mischel, "Wundt and the Conceptual Foundations of Psychology," *Philosophy and Phenomenological Research* 31 (September 1970): 1–26. For Titchener's point of view see his articles, "The Postulates of a Structural Psychology," p. 459, and "Wundt's Psychology of the Will," *Proceedings of the International Congress of Education of the World's Columbian Exposition, Chicago, July 25–28, 1893,* pp. 705–12. This article offers an English summary of Oswald Külpe's "Die Lehre vom Willen in der neueren Psychologie." Külpe's article is the fullest discussion of the various positions on the will in German psychology in the late 1880s. For Wundt's views see his *Physiologische Psychologie* (in the 2d ed., sec. 5 is on the will and will-acts; see esp. p. 378ff.) and various of his articles in *Philosophische Studien,* esp. "Zur Lehre vom Willen," 1 (1882): 337–78, and "Zur Lehre von den Gemuthsbewegungen," 7 (1890): 335–93.

32. Wundt, "Ueber psychische Causalität und das Princip des psychophysischen Parallelismus," *Philosophische Studien* 10 (1894): 123–24; Edward König, *W. Wundt: Seine Philosophie und Psychologie* (Stuttgart: Fr. Frommanns Verlag E. Hauff, 1901), p. 25 and *passim.* See also Wolfgang G. Bringmann, William D. G. Balance, and Rand B. Evans, "Wilhelm Wundt, 1832–1920: A Brief Biographical Sketch," *Journal of the History of the Behavioral Sciences* 11 (July 1975): 287–97.

33. Wundt, *Grundzüge der physiologischen Psychologie,* 2d ed., 2 vols. (Leipzig: W. Engelmann, 1880), 1:205ff. For a treatment of the historical tradition of apperception, see Otto Staude, "Der Begriff der Apperception in der neueren Psychologie," *Philosophische Studien* 1 (1882): 149–212.

34. Wundt, *Ethics: An Investigation of the Facts and Laws of the Moral Life,* 2d ed., 3 vols., trans. Edward Bradford Titchener et al. (New York: Macmillan Co., 1901), 3:40ff. On mental causality, see also Wundt, "Ueber psychische Causal-

ität." My description of Laplace's world-formula is from Merz, *European Thought in the Nineteenth Century,* 3:551.

35. HM, *Beiträge zur experimentellen Psychologie,* 4 vols. (Freiburg i. B.: J. C. B. Mohr [Paul Siebeck], 1889–92), 1:36. On Hume, see William James, *The Principles of Psychology,* 2 vols. (New York: Henry Holt, 1890), 1:350–53.

36. HM, *Willenshandlung,* pp. 96, 62, and *passim;* HM, *Beiträge,* 1:23; 4:228. Münsterberg's denial of a distinct mental element of "feeling" differed from the Wundtian orthodoxy, but was not unique. Among German experimentalists, Theodore Ziehen and Sigmund Exner held similar views. See Titchener, "Structural Psychology," p. 458.

37. Victor Henri, "Revue générale sur le sens musculaire," *L'année psychologique* 5 (1898): 399–557; E. G. Jones, "The Development of the 'Muscular Sense' Concept during the Nineteenth Century and the Work of H. Charlton Bastian," *Journal of the History of Medicine* 27 (July 1972): 298–311; Edwin G. Boring, *Sensation and Perception in the History of Experimental Psychology* (New York: Appleton-Century-Crofts, 1942), chap. 14, esp. pp. 524–35. On Müller's importance, which Boring misses, see Young, *Mind, Brain, and Adaptation,* pp. 114–18. See also James, *Principles of Psychology,* 2:522–28.

38. John Dewey, "The Reflex Arc Concept in Psychology," *Psychological Review* 3 (July 1896): 357–90; D. C. Phillips, "James, Dewey, and the Reflex Arc," *Journal of the History of Ideas* 32 (October–December 1971): 555–68.

39. HM, *Ueber Aufgaben und Methoden der Psychologie,* Gesellschaft für psychologische Forschung, Schriften, no. 1 (Leipzig, 1893), p. 223; James, *Principles of Psychology,* 2:492ff. Münsterberg's volume first appeared separately in 1891.

40. James, *Talks to Teachers on Psychology and to Students on Some of Life's Ideals* (Boston: Henry Holt and Co., 1899), p. 99; Edouard Claparède, in *A History of Psychology in Autobiography,* ed. Carl Murchison and Edwin G. Boring, 6 vols. (Worcester, Mass.: Clark University Press, 1930–61), 1:70.

41. HM, *Willenshandlung,* p. 118 and *passim;* James, *Principles of Psychology,* 2:501. Both R. H. Lotze and Herbert Spencer had also stressed the prior existence of a memory image in the sense of will. See Jones, "Development of the 'Muscular Sense' Concept," pp. 303–4.

42. HM, *Willenshandlung,* p. 20.

43. James, *Principles of Psychology,* vol. 2, chap. 26. For other American views besides James's, see James R. Angell, "The Influence of Darwin on Psychology," *Psychological Review* 16 (May 1909): 157; James Mark Baldwin, "Consciousness and Evolution," *Science* n.s. 2 (23 August 1895): 223; Dewey, "The Interpretation of the Savage Mind," *Psychological Review* 9 (May 1902): 219.

44. HM, "Die Association successiver Vorstellungen," *Zeitschrift für Psychologie und Physiologie der Sinnesorgane* 1 (1890): 99–107; HM, *Willenshandlung,* p. 23. James took note of Münsterberg's argument, which he did not accept, in *Principles of Psychology,* 2:590n.

45. Cassirer, *Problem of Knowledge,* pp. 3–4.

46. HM, *Ursprung der Sittlichkeit,* p. 23ff. The volume of literature on nineteenth-century ethics is enormous; Merz, *European Thought in the Nineteenth Century,* vol. 4, chap. 8, is especially useful.

47. HM, *Ursprung der Sittlichkeit,* pp. 39, 85–86, 111–12.

48. HM, *Willenshandlung,* p. 50. See also HM, *Ursprung der Sittlichkeit,* p. 102ff.

49. HM, *Willenshandlung,* p. 42.
50. HM, *Ursprung der Sittlichkeit,* p. 102.
51. Ibid., p. 117.

Chapter 4

1. James to HM, 21 February 1892, JP; James to Henry James, 11 April 1892, in *The Letters of William James,* ed. Henry James, 2 vols. (Boston: Atlantic Monthly Press, 1920), 1:318.

2. James to HM, 21 February 1892, JP. The fullest account of psychology at Harvard is given in Bruce Kuklick, *The Rise of American Philosophy: Cambridge, Massachusetts, 1860–1930* (New Haven: Yale University Press, 1977). See also Sheldon M. Stern, "William James and the New Psychology at Harvard," in *Social Sciences at Harvard, 1860–1920: From Inculcation to the Open Mind,* ed. Paul Buck (Cambridge, Mass.: Harvard University Press, 1965), pp. 175–222; and Ralph Barton Perry, "Psychology, 1876–1929," in *The Development of Harvard University since the Inauguration of President Eliot, 1869–1929,* ed. Samuel Eliot Morison (Cambridge, Mass.: Harvard University Press, 1930), pp. 216–22. On the "new psychology" in America, see especially Dorothy Ross, *G. Stanley Hall: The Psychologist as Prophet* (Chicago: University of Chicago Press, 1972); Frank M. Albrecht, "The New Psychology in America" (Ph.D. dissertation, Johns Hopkins University, 1960); and Thomas M. Camfield, "The Professionalization of American Psychology, 1870–1917," *Journal of the History of the Behavioral Sciences* 9 (January 1973): 66–75.

3. Edmund D. Delabarre, "A Student's Impressions of James in the Late '80's," *Psychological Review* 50 (January 1943): 126; Mary Whiton Calkins in *A History of Psychology in Autobiography,* ed. Carl Murchison and Edwin G. Boring, 6 vols. (Worcester, Mass.: Clark University Press, 1930–61), 1:33; James to HM, 2 July and 27 August 1890, MP. In Paris, Münsterberg and James shared an interest in hypnotism, to which the conference had been in part dedicated. For Münsterberg's views on hypnotism at this time, see especially his review of Max Dessoir's *Bibliographie des modernen Hypnotismus* and his *Compte Rendu* of the conference, both in the first volume of his *Pamphlets,* held by Widener.

4. James to HM, 8 July 1901, JP; James to HM, undated fragment (c. 1892), MP.

5. James Mark Baldwin, *Between Two Wars, 1861–1921: Being Memories, Opinions and Letters Received,* 2 vols. (Boston, Mass.: Stratford Co., 1926), 1:35–36; James to Henry James, 11 April 1892, in *The Letters of William James,* ed. Henry James, 2 vols. (Boston: Atlantic Monthly Press, 1920), 1:318. The standard work on the influence of the German university and scholarship in America is Jurgen Herbst, *The German Historical School in American Scholarship: A Study in the Transfer of Culture* (Ithaca, N.Y.: Cornell University Press, 1965). See also Charles Franklin Thwing, *The American and the German University: One Hundred Years of History* (New York: Macmillan Co., 1928). Laurence R. Veysey, *The Emergence of the American University* (Chicago: University of Chicago Press, 1965), chap. 3, tells the same story but is more skeptical about the importance of the German influence on American academic structure. In this regard see especially Veysey's "From Germany to America," *History of Education Quarterly* 13 (Winter 1973): 401–7, which argues that American bureaucratic and industrial models were far more important for the structure of American higher education

than was the German university. On the transfer of psychology from Germany to America, see R. G. A. Dolby, "The Transmission of Two New Scientific Disciplines from Europe to North America in the Late Nineteenth Century," *Annals of Science* 34 (May 1977): 287–310.

6. HM, "Twenty-Five Years in America: The First Chapter of an Unfinished Autobiography," *Century Illustrated Magazine* 94 (May 1917): 35–36; James to Josiah Royce, 22 June 1892, in *The Thought and Character of William James* by Ralph Barton Perry, 2 vols. (Boston: Little, Brown & Co. 1935), 2:141. The description of America as a "land of unlimited possibilities" is from the title of Ludwig Goldberger's *Das Land der unbegrenzten Möglichkeiten: Beobachtungen über das Wirtschaftsleben der Vereinigten Staaten von Amerika* (Berlin: F. Fontane & Co., 1903). On the view of America in German popular literature, see especially *Reallexicon der deutschen Literaturgeschichte,* 2d ed., s.v. "Amerikanische Literatur," by Horst Oppel, esp. pp. 50–55.

7. HM to James, 29 April 1892, JP; HM to James, 28 July 1892, MP.

8. William O. Krohn, "Facilities in Experimental Psychology at the Various German Universities," *American Journal of Psychology* 4 (August 1892): 587; idem, "Facilities in Experimental Psychology in the Colleges of the United States," *Report of the Commissioner of Education, 1890–1891,* 2:1139; HM, "The New Psychology and Harvard's Equipment for Teaching It," *Harvard Graduates' Magazine* 1 (January 1893): 204. Jacques Loeb, the Swiss biologist, told James in 1896 that he found academic conditions "far healthier" in America than in Germany. James to HM, 2 September 1896, JP. Mattoon M. Curtis, "The Present Condition of the German Universities," *Educational Review* 2 (June 1891): 30–31, makes the point that the expansion of the German universities had peaked.

9. HM, *Ueber Aufgaben und Methoden,* p. 231.

10. HM, "Twenty-Five Years," p. 37; HM to James, 29 April 1892, JP; James to HM, 3 May 1892, JP. Carl Stumpf, a leading experimental psychologist then at Munich, urged Münsterberg to take the Harvard position. Stumpf to James, 30 June 1892, JP. See also additional letters between James and Münsterberg in their respective manuscript collections.

11. HM, *Die Amerikaner,* 2 vols. (Berlin: Ernst Siegfried Mittler und Sohn, 1904), 1:iv. Edwin Holt did not include this statement in his authorized American translation of the work.

12. G. Stanley Hall, *Aspects of German Culture* (Boston: James R. Osgood, 1891), p. 149. DuBois-Reymond was apparently the first German to use the term "Amerikanisierung," which he characterized as "the frightful overrunning and permeation of European culture with realism and the wildly increasing predominance of technology." See Otto Basler, "Amerikanismus: Geschichte des Schlagwortes," *Deutsche Rundschau* 214 (August 1930): 142–46; and Fritz Stern, *The Politics of Cultural Despair: A Study in the Rise of the Germanic Ideology* (Berkeley, Calif.: University of California Press, 1961), pp. 169–71.

13. HM, *The Americans,* trans. Edwin B. Holt (New York: McClure, Phillips & Co., 1905), pp. 349–50; MM. *Hugo Münsterberg,* p. 41ff.; Wundt to HM, 29 March 1896, MP; HM, "Twenty-Five Years," p. 37ff.; Charles M. Bakewell in *George Herbert Palmer, 1842–1933: Memorial Addresses,* ed. Harvard University, Department of Philosophy (Cambridge: Harvard University Press, 1935), p. 6.

14. *Annual Report of the President of Harvard University, 1892–3,* pp. 62–63; HM to James [5 November 1892?], JP, and later correspondence. On the early Harvard laboratory, see HM, "The New Psychology and Harvard's Equipment

for Teaching It," *Harvard Graduates' Magazine* 1 (January 1893): 201–9, and Herbert Nichols, "The Psychological Laboratory at Harvard," *McClure's Magazine* 1 (October 1893): 399–409.

15. Royce to James, 18 December 1892, in *Letters of William James,* ed. Henry James, 1:332; James to Dickinson Miller, 19 November 1893, JP; James Mark Baldwin, "Psychology, Past and Present," *Psychological Review* 1 (July 1894): 384; James McKeen Cattell, "The Advance of Psychology," *Science* n.s. 9 (21 October 1898): 537. At least at first, Wundt apparently disagreed with the assessment. He told some visiting Americans in 1893 that Titchener's laboratory at Cornell and James Angell's at the University of California were the only two laboratories in America that he could recommend. James to HM, 13 April 1893, JP.

16. James to Royce, 22 June 1892, in *William James,* by Perry, 1:141; Palmer to HM, 8 September 1893, MP; HM to Eliot, 12 September 1902, Eliot Papers, Harvard University Archives (hereafter EP); *Annual Report of the President, 1893–4,* pp. 57–59; *1894–5,* pp. 58–59.

17. HM to James, 28 July 1891, JP; HM, "Twenty-Five Years," p. 41. Münsterberg did publish an answer to Müller's critique in his pamphlet, "Professor G. E. Müller's 'Berechtigung' in der *Zeitschrift für Psychologie und Physiologie der Sinnesorgane* Bd. IV" (Boston: Carl H. Heintzmann, 1893). See HM, *Pamphlets.*

18. MM, *Hugo Münsterberg,* p. 50 and *passim;* HM, "Lebenslauf"; HM to James, 22 June 1893, JP; HM to Eliot, 2 February 1894, EP.

19. MM, *Hugo Münsterberg,* chap. 4; HM, "Lebenslauf"; HM to Cattell, 20 September 1894, Cattell Papers.

20. On American attitudes toward nature during this period, see Peter J. Schmitt, *Back to Nature: The Arcadian Myth in Urban America* (New York: Oxford University Press, 1969), and Roderick Nash, *Wilderness and the American Mind,* rev. ed. (New Haven: Yale University Press, 1973).

21. HM, "Der Amerikaner: Eine Weltausstellungsbetrachtung," *Vossische Zeitung* (Berlin), 3 August 1893.

22. HM to Eliot, 14 September 1894, EP; HM to James, 14 September 1894, JP.

23. HM to Eliot, 14 September 1894, EP; James to Eliot, 21 February [1897], EP.

24. HM to James, 8 June 1896, JP. See also HM to James, 24 January 1896, JP; and HM, "Twenty-Five Years," pp. 41–42.

25. Ernest Gagliardi et al., *Die Universität Zürich 1833–1933 und ihre Vorläufer, Festschrift zur Jahrhundertfeier* (Zurich: Verlag der Erziehungsdirektion, 1938), pp. 706, 844, 844n. For Wundt's letter of recommendation, see Wolfgang Bringmann and William D. G. Balance, "Wundt versus Münsterberg: Roback's Version Challenged," *American Psychologist* 28 (September 1973): 849–50. See also HM to Eliot, 2 February 1897, EP.

26. Gagliardi, *Universität Zürich,* pp. 844–45; HM to Eliot, 24 March 1897, EP; William D. G. Balance, "Frustrations and Joys of Archival Research," *Journal of the History of the Behavioral Sciences* 11 (January 1975): 37–40. Balance, who has examined the Zurich files on this incident, offers the most complete account. He discredits the contention of Münsterberg's student, Aaron Roback, that Wundt incited anti-Semitic prejudice against Münsterberg. Abraham Aaron Roback, *History of American Psychology* (New York: Library Publishers, 1952), p. 194. See also Wundt to HM, 29 March 1896, MP.

27. HM, "Lebenslauf"; HM to [University of Zurich], undated fragment, MP; Gagliardi, *Universität Zürich,* pp. 844–45.

28. Carl Stumpf to James, 13 October 1896, JP; HM to Eliot, 3 March 1897, MP; Wundt to HM, 29 March 1896, MP.

29. Wundt to HM, 29 March 1896, MP.

30. Baldwin to HM, 15 October 1896, and 30 March 1897, MP.

31. James to HM, 9 April 1897, MP; HM to Eliot, 2 February 1897, EP; Eliot to HM, 3 March 1897, and 15 January 1897, MP.

32. HM to Eliot, 24 March 1897, EP; Wundt to HM, 29 March 1896, MP.

Chapter 5

1. HM, "Twenty-Five Years," p. 42.

2. See Chapter 6 of this study.

3. Henry A. Murray, "What Should Psychologists Do about Psychoanalysis," *Journal of Abnormal Behavior* 35 (April 1940): 152; Wundt to Vetter in Bringmann and Balance, "Wundt versus Münsterberg," p. 849; Wundt to HM, 29 March 1896, MP; James to Stumpf, 24 June 1892, JP; Cattell to HM, 22 May 1907, MP; Laurence R. Veysey, *The Emergence of the American University* (Chicago, Ill.: University of Chicago Press, 1965), p. 231.

4. All three reminiscences are from *A History of Psychology in Autobiography,* ed. Carl Murchison and Edwin G. Boring, 6 vols. (Worcester, Mass.: Clark University Press, 1930–61). The Calkins comment appears in 1:33; the Dunlap in 2:41; and the Yerkes in 2:389.

5. George Herbert Palmer, "Philosophy," in *The Development of Harvard University since the Inauguration of President Eliot, 1869–1929,* ed. Samuel Eliot Morison (Cambridge, Mass.: Harvard University Press, 1930), p. 17; Frank Angell, review of *Hugo Münsterberg: His Life and Work,* by Margaret Münsterberg, in *Psychological Bulletin* 19 (August 1922): 125; Gordon Allport in *Psychology in Autobiography,* ed. Murchison and Boring, 5:6; Marianne Weber, *Max Weber: Ein Lebensbild* (Tübingen: J. C. B. Mohr [Paul Siebeck], 1926, pp. 292ff.

6. Rollo Brown, *Harvard Yard in the Golden Age* (New York: Current Books, 1948), p. 49.

7. Palmer, "Philosophy," in *Development of Harvard University,* ed. Morison, p. 18. Details of the various feuds can be found in the letters between the participants. See the Münsterberg, James, Eliot, and Lowell papers.

8. On community as a theme in the Progressive period, see especially R. Jackson Wilson, *In Quest of Community: Social Philosophy in the United States, 1860–1920* (New York: John Wiley & Sons, 1968); and Jean B. Quandt, *From the Small Town to the Great Community: The Social Thought of Progressive Intellectuals* (New Brunswick, N.J.: Rutgers University Press, 1970).

9. HM, *American Traits,* p. 198.

10. Ibid., pp. 154, 80.

11. HM, *Ursprung der Sittlichkeit,* pp. 74–78.

12. HM, *American Problems from the Point of View of a Psychologist* (New York: Moffat, Yard & Co., 1910), p. 19

13. HM, *American Traits,* pp. 149, 136, 146, 144, 139, 129, 158.

14. Ibid., p. 135.

15. Roosevelt to HM, 3 June 1901, Theodore Roosevelt Papers, Library of Congress. On the concern of Americans over virility and the fear of the feminiza-

tion of society in the Progressive years, see especially Peter Filene, *Him/Her/Self: Sex Roles in Modern America* (New York: Harcourt Brace Jovanovich, 1975), chap. 3; James R. McGovern, "David Graham Phillips and the Virility Impulse of Progressives," *New England Quarterly* 39 (September 1966); and Roderick Nash's introduction to *Call of the Wild: 1900–1916* (New York: G. Braziller, 1970). On "feminization" as a theme of nineteenth-century America, see Ann Douglas, *The Feminization of American Culture* (New York: Alfred A. Knopf, 1977).

16. Roosevelt to HM, 3 June 1901, Roosevelt Papers; MM, *Hugo Münsterberg,* p. 76.

17. Roosevelt to HM, 3 June 1901, Roosevelt Papers; HM, "Uber die Befähigung des weiblichen Geschlectes zum wissenschaftlichen Studium und Berufe," in *Die akademische Frau,* ed. Arthur Kirchoff (Berlin: Hugo Steinetz Verlag, 1897), pp. 9–12. This speech was reprinted as chapter 16 of HM, *Aus Deutsch-Amerika* (Berlin: Ernst Siegfried Mittler und Sohn, 1909). See also HM, *American Traits,* chap. 4.

18. Ibid., p. 154.

19. Ibid., pp. 164–65.

20. On educational reform in this period, see Lawrence A. Cremin, *The Transformation of the School: Progressivism in American Education, 1876–1957* (New York: Alfred A. Knopf, 1961); Dorothy Ross, *G. Stanley Hall: The Psychologist as Prophet* (Chicago, Ill.: University of Chicago Press, 1972), chaps. 7 and 15; James Dale Hendricks, "The Child Study Movement in American Education, 1880–1910: A Quest for Educational Reform through a Systematic Study of the Child" (Ph.D. dissertation, Indiana University, 1968). For more skeptical views, see Michael B. Katz, *Class, Bureaucracy, and Schools: The Illusion of Educational Change in America* (New York: Praeger Publishers, 1971), pp. 113–25; and Robert Church and Michael W. Sedlak, *Education in the United States: An Interpretive History* (New York: Free Press, 1976), chap. 9.

21. Nicholas Murray Butler, editorial in *Education Review* 15 (March 1898): 298–300; William Torrey Harris to HM, 22 April 1898, MP. For Münsterberg's early views on education, see especially his "The New Psychology," in *The Old Psychology and the New,* ed. Larkin Dunton (Boston: New England Publishing Co., 1895), pp. 14–26; "The Danger from Experimental Psychology," *Atlantic Monthly* 81 (February 1898): 159–67; "Psychology and Education," *Educational Review* 16 (September 1898): 105–32 (reprinted in *Psychology and Life* [New York: Houghton Mifflin Co., 1899]); "School Reform," *Atlantic Monthly* 85 (May 1900): 656–69 (reprinted in *American Traits).*

22. HM, *American Traits,* p. 66.

23. HM, *American Problems,* p. 16; HM, *American Traits,* pp. 68–69.

24. Ibid., pp. 67–68; HM, *American Problems,* pp. 16–17. For James on habit, see his *Principles of Psychology,* 2 vols. (New York: Henry Holt, 1890), vol. 1, chap. 4.

25. HM, *American Traits,* p. 87 and *passim.*

26. HM, *The Americans,* pp. 405–6; HM, "The American College for Germany," *Science* n.s. 26 (20 September 1907): 361–68; HM, *American Traits,* pp. 161–62.

27. Alfred Bushnell Hart, "The Present and the Future," *Harvard Graduates' Magazine* 4 (September 1895): 83; HM to Eliot, 15 June 1894, EP.

28. HM to Eliot, 30 August 1894, and 8 October 1898, EP.

29. HM to Eliot, 19 February 1906, and 8 October 1898, EP. See also HM, "Prizes at the Top," *Journal of Education* 67 (26 March 1908): 342–43.

30. Hugh Hawkins, *Between Harvard and America: The Educational Leadership of Charles W. Eliot* (New York: Oxford University Press, 1972), p. 352n; HM to Eliot, 14 October 1898, and 19 February 1906, EP.

31. HM, *American Traits,* pp. 104, 113, 94, and *passim.*

32. Ibid., pp. 114–15. Münsterberg wrote the entries on "History, Logic of," "Germany–History of Science and Philosophy," "Germany–The University System," and "Sciences–Classification of," in the 1907 edition of *The Americana: A Universal Reference Library.*

33. Edward A. Ross, *Social Psychology: An Outline and Source Book* (New York: Macmillan Co., 1908), pp. 173–74; Roosevelt to HM, 7 May 1901, Roosevelt Papers.

34. HM, *American Problems,* p. 53.

Chapter 6

1. Antonio Aliotta, *The Idealistic Reaction against Science,* trans. Agnes McCaskill (London: Macmillan Co., 1914). In addition, see H. Stuart Hughes, *Consciousness and Society: The Reorientation of European Social Thought, 1890–1930* (New York: Random House, 1958); Frank Miller Turner, *Between Science and Religion: The Reaction to Scientific Naturalism in Late Victorian England* (New Haven: Yale University Press, 1974); Georg C. Iggers, *The German Conception of History: The National Tradition of Historical Thought from Herder to the Present* (Middletown, Conn.: Wesleyan University Press, 1968). The Dilthey quotation is from p. 144 of Iggers.

2. HM, "Diary for the Month of March 1900," p. 1, Münsterberg File, Harvard University Archives.

3. William Stern, "Hugo Münsterberg," p. 186. I have changed the translation slightly.

4. Fritz-Joachim von Rintelen, *Contemporary German Philosophy and Its Background* (Bonn: H. Bouvier u. Co. Verlag, 1970), p. 24; Wilhelm Windelband, *A History of Philosophy,* vol. 2: *Renaissance, Enlightenment, and Modern,* trans. James H. Tufts (New York: Macmillan Co., 1901), p. 680. In addition to these volumes, see the following on the Sud-Baden school: Aliotta, *Idealistic Reaction against Science,* pt. 2, chap. 3; Hughes, *Consciousness and Society,* pp. 188–91; Iggers, *German Conception of History, pp. 144–59.*

5. Max Dessoir, "Zur Erinnerung an Hugo Münsterberg," in *Grundzüge der Psychologie,* by HM, 2d ed. (Leipzig: Verlag von Johann Ambrosius Barth, 1918), p. xiii.

6. HM, "The New Psychology," pp. 14–15.

7. HM, "Danger from Experimental Psychology," pp. 159–67; HM, "The New Psychology," p. 23.

8. James McKeen Cattell, "Professor Münsterberg on 'The Danger from Experimental Psychology,'" *Psychological Review* 5 (May 1898): 411–13; Edward Thorndike, "What Is a Psychical Fact," *Psychological Review* 5 (November 1898): 645–50; John Dewey, "Psychology and Social Practice," *Psychological Review* 9 (March 1902): 105–24; Joseph Jastrow, "Some Currents and Undercurrents in Psychology," *Psychological Review* 8 (January 1901): 24.

9. HM, *The Eternal Values* (New York: Houghton Mifflin Co., 1909), p. 83.

10. See James to HM, 18 June 1900, JP.

11. Rickert, review of *Grundzüge der Psychologie* in *Deutsche Literaturzeitung* 12 (6 April 1901): 842; Fritz Medicus, review in *Kantstudien* 8 (April 1903): 121; Stern, review in *Zeitschrift für Psychologie und Physiologie der Sinnesorgane* 29 (1902): 262–70; Max Weber, *Roscher und Knies: The Logical Problems of Historical Economics,* trans. Guy Oakes (New York: Free Press, 1975), pp. 129–54.

12. HM, *Grundzüge der Psychologie* (Leipzig: Johann Ambrosius Barth, 1900), pp. 45, 50–51.

13. See HM, *Eternal Values,* chap. 6.

14. HM, *Grundzüge der Psychologie,* pp. 41–42, 60ff.

15. HM, *Psychology and Life,* pp. 219–20. See also HM, *Grundzüge der Psychologie,* chap. 3.

16. HM, *Psychology: General and Applied* (New York: D. Appleton & Co., 1914), p. 12.

17. HM, *Grundzüge der Psychologie,* pp. 65ff, 104ff. For a family tree of science based upon this division, see HM, "The Position of Psychology in the System of Knowledge," in *Harvard Psychological Studies,* ed. HM (New York: Macmillan Co., 1903): 641–54.

18. HM, *On the Witness Stand: Essays on Psychology and Crime* (New York: McClure Co., 1908), pp. 119–21.

19. HM, *Grundzüge der Psychologie,* pp. 59–60, 54.

20. Ibid., sec. 2, esp. chap. 8; Cattell, "Professor Münsterberg," pp. 411–13.

21. Alfred E. Taylor, "Mind and Body in Recent Psychology," *Mind* n.s. 29 (October 1904): 502; HM, *Grundzüge der Psychologie,* pp. 255–59 and *passim.*

22. Ibid., sec. 3, esp. p. 494ff.

23. HM, "Psychological Atomism," *Psychological Review* 7 (January 1900): 8; HM, *Grundzüge der Psychologie,* p. 415ff. See also Alfred E. Taylor, *Elements of Metaphysics* (London: Methuen & Co., 1903), pp. 303–4.

24. HM, *Grundzüge der Psychologie,* pp. 548–49 and *passim.* For explications of the Action Theory in English, see HM, "The Physiological Basis of Mental Life," *Science* n.s. 9 (24 March 1899): 442–47, and HM, *Psychology: General and Applied,* bk. 1, pt. 2.

25. HM, *Grundzüge der Psychologie,* p. 530.

26. Thorndike, *The Elements of Psychology* (New York: A. G. Seiler, 1905), p. 203. John Dewey, *Human Nature and Conduct: An Introduction to Social Psychology* (New York: Henry Holt and Co., 1922), pp. 177, 25.

27. HM, *Grundzüge der Psychologie,* p. 549; HM, *Psychology: General and Applied,* pp. 136, 143.

28. Ibid., p. 327.

29. HM, *Philosophie der Werte: Grundzüge einer Weltanschauung* (Leipzig: J. A. Barth, 1908), *passim.*

30. Iggers, *German Conception of History,* p. 157.

31. HM, *Psychology: General and Applied,* pp. 15–16, 312, 304.

32. Wilhelm Dilthey, *Meaning in History: Dilthey's Thoughts on History and Society,* ed. Hans Peter Rickman (London: Allen and Unwin, 1961), pp. 67–68; Weber, *Roscher und Knies,* p. 187; HM, *Psychology: General and Applied,* p. 313.

33. Stern, "Hugo Münsterberg," p. 187; HM, *Psychology: General and Applied,* pp. 307–8.

34. White, *Social Thought in America: The Revolt against Formalism,* rev. ed. (Boston: Beacon Press, 1957), *passim.*

35. John Dewey, review of *Eternal Values,* by HM, *Philosophical Review* 19 (March 1910): 110.

36. James to Baldwin, 20 November 1899, in James Mark Baldwin, *Between Two Wars, 1861–1921: Being Memories, Opinions and Letters Received,* 2 vols. (Boston, Mass.: Stratford Co., 1926), 2:216–217. For popularized versions of Münsterberg's philosophy, see HM, *The Eternal Life* (New York: Houghton Mifflin Co., 1905), and HM, *Science and Idealism* (New York: Houghton Mifflin Co., 1906).

37. HM, *Eternal Values,* p. vii; F. C. S. Schiller, review of *Psychology and Life,* by HM, *Mind* n.s. 8 (October 1899): 540–43; HM to Cattell, 1 November 1899, MP. On the furor over Schiller's review, see Baldwin, *Between Two Wars,* 1:87–88.

38. HM, "Lebenslauf."

Chapter 7

1. HM to Eliot, 7 December 1908, EP; HM to Friedrich Schmidt [-Ott] (Prussian Ministry of Education), 17 September 1910, MP.

2. Alfred Vagts, *Deutschland und die Vereinigten Staaten in der Weltpolitik,* 2 vols. (New York: Macmillan Co., 1935), 2:1932. On German policy toward America, see, in addition to Vagts, Edward B. Parsons, "The German-American Crisis of 1902–1903," *The Historian* 33 (May 1971): 436–52; Dexter Perkins, *A History of the Monroe Doctrine,* rev. ed. (Boston: Little, Brown & Co., 1955), pp. 208–26; and Johann Heinrich von Bernstorff, *My Three Years in America* (New York: Charles Scribner's Sons, 1920), p. 23. On Althoff and cultural diplomacy, see Arnold Sachse, *Friedrich Althoff und sein Werk* (Berlin: E. S. Mittler & Sohn, 1928), pp. 171–72, 309, and *passim;* Vagts, *Deutschland und die Vereinigten Staaten,* 2:2003ff.; Brigitte Schroeder-Gudehus, "Caractéristiques des relations scientifiques internationales, 1870–1914," *Cahiers d'histoire mondiale* 10 (1966–1967): 161–77; Paul Forman, "Scientific Internationalism and the Weimar Physicists: The Ideology and Its Manipulation in Germany after World War I," *Isis* 64 (June 1973): 150–80.

3. Harnack to HM, 29 September 1908, MP. Münsterberg received the Order of the Crown of Prussia, second class, and the Order of the Red Eagle, third and second class. See HM to [?], 29 November 1902, Münsterberg file, Harvard University Archives; von Hüdt (Ministry of Cultural, Academic, and Medical Affairs) to HM, 22 December 1905, MP; *Boston Transcript,* 23 August 1911.

4. Schmidt to HM, 16 January 1894, MP; HM, *Die Amerikaner,* 2 vols. (Berlin: Ernst Siegfried Mittler & Sohn, 1904). From his first days in Cambridge, Münsterberg had planned a book on America. See HM to James, 9 October 1892, JP.

5. HM, *American Traits,* pp. x–xi.

6. Schmidt to HM, 16 January 1894, MP; HM, "The Helmholtz Memorial," *Science* n.s. 1 (17 May 1895): 547–48. Münsterberg's article had been published in the *Illinois Staatszeitung.*

7. Holleben is quoted by Vagts, *Deutschland und die Vereinigten Staaten,*

2:2003; 1:585. See also the extensive collection of Holleben letters in the Münsterberg papers.

8. See for example HM, "The Germans and the Americans," *Atlantic Monthly* 84 (September 1899): 396–409 (reprinted in *American Traits*).

9. On Münsterberg's relations with Holleben, see for example Holleben to HM, 14 April 1899, 20 May 1899, 1 January 1900, and 30 November 1900, MP. On the question of an honorary degree for Holleben, see HM to Eliot, 10 May 1899, 8 May 1900, and 30 March 1901, EP. Münsterberg called the honorary Harvard doctorate "the highest and rarest order of the country." HM, *Aus Deutsch-Amerika* (Berlin: Ernst Siegfried Mittler & Sohn, 1909), p. 19.

10. Francke to HM, 19 January and 5 April 1898, MP; Francke, "Deutsche Kultur in den Vereinigten Staaten und das Germanische Museum der Harvard Universität," *Deutsche Rundschau* 28 (April 1902): 127. In fairness to Francke, on the whole a sympathetic figure, it should be mentioned that he intended this assertion to encourage support for the museum in Germany, and he included Anglo-Saxons among the Teutonic peoples. On the founding of the museum, see especially Eliot's account in Albert Bernhardt Faust, *The German Element in the United States with Special Reference to Its Political, Moral, Social and Educational Influence*, 2d ed., 2 vols. (New York: Steuben Society of America, 1927), 1:686–88.

11. HM, *American Traits*, p. 18. See also Münsterberg's uncomplimentary remarks on German-Americans in *Die Amerikaner*, 1:36ff. On the generally unfavorable attitude of the German Foreign Office toward German-Americans, see Vagts, *Deutschland und die Vereinigten Staaten*, 1:600ff.; 2:1920–21. A perceptive essay on the attitudes of the German-Americans is G. A. Dobbert, "German-Americans between New and Old Fatherland, 1870–1941," *American Quarterly* 19 (Winter 1967): 663–80.

12. Francke, "Deutsche Kultur," p. 140. See also Francke, "Foreword to the First Edition," *Handbook of the Germanic Museum*, 6th rev. ed. (Cambridge, Mass.: Harvard University Press, 1927).

13. Clara Eve Schieber, *The Transformation of American Sentiment toward Germany, 1870–1914* (Boston: Cornhill Publishing Co., 1923), p. 240 and *passim;* HM to Eliot, 23 January and 31 January 1902, EP; Eliot to HM, 5 December 1908, MP. Writing to Eliot on 11 November 1908, EP, Münsterberg recalled: "You told me with absolute firmness that it was impossible for you to receive Prince Henry personally and that an honorary degree was out of the question."

14. MM, *Hugo Münsterberg*, pp. 83–86.

15. On the prince's visit to Harvard, see "Prince Henry's Visit," *Harvard Graduates' Magazine* 10 (June 1902): 566–73. Eliot's speeches at the degree ceremony and at the Boston banquet can be found in Charles W. Eliot, *The Road toward Peace* (Boston: Houghton Mifflin Co., 1915), pp. 221–28. It is significant that Eliot saw fit to reprint these speeches in a pro-Allies book published during World War I. In it Eliot asserted, "Germany must be defeated" (p. 114).

16. Schieber, *Transformation of American Sentiment*, pp. 250–51 and *passim;* Emil Witte, *Aus einer deutschen Botschaft: Zehn Jahre deutsch-amerikanischer Diplomatie* (Berlin: Zeitbilder-Verlag, 1907), pp. 194–99; HM, *Aus Deutsch-Amerika*, p. 237. This passage originally appeared in the German periodical *Die Woche.*

17. Vagts, *Deutschland und die Vereinigten Staaten*, vol. 2, chap. 15; Parsons, "The German-American Crisis," *passim.* The extent of Roosevelt's involvement in

this incident has been the subject of considerable historical debate. See especially Perkins, *Monroe Doctrine*, pp. 216–27, and Howard Beale, *Theodore Roosevelt and the Rise of America to World Power* (Baltimore: Johns Hopkins Press, 1956), pp. 143–46. The quotation from the press is in Thomas A. Bailey, *A Diplomatic History of the American People*, 8th ed. (New York: Appleton-Century-Crofts, 1969), p. 503. Münsterberg described his and Holleben's role in HM to Oswald Garrison Villard, 6 February 1903, Villard Papers, Houghton Library, Harvard University, and HM to Roosevelt, 26 January 1903, Roosevelt Papers.

18. Quoted in Vagts, *Deutschland und die Vereinigten Staaten*, 2:1596–97.

19. Ibid., 2:1751. Münsterberg's plan was not nearly so outlandish as it seems today. Early in the century university presidents were major public figures. Eliot—as president of Harvard—was a national moral leader, and his speeches were more widely read during this period than anyone's, "save the Presidents of the United States themselves." See Burton J. Bledstein, *The Culture of Professionalism: The Middle Class and the Development of Higher Education in America* (New York: W. W. Norton & Co., 1976), p. 132.

20. Quoted in Alfred Vagts, *Deutsch-amerikanische Rückwanderung: Probleme, Phänomene, Statistik, Politik, Soziologie, Biographie* (Heidelberg: Carl Winter, 1960), pp. 147–48.

21. Vagts, *Deutschland und die Vereinigten Staaten*, 2:1597; HM to Roosevelt, 14 January and 26 January 1903, Roosevelt to HM, 29 January 1903, Roosevelt Papers.

22. S. M. Buck, letter to the editor, *New York American*, 15 March 1902. Emil Witte reprinted Buck's letter and added his own charges in *Aus einer deutschen Botschaft*, pp. 210, 173–75. He had already made similar charges to Eliot. See Witte to Eliot, 15 October 1901, EP. Witte had been dismissed from the German embassy in the summer of 1901, allegedly for embezzlement. He unsuccessfully attempted to bribe Holleben and Münsterberg, and his expose, which he published himself, expressed a personal grudge. In some cases his facts were demonstrably false, in others unsubstantiated. Münsterberg denied Buck's charges in the *New Yorker Staatszeitung* and Witte's in a letter to Roosevelt, who had seen Witte's evidence after it had been seized by American agents. See HM to Roosevelt, 22 February 1902, Roosevelt Papers, and HM to Lawrence Lowell, 5 February 1915, MP.

23. On the International Congress, see A. W. Coates, "American Scholarship Comes of Age: The Louisiana Purchase Exposition of 1904," *Journal of the History of Ideas* 22 (July-September 1961): 404–17; George Haines and Frederick Jackson, "A Neglected Landmark in the History of Ideas," *Mississippi Valley Historical Review* 34 (September 1947): 201–20; Jurgen Herbst, *The German Historical School in American Scholarship: A Study in the Transfer of Culture* (Ithaca, N.Y.: Cornell University Press, 1965), p. 214; Jean B. Quandt, *From the Small Town to the Great Community: The Social Thought of Progressive Intellectuals* (New Brunswick, N.J.: Rutgers University Press, 1970), p. 122ff.; MM, *Hugo Münsterberg*, p. 95ff.

24. "Committee on Plan and Scope for International Congress of Science and Art," New York, 19 January 1903, MP; Small as cited by Coates, "American Scholarship," p. 407. Münsterberg summarized his plan in "The Scientific Plan of the Congress," in *Congress of Arts and Science, Universal Exposition, St. Louis, 1904*, ed. Howard J. Rogers, 10 vols. (Boston: Houghton Mifflin and Co., 1905–7), 1:85–134; HM, "The International Congress of Arts and Science,"

Journal of Philosophy, Psychology and Scientific Method 1 (7 January 1904): 1–8; and HM, "The St. Louis Congress of Arts and Science," *Atlantic Monthly* 91 (May 1903): 671–84.

25. Dewey criticized Münsterberg's plan in *Science* n.s. 18 (28 August 1903): 276–78 and (20 November 1903): 656–66. See also the letters of Robert S. Woodward and Münsterberg in *Science* 18 (4 September 1903): 302–3; (30 October 1903): 559–63; (18 December 1903): 788–89; Herbst, *German Historical School,* p. 214; and Quandt, *Small Town to the Great Community,* p. 122ff.

26. See HM to William Rainey Harper, 5 February 1903, MP.

27. Coates, "American Scholarship," p. 412; Simon Newcomb to HM, telegram, 14 March 1904, MP; Theodor Lewald (German Commissioner for the World's Fair) to HM, 22 April 1904, MP. Svante Arrhenius, the Swedish physicist and chemist who won a Nobel Prize in 1903, indicated in a letter to Münsterberg the degree of national pride involved in the make-up of the Congress and the extent of the German government's interest in the matter. He wrote: "In Germany, people are very proud of the American recognition of Germany at the expense of small countries, and the state takes over the whole affair." As a Swede, he found consolation in the fact that only a single Dutch representative was asked. Arrhenius to HM, 17 January 1904, MP.

28. Simon Newcomb to HM, 31 August and 24 August 1904, MP. The German Foreign Office, which was generally critical of the value of academic exchanges and *Kulturpolitik* as instruments of diplomacy, was not initially enthusiastic. See Vagts, *Deutschland und die Vereinigten Staaten,* 2:1921n. But the Prussian Ministry of Education backed it enthusiastically. See Lewald to HM, 20 April and 22 April 1904; Wilhelm Windelband to HM, 7 May 1904, MP.

29. Haines and Jackson, "Neglected Landmark," pp. 201–2; Coates, "American Scholarship," p. 416; Marianne Weber, *Max Weber: Ein Lebensbild* (Tübingen: J. C. B. Mohr [Paul Siebeck], 1926), p. 329.

30. HM to Benno Erdmann, 26 April 1911, MP. In 1910 Münsterberg referred to the "unsatisfactory participation in international congresses." HM to Karl Breul, 27 October 1910, MP.

31. Francke, *Deutsche Arbeit in Amerika: Erinnerungen* (Leipzig: Felix Meiner Verlag, 1930), p. 40. Francke's guests were Jakob Minor of the University of Vienna and August Sauer of Prague. See also Marianne Weber's comment on sparse attendance for foreign speakers in *Max Weber,* p. 329.

32. HM to Eliot, 12 September 1902, EP; Newcomb to HM, 16 August 1904, MP. See also HM to Frederick Holls, 4 October, 29 November, and 7 December 1902, Holls Papers, Baker Library, Columbia University.

33. HM to Cattell, 23 September 1902, Cattell Papers.

34. Herbst, *German Historical School,* p. 213; William James to James Ward, 31 July 1905, in Ralph Barton Perry, *The Thought and Character of William James,* 2 vols. (Boston: Little, Brown, 1935), 2:151; Max Dessoir, "Zur Erinnerung an Hugo Münsterberg," in *Grundzüge der Psychotechnik,* by HM, p. xiv; *Geheimrat* Elster to HM, 14 March 1905, MP.

35. Rickert to HM, telegram [March 1905], Cattell to HM, 7 April 1905, HM to Elster, telegram, 30 March 1905, MP; HM, "Twenty-Five Years," pp. 45–46; MM, *Hugo Münsterberg,* pp. 125–29.

36. HM to Elster, telegram, 11 April 1905, Hensel to HM, 14 May 1905, MP. Münsterberg mentioned the Breslau and Göttingen offers in HM to Eliot, 2 October 1905, EP, and HM to Lowell, 21 October 1909, MP. In a letter to Wundt (13

May 1911, MP), Münsterberg referred to the Göttingen offer, as well as one at Bonn, which was opposed by the faculty because the retiring Benno Erdmann preferred Oswald Külpe.

37. HM to Eliot, 30 May 1901, EP; James to HM, 8 July 1901, MP. See also HM to Roosevelt, 31 May 1901, Roosevelt to HM, 3 June 1901, and HM to Roosevelt, 5 June 1901, Roosevelt Papers.

38. James to Gardner, 21 June 1899, JP; James to HM, 17 November 1899, James to HM, 3 August 1901, MP. See also James Mark Baldwin, *Between Two Wars, 1861–1921: Being Memories, Opinions and Letters Received*, 2 vols. (Boston, Mass.: Stratford Co., 1926), 2:214–17. Münsterberg's early articles on mysticism were: "Professor Hyslop on Mysticism," *Psychological Review* 6 (July 1899): 408–10, and "Psychology and Mysticism," *Atlantic Monthly* 83 (January 1899): 67–85.

39. James to HM, 27 December 1905, JP.

40. Eliot to James, 29 December 1905, HM to Eliot, 11 November 1908, EP. Further correspondence on this affair can be found in the Eliot, James, and Münsterberg papers. See also Perry, *William James,* 2:151–52.

41. Eliot to HM, 8 April 1908, MP.

42. On the origins of the exchange program, I have found useful an unpublished article made available to me by its author: Brigitte Schroeder-Gudehus, "Echanges universitaires et politique culturelle extérieure, 1905–1914" (December 1975). See also Jerome D. Greene (Secretary of Harvard) to James B. Scott (Office of the Solicitor, U.S. Department of State), 3 May 1909, Lowell Papers, Series 1909–1914, Box 493; Albert Bernhard Faust, *Das Deutschtum in den Vereinigten Staaten in seiner Bedeutung für die amerikanische Kultur* (Leipzig: B. G. Teubner, 1912), pp. 213–17, 219ff.; Francke, *Deutsche Arbeit,* p. 46ff.; John W. Burgess, *Reminiscences of an American Scholar: The Beginnings of Columbia University* (New York: Columbia University Press, 1934), chap. 12; Friedrich Schmidt-Ott, *Erlebtes und Erstrebtes, 1860–1950* (Wiesbaden: Franz Steiner Verlag, 1952), pp. 107–15; Sachse, *Althoff, passim.*

43. See HM to Eliot, 25 December 1905, and 26 February 1906, EP; Schmidt to HM, 2 January 1906, 27 June 1906, and 6 April 1907, MP.

44. Eliot to HM, 6 November 1908, MP. Münsterberg's article appeared as "Professorenaustausch" in *Aus Deutsch-Amerika,* pp. 16–33. The reference to Kühnemann is on p. 24.

45. Eliot to HM, 16 November 1908, MP. This letter answered HM to Eliot, 11 November 1908, EP.

46. HM to Eliot, 17 November 1908, EP. The correspondence continued through 12 January 1909.

Chapter 8

1. HM, *Business Psychology* (Chicago: LaSalle Extension University, 1915), p. 19; HM, *American Traits,* pp. 193–94. On the question of expertise in Progressive America, see Chapter 1, note 8, of this study.

2. On the relation of science and industry in Germany, see especially Peter Borscheid, *Naturwissenschaft, Staat und Industrie in Baden (1848–1914)* (Stuttgart: Ernst Klett Verlag, 1967); Frank R. Pfetsch, *Zur Entwicklung der Wissenschaftspolitik in Deutschland, 1750–1914* (Berlin: Duncker und Humblot, 1974).

3. L. William Stern, *Über Psychologie der individuellen Differenzen. (Ideen an*

einer 'Differentiellen Psychologie.') (Leipzig: Johann Ambrosius Barth, 1900), pp. 37, v; HM, "How Men Differ," unpublished typescript, MP. On the increasing interest of experimentalists in the question of mental testing and individual differences, see any of the standard histories of psychology, for example, Edwin G. Boring, *A History of Experimental Psychology,* 2d ed. (New York: Appleton-Century-Crofts, 1950), chaps. 18–19 *passim.* On the origins of mental testing, Kimball Young, "The History of Mental Testing," *Pedagogical Seminary* 31 (March 1923): 1–47, remains as good a source as any.

4. Christian A. Ruckmich, "The History and Status of Psychology in the United States," *American Journal of Psychology* 23 (October 1912): 529–30.

5. James McKeen Cattell, "The Conception and Methods of Psychology," *Popular Science Monthly* 66 (December 1904): 186.

6. Carl E. Seashore, "The Measurement of a Singer," *Science* 35 (February 9, 1912): 201. Max Meyer compared the state of applied psychology in America and European universities in "Der gegenwärtige Stand der angewandten Psychologie in den einzelnen Kulturländern, x. Vereinigte Staaten von Amerika," *Zeitschrift für angewandten Psychologie* 1 (1908): 470–72. Not much has been written on the history of applied psychology, but see Friedrich Dorsch, *Geschichte und Probleme der angewandte Psychologie* (Berne: Verlag Hans Huber, 1963), and Maurice Reuchlin, "Naissance de la psychologie appliqué," *Traité de psychologie appliqué,* ed. Maurice Reuchlin (Paris: Presses universitaries de France, 1971), 1:1–48. For a discussion of the beginnings of applied psychology in America, see Donald S. Napoli, "The Architects of Adjustment: The Practice and Professionalization of American Psychology, 1920–1945" (Ph.D. dissertation, University of California, Davis, 1975), chap. 1.

7. Stern, *Individuellen Differenzen;* Stern, "Angewandte Psychologie," *Beiträge zur Psychologie der Aussage* 1 (1903–4): 11–12, 19–33. On Stern, see his autobiography in *A History of Psychology in Autobiography,* ed. Carl Murchison and Edwin G. Boring, 6 vols. (Worcester, Mass.: Clark University Press, 1930–1961), 1:335–88; Gordon Allport, "The Personalistic Psychology of William Stern," *Historical Roots of Contemporary Psychology,* ed. Benjamin B. Wolman (New York: Harper & Row, 1968), pp. 321–37; and Francis P. Hardesty, "Louis William Stern: A New View of the Hamburg Years," *Annals of the New York Academy of Sciences* 270 (28 April 1976): 31–44. Edward Titchener briefly noted the inroads of applied psychology into German academia in "The Past Decade in Experimental Psychology," *American Journal of Psychology* 21 (July 1910): 406–8.

8. Stern, "Angewandte Psychologie," p. 10; Jacob Z. Jacobson, *Scott of Northwestern: The Life Story of a Pioneer in Psychology and Education* (Chicago: Louis Mariano, Publisher, 1951), p. 70; HM, *American Traits,* p. 57.

9. HM, *Grundzüge der Psychotechnik* (Leipzig: Johann Ambrosius Barth, 1914), pp. 30–31; HM to Lawrence Lowell, 3 May 1916, Lowell Papers, Series 1914–17, Box 231.

10. Many of Münsterberg's essays were soon republished in *American Patriotism and Other Social Studies* (New York: Moffat, Yard & Co., 1913), *American Problems,* and *Psychology and Social Sanity* (New York: Doubleday, Page & Co., 1914). His full-length books in English were: *On the Witness Stand: Essays on Psychology and Crime* (New York: McClure Co., 1908); *Psychotherapy* (New York: Moffat, Yard & Co., 1909); *Psychology and the Teacher* (New York: D. Appleton & Co., 1909); *Psychology and Industrial Efficiency* (New York: Houghton Mifflin Co., 1913); and *The Photoplay: A Psychological Study* (New York: D. Ap-

pleton & Co., 1916). Texts for three of his correspondence courses were published: *Vocation and Learning* (St. Louis: People's University, 1912), *Business Psychology,* and *The Acquirement of Abilities* (Chicago: LaSalle Extension University). On his work on film, see Chapter 9 of this study.

11. HM, "The Field of Applied Psychology," *Psychological Bulletin* 6 (15 February 1909): 49–50; HM, *Grundzüge der Psychotechnik,* p. v; Cattell to HM, 18 March 1914, MP.

12. HM to James, 24 January 1896, JP; Lightner Witmer, "Mental Healing and the Emmanuel Movement," *Psychological Clinic* 2 (15 January 1909): 241. Witmer's article, which attacked James and Royce in equally scathing terms, precipitated a minor controversy in the psychological community. See Ralph Barton Perry, *The Thought and Character of William James,* 2 vols. (Boston, Mass.: Little, Brown, 1935), 2:153.

13. HM, *On the Witness Stand,* pp. 139–44; J. Sanderson Christison, *The Tragedy of Chicago: A Study in Hypnotism* (Chicago: By the author [1906]).

14. Quoted in the *Chicago Tribune,* 13 June 1906.

15. HM, *On the Witness Stand,* pp. 141–42; *Chicago Tribune,* 23 June 1906. Harry Olson, the assistant prosecutor in the Ivens case and the founder of a Psychopathic Laboratory connected to the Chicago municipal court, wrote Münsterberg nearly ten years later that the confession was true, but the judgment unfortunate. "Dementia praecox was not known at the time of the trial in question, and the alienist called to the witness-stand had little knowledge of psychology . . . ," he wrote. "While you did not see the case, you seemed to have understood from the testimony in the case, shown you, what the situation was." Harry Olson to HM, 16 May 1916, MP.

16. HM, *On the Witness Stand,* pp. 44–45 and *passim.*

17. Ibid., pp. 55–56, 48, 63.

18. Helpach is quoted in Hannah S. Decker, *Freud in Germany: Revolution and Reaction in Science, 1893–1907* (New York: International Universities Press, 1977), p. 109. On developments in French and German psychiatry, see Gregory Zilboorg and George W. Henry, *A History of Medical Psychology* (New York: W. W. Norton & Co., 1941), p. 361ff.; Ernest Jones, *The Life and Work of Sigmund Freud,* 3 vols. (New York: Basic Books, 1953–57), vol. 1, chap. 12; and Decker, *Freud in Germany,* p. 177ff.

19. Freiherr Albert von Schrenck-Notzing, *Uber Suggestion und Erinnerungsfälschung im Berchthold-Process* (Leipzig: Johann Ambrosius Barth, 1897), pp. 69, 74. Münsterberg briefly refers to his work with Schrenck-Notzing in HM to Leonard Troland, 24 March 1916, MP, and in his "Lebenslauf."

20. Schrenck-Notzing, *Uber Suggestion,* pp. 8–9. Alienists, of course, had for years appeared as experts on insanity. See, for example, Charles Rosenberg, *The Trial of the Assassin Guiteau* (Chicago: Chicago University Press, 1968).

21. For Stern's work on testimony, see especially his article, "Aussagestudium," *Beiträge zur Psychologie der Aussage* 1 (1903–4): 46–78. He summarized his work for an American audience at the famous Clark Conference, where Sigmund Freud also spoke. Stern, "Abstracts of Lectures on the Psychology of Testimony and on the Study of Individuality," *American Journal of Psychology* 21 (April 1910): 270–82.

22. Alfred Binet, "La science du témoignage," *L'année psychologique* 11 (1905): 128–36; Edouard Claparède, "La psychologie judiciaire," *L'année psychologique* 12 (1906): 274–302; George M. Beard, "The Scientific Study of Human Testi-

mony," *Popular Science Monthly* 13 (June 1878): 175; ibid. (July 1878): 332; Cattell, "Measurements of Accuracy of Recollection," *Science* n.s. 2 (6 December 1895): 765–66; Guy Montrose Whipple, "The Observer as Reporter: A Survey of the 'Psychology of Testimony,'" *Psychological Bulletin* 6 (15 May 1909): 153–70.

23. HM, *On the Witness Stand,* pp. 15–69 and *passim.*

24. Ibid., pp. 28–32, 63–64.

25. Charles C. Moore, "Yellow Psychology," *Law Notes* 11 (October 1907): 125.

26. For example, see Herbert C. Smythe to HM, 24 October 1910; A. Ames to HM, 1 June 1912; and HM to Charles Durfee, 17 December 1913, MP. The first murder trial was of Haywood in 1907; the second was of Albert J. Roper in Somerville, Massachusetts, in 1916. On the latter, see HM, "The Psychologist in Court," unpublished typescript, MP.

27. Robert Buckhout, "Eyewitness Testimony," *Jurimetrics Journal* 15 (Spring 1975): 186. This essay originally appeared in *Scientific American* in December 1974.

28. On the history of lie-detection, see L. A. Geddes, "History of the Polygraph, an Instrument for the Detection of Deception," *Biomedical Engineering* 8 (April 1975): 154–56, and Paul V. Trovillo, "A History of Lie Detection," *American Journal of Police Science* 29 (March-April 1939): 848–81, and (May-June 1939): 104–19.

29. On the Haywood trial, see Joseph R. Conlin, *Big Bill Haywood and the Radical Union Movement* (Syracuse, N.Y.: Syracuse University Press, 1969), pp. 52–79; David H. Grover, *Debates and Dynamiters: The Story of the Haywood Trial* (Corvallis, Ore.: Oregon State University Press, 1964); and Philip S. Foner, *History of the Labor Movement in the United States,* vol. 4: *The Industrial Workers of the World, 1905–1917* (New York: International Publishers, 1965), pp. 40–59.

30. Conlin, *Big Bill Haywood,* pp. 73, 77–78, and *passim;* Grover, *Debates and Dynamiters,* pp. 80–81; Foner, *History of the Labor Movement,* 4:51–59; HM, "Experiments on Harry Orchard," unpublished typescript, MP, pp. 2–4.

31. HM, *On the Witness Stand,* pp. 93–97. The initial work in word association as a means of detecting lies was Max Wertheimer and Julius Klein, "Psychologische Tatbestanddiagnostik," *Archiv für Kriminal-Anthropologie und Kriminalistik* 15 (1904): 72–113, and Carl Gustav Jung, "The Psychological Diagnosis of Evidence," *Collected Works of Carl Jung,* trans. Leopold Stein (Princeton, N.J.: Princeton University Press, 1973), 2:318–52. Jung's essay first appeared in 1905. Freud offered a cautious discussion of the procedure in "Psychoanalysis and the Establishment of the Facts in Legal Proceedings," *The Standard Edition of the Complete Psychological Works of Sigmund Freud,* ed. James Strachey, 24 vols. (London: Hogarth Press, 1953–74), 9:103–14. See also Stern, "Selbstverrat durch Assoziation," *Beiträge zur Psychologie der Aussage* 2 (1905–6): 150–55; and Stern and F. Kramer, "Selbstverrat durch Assoziation, Experimentelle Untersuchungen," *Beiträge zur Psychologie der Aussage* 2 (1905–6): 1–32. Münsterberg's student, Harold E. Burtt, devoted a chapter to the association method of lie detection in 1931 in his *Legal Psychology* (New York: Prentice-Hall, 1931).

32. HM, "Experiments on Harry Orchard," pp. 20, 7.

33. *Boston Herald,* 3 July 1907; MM, *Hugo Münsterberg,* pp. 148–49.

34. HM, letter to the editor, *Nation* 85 (18 July 1907): 55.

35. HM to *McClure's Magazine,* 14 July 1907, MP. Theodore Roosevelt, after the decision, privately wrote, "There has been a gross miscarriage of justice, to my

mind, out in Idaho in the acquittal of Haywood." Foner, *History of Labor Movement,* 4:59. Conlin's recent account of the case considers the question of Haywood's complicity "unresolved" *(Big Bill Haywood,* p. 224n). Foner absolves him. In any case, the state did not provide significant evidence corroborating Orchard's confession, as Idaho law required.

36. HM, *On the Witness Stand,* pp. 101–2, 92, 113–14.

37. Ibid., pp. 109, 82.

38. Edwin B. Holt, *The Freudian Wish and Its Place in Ethics* (New York: Henry Holt and Co., 1915), p. 38. Holt made this remark in an only slightly veiled case study, in which Münsterberg was presented as a businessman. See Chapter 11, note 51, of this study. Eliot also commented on Münsterberg's veracity. "Your public speeches," he wrote, "are not infrequently quite unlike your private utterances, doubtless because you think it inexpedient or improper to say in public what you really think." Eliot to HM, 16 November 1908, MP.

39. HM to Holt, 3 April 1916, MP.

40. Hugo Reisinger to HM, 23 March 1908, and 16 May 1908, MP.

41. Adolphus Busch to HM, 23 August 1908, MP; Gustave Pabst to HM, 19 March 1912, MP. The prohibition article was HM, "Prohibition and Social Psychology," *McClure's Magazine* 31 (August 1908): 438–44.

42. HM to Lowell, 23 June 1909, MP. For an example of the rumors of a payoff, see George M. Hammell to HM, 5 August 1908, MP.

43. B. F. Skinner, *Science and Human Behavior* (New York: Macmillan Co., 1953), p. 282.

44. HM, *On the Witness Stand,* pp. 131–32 and *passim.*

45. See William Marston, "Psychological Possibilities in the Deception Tests," *Journal of the American Institute of Criminal Law and Criminology* 11 (February 1921): 550–70; idem, "Systolic Blood Pressure Symptoms of Deception," *Journal of Experimental Psychology* 2 (April 1917): 117–63; idem, "Reaction-Time Symptoms of Deception," *Journal of Experimental Psychology* 3 (February 1920): 72–87; Herbert S. Langfeld, "Psychophysical Symptoms of Deception," *Journal of Abnormal Psychology* (December 1920–March 1921): 319–28.

46. John H. Wigmore, "Professor Münsterberg and the Psychology of Evidence," *Illinois Law Review* 3 (February 1909): 399–445.

47. On the history of vocational guidance, see especially John M. Brewer, *History of Vocational Guidance: Origins and Early Development* (New York: Harper & Brothers, 1942). On phrenology and vocation, see Madeleine B. Stern, *Heads and Headlines: The Phrenological Fowlers* (Norman, Okla.: University of Oklahoma Press, 1971), pp. 37–39, 212–13, and *passim.*

48. Frank Parsons, *Our Country's Needs: Or the Development of a Scientific Industrialism* (Boston: Arena Publishing Co., 1894), pp. 69, xvi.

49. Frank Parsons, "The Vocation Bureau," *Arena* 40 (July 1908): 3. On Parsons, see Arthur Mann, *Yankee Reformers in the Urban Age* (Cambridge, Mass.: Harvard University Press, 1954), pp. 126–44; and Howard V. Davis, *Frank Parsons: Prophet, Innovator, Counselor* (Carbondale, Ill.: University of Southern Illinois Press, 1969). On the Vocation Bureau, see Brewer, *Vocational Guidance,* chap. 5, and Edmund G. Williamson, *Vocational Counseling: Some Historical, Philosophical, and Theoretical Perspectives* (New York: McGraw-Hill Book Co., 1965), pp. 72–81. For a more skeptical view, see Marvin Lazerson, *Origins of the Urban School: Public Education in Massachusetts, 1870–1915* (Cambridge, Mass.: Harvard University Press, 1971), p. 190ff.

50. For recent studies of the role of business leaders in Progressive reform, see James Weinstein, *The Corporate Ideal in the Liberal State: 1900–1918* (Boston: Beacon Press, 1968); and James Gilbert, *Designing the Industrial State: The Intellectual Pursuit of Collectivism in America* (Chicago: Quadrangle Books, 1972).

51. Cattell, "The Progress of Psychology," *Popular Science Monthly* 43 (September 1893): 784; idem, "Homo Scientificus Americanus," *Science* n.s. 18 (10 April 1903): 569; HM, "Zur Individualpsychologie," *Centralblatt für Nervenheilkunde und Psychiatrie* 14 (May 1891): 196–98; J. M. Lahy, "La supériorité professionelle chez les conducteurs de tramways dans ses rapports avec la consommation d'énergie électrique," *La technique moderne* 7 (December 1913): 388–90.

52. Parsons, *Choosing a Vocation* (New York: Houghton Mifflin Co., 1909), chap. 3 and *passim;* HM, *Psychology and Industrial Efficiency*, pp. 43–45 and *passim*.

53. Ibid., pp. 36, 128.

54. Ibid., p. 128.

55. HM, *American Problems*, pp. 32–34; HM, *Psychology and Industrial Efficiency*, pp. 43–45 and *passim;* HM, "How Men Differ," p. 5. Compare Münsterberg's remark to Edward L. Thorndike's: "There is excellent reason to believe that it is literally true that the result of two hours' tests properly chosen from those already tested gives a better diagnosis of an educated adult's general intellectual ability than the result of the judgments of two teachers or friends who have observed him in the ordinary course of life each for a thousand hours" (Thorndike, "Educational Diagnosis," *Science* n.s. 37 [24 January 1913]: 139).

56. See Lucy C. Cogan, Agnes Conklin, and H. L. Hollingworth, "An Experimental Study of Self-Analysis, Estimates of Associates, and the Results of Tests," *School and Society* 11 (31 July 1915): 171–79; Walter Dill Scott, "The Scientific Selection of Salesmen," *Advertising and Selling* 25 (October 1915): 5–6, 94–96; HM, "How Men Differ," pp. 12–13. See also H. L. Hollingworth, *Vocational Psychology: Its Problems and Methods* (New York: D. Appleton & Co., 1916), chaps. 6 and 7.

57. HM, *Business Psychology*, p. 287. Compare Münsterberg's position with the industrial psychologist Morris Viteles's, who wrote in 1934: "Although variability in the human race results from the interaction of heredity and environment, heredity appears to be the determining factor in accounting for individual differences" (Viteles, *The Science of Work* [New York: W. W. Norton & Co., 1934], p. 329).

58. Stratton D. Brooks, "Vocational Guidance," *School Review* 19 (January 1911): 44.

59. HM, *Business Psychology*, p. 288; HM, *On the Witness Stand*, p. 241; HM, *Grundzüge der Psychotechnik*, p. 238.

Chapter 9

1. HM et al., *Subconscious Phenomena* (Boston: R. G. Badger, 1910), gathers together the essays of all the contributors to the *Journal of Abnormal Psychology* symposium. On Putnam, Prince, and the "Boston School," see Nathan G. Hale, Jr., *Freud and the Americans: The Beginnings of Psychoanalysis in the United States, 1876–1917* (New York: Oxford University Press, 1971), and Nathan G. Hale, Jr., ed., *James Jackson Putnam and Psychoanalysis: Letters between Putnam*

and Freud (Cambridge, Mass.: Harvard University Press, 1971). Münsterberg was appropriately discreet on the identity of his patients, but among them was the German-American poet, George Sylvester Viereck. Viereck briefly described hypnotic therapy from Münsterberg in his comments on chapter 35 of "The Stormy Petrel," Elmer Gertz's unpublished biography of him. For these comments, see Elmer Gertz Papers, Library of Congress, Box 129.

2. HM, *Psychology and Social Sanity,* p. 229.

3. Philip Rieff, *The Triumph of the Therapeutic: The Uses of Faith after Freud* (New York: Harper & Row, 1966), chap. 3.

4. Hale, *Freud and the Americans,* chap. 9; Gail Thain Parker, *Mind Cure in New England: From the Civil War to World War I* (Hanover, N.H.: University Press of New England, 1973), pt. 1; Donald B. Meyer, *The Positive Thinkers: A Study of the American Quest for Health, Wealth and Personal Power from Mary Baker Eddy to Norman Vincent Peale* (New York: Doubleday & Company, 1965), pt. 1; Gregory Zilboorg and George W. Henry, *A Medical History of Psychology* (New York: W. W. Norton & Co., 1941), chaps. 9 and 10. Otto Marx describes one of Prince's more sensational cases in "Morton Prince and the Dissociation of a Personality," *Journal of the History of the Behavioral Sciences* 6 (April 1970): 120–30.

5. HM, *Psychotherapy,* pp. x, 160–162.

6. Ibid., pp. 160, 162–163 and *passim.*

7. Ibid., pp. 75–76 and *passim.*

8. Ibid., pp. 167, 217, 85.

9. Ibid., pp. 258, 284–86, 295–96.

10. Ibid., pp. 162–63, 84; HM, *On the Witness Stand,* pp. 238–39.

11. Sigmund Freud, *Introductory Lectures on Psychoanalysis,* quoted in Paul Roazen, *Freud and His Followers* (New York: Alfred A. Knopf, 1974), p. 113.

12. Ernest Jones, *The Life and Work of Sigmund Freud,* 3 vols. (New York: Basic Books, 1953–57), 3:28n; William McGuire, ed., *The Freud/Jung Letters: The Correspondence,* trans. Ralph Manheim and R. F. C. Hull (Princeton, N.J.: Princeton University Press, 1974), pp. 229, 445. Hannah S. Decker, *Freud in Germany: Revolution and Reaction in Science, 1893–1907* (New York: International Universities Press, 1977), discusses the reaction of orthodox German psychologists and psychiatrists to Freudian theory. See also Jones, *Sigmund Freud,* and Henri F. Ellenberger, *The Discovery of the Unconscious* (New York: Basic Books, 1970). Münsterberg referred to Jung's charge of plagiarism and defended himself in HM to Eliot, 29 October 1907, MP.

13. HM, "Muensterberg vigorously Renounces Red Light Drama," *New York Times,* 14 September 1913, sec. 5, p. 4; HM, *Psychology and Social Sanity,* p. 14 and *passim.*

14. Sigmund Freud, *"Civilized" Sexual Morality and Modern Nervous Disorder* (1908), in *The Standard Edition of the Complete Psychological Works of Sigmund Freud,* ed. James Strachey, 24 vols. (London: Hogarth Press, 1953–74), 9:191. For a discussion of Freud in this context, see Rieff, *Triumph of the Therapeutic,* chaps. 1, 2, and 4; Russell Jacoby, *Social Amnesia: A Critique of Contemporary Psychology from Adler to Laing* (Boston: Beacon Press, 1975), esp. chap. 6; Richard King, *The Party of Eros: Radical Social Thought and the Realm of Freedom* (Chapel Hill, N.C.: University of North Carolina Press, 1972).

15. Hale, *Freud and the Americans,* chap. 10; David J. Pivar, *Purity Crusade, Sexual Morality, and Social Control, 1868–1900* (Westport, Conn.: Greenwood

Press, 1973); Peter G. Filene, *Him/Her/Self: Sex Roles in Modern America* (New York: Harcourt Brace Jovanovich, 1975), chap. 3.

16. HM, *Psychology and Social Sanity,* pp. 12–13 and *passim;* HM, "Red Light Drama," p. 4.

17. HM, *Psychotherapy,* pp. 272–74.

18. Ibid., pp. 250–52.

19. Ibid., p. 396.

20. Freud, *Five Lectures on Psycho-analysis* (1909), in *Standard Edition,* 11:36; Freud, *The Question of Lay Analysis,* quoted in Roazen, *Freud and His Followers,* p. 204; Josef Breuer and Freud, *Studies in Hysteria* (1895), in *Standard Edition,* 2:305.

21. Freud, *Civilization and Its Discontents* (1930), in *Standard Edition,* 21:123–24. Freud first used the word *Uber-Ich* in 1923 in *The Ego and the Id.* Ernest Jones argued that Freud was unaware of Münsterberg's earlier use of it. Jones, *Sigmund Freud,* 3:282n. For a discussion of the American reception of Freud, see F. H. Matthews, "The Americanization of Sigmund Freud: Adaptations of Psychoanalysis before 1917," *Journal of American Studies* 1 (April 1967): 39–62; Roazen, *Freud and His Followers,* pt. 7, chaps. 8 and 9; John C. Burnham, *Psychoanalysis and American Medicine, 1894–1918* (New York: International Universities Press, 1967); and Hale, *Freud and the Americans.*

22. HM, *On the Witness Stand,* p. 156. Münsterberg also made the claim on dreams in HM to Edwin B. Holt, 30 March 1916, MP.

23. HM, *Ueber Aufgaben und Methoden,* p. 168. See also James Mark Baldwin, *Between Two Wars, 1861–1921: Being Memories, Opinions and Letters Received,* 2 vols. (Boston, Mass.: Stratford Co., 1926), 1:89.

24. Holt, *Freudian Wish,* p. 38; *Deutsches Biographisches Jahrbuch* (1925), s.v. "Münsterberg, Hugo," by Max Dessoir, p. 242; HM, "Der Staub," *Verse,* pp. 4–7.

25. Ralph Barton Perry, *The Thought and Character of William James,* 2 vols. (Boston: Little, Brown, 1935), 2:674; HM, "Lebenslauf."

26. James to Royce, 22 June 1872, in Perry, *William James,* 2:141.

27. HM to James, 4 July 1901, JP; Palmer to HM, 1 December 1902, MP.

28. HM, *Psychotherapy,* pp. 282–83.

29. HM, *American Problems,* p. 3. On Beard and neurasthenia, see Charles E. Rosenberg, *No Other Gods: On Science and American Social Thought* (Baltimore: Johns Hopkins University Press, 1976), chap. 5; Meyer, *Positive Thinkers,* esp. chap. 1; Hale, *Freud and the Americans,* chaps. 3 and 9; S. P. Fullinwider, "Neurasthenia: The Genteel Caste's Journey Inward," *Rocky Mountain Social Science Journal* 11 (April 1974): 1–9; Barbara Sicherman, "The Uses of Diagnosis: Doctors, Patients, and Neurasthenia," *Journal of the History of Medicine* 32 (January 1977): 33–54.

30. George M. Beard, *American Nervousness: Its Causes and Consequences* (New York: G. P. Putnam's Sons, 1881), p. 138 and *passim.*

31. Kraft-Ebing is quoted in Freud, *"Civilized" Sexual Morality, Standard Edition,* 9:185. For a discussion of Freud and Beard on neurasthenia, see M. B. MacMillan, "Beard's Concept of Neurasthenia and Freud's Concept of the Actual Neurosis," *Journal of the History of the Behavioral Sciences* 12 (October 1976): 376–90.

32. HM, *American Traits,* p. 26; HM, *American Problems,* pp. 21, 15–17.

33. HM, *American Problems,* pp. 4–6 and *passim;* HM, "America's National

Disease Nervousness Is All an Illusion," *Jersey City Journal,* 30 September 1909. There is a clipping of this article in the Münsterberg Papers.

34. David Riesman, *The Lonely Crowd: A Study of the Changing American Character* (New Haven: Yale University Press, 1950), *passim.*

35. HM, *Psychology and Social Sanity,* p. 68.

36. HM, *Psychology and Industrial Efficiency,* p. 232; HM, *American Problems,* p. 86.

37. HM, *Psychology: General and Applied,* pp. 256–57; HM, *On the Witness Stand,* pp. 187–88.

38. HM, *American Problems,* pp. 170–73; HM, *Psychology and Industrial Efficiency,* pt. 3. On advertising see David P. Kuna, "The Concept of Suggestion in the Early History of Advertising Psychology," *Journal of the History of the Behavioral Sciences* 12 (October 1976): 347–53; Daniel Andrew Pope, "The Development of National Advertising, 1865–1920" (Ph.D. dissertation, Columbia University, 1973).

39. HM, *Psychology and Social Sanity,* p. 229 and *passim.*

40. On the efforts of advertisers to bring about a culture of consumerism, see Stuart Ewen, *Captains of Consciousness: Advertising and the Social Roots of the Consumer Culture* (New York: McGraw-Hill Book Co., 1976).

41. HM, *Grundzüge der Psychotechnik,* p. 610.

42. Johan Huizinga, *Homo Ludens: A Study of the Play-Element in Culture* (Boston: Beacon Press, 1955), pp. 191–92; HM, *Psychology: General and Applied,* pp. 454–55.

43. Max Horkheimer and Theodor W. Adorno, *Dialectic of Enlightenment,* trans. John Cumming (New York: Seabury Press, 1972), p. 124. On aesthetic theory in the nineteenth century, see John T. Merz, *A History of European Thought in the Nineteenth Century,* 4 vols. (Edinburgh: William Blackwood & Sons, 1896–1914), vol. 4, chap. 7.

44. HM, *Psychology: General and Applied,* pp. 455–59 and *passim.* Theodor Ziehen confirmed Münsterberg's claim (*Grundzüge der Psychotechnik,* p. 627) that his Harvard laboratory was the only one in the world to maintain continuous experimentation in the psychology of aesthetics. See Ziehen, "Zur Errinerung an Hugo Münsterberg," *Zeitschrift für Asthetik und allgemeine Kunstwissenschaft* 12 (1917): 237–28.

45. HM, *Psychology: General and Applied,* p. 462.

46. Merz, *History of European Thought,* 4:9–20; Donald W. Crawford, *Kant's Aesthetic Theory* (Madison, Wis.: University of Wisconsin Press, 1974).

47. HM, *The Principles of Art Education: A Philosophical, Aesthetic and Psychological Discussion of Art Education* (New York: Prang Educational Co., 1905), pp. 112, 31.

48. George L. Mosse, *The Nationalization of the Masses: Political Symbolism and Mass Movement in Germany from the Napoleonic Wars through the Third Reich* (New York: Howard Fertig, 1975), pp. 22–23.

49. HM, *Photoplay,* pp. 161, 142–44, 150. Italics in original.

50. Ibid., pp. 160–61, 157, 164 and *passim.*

51. HM, "Interview for Paramount Co.," 25 April 1916, MP; HM, "Why We Go to the 'Movies,' " *Cosmopolitan* 60 (December 1915): 23–24; HM, *Psychology: General and Applied,* p. 454. See also HM, "Peril to Childhood in the Movies," *Mother's Magazine* 12 (February 1917): 109–10, 158–59.

52. HM, "Why We Go to the 'Movies,' " p. 25; MM, *Hugo Münsterberg,* pp.

281–87. On Münsterberg and the film, see especially Donald Fredericksen, "The Aesthetic of Isolation in Film Theory: Hugo Münsterberg" (Ph.D. dissertation, University of Iowa, 1973). Richard Griffith's introduction to *The Film: A Psychological Study,* by Münsterberg (New York: Dover Publications, 1970), a recent re-edition of *Photoplay,* adds little to Margaret Münsterberg's account and suffers from factual inaccuracies.

53. Münsterberg claimed that "Testing the Mind"—which consisted of numerous separate installments, bearing such titles as "Are You Fitted for Your Job?" "Does Your Mind Work Quickly?" and "Can You Judge Well What Is Beautiful and What Is Ugly?"—was seen by two million theatergoers. HM to Samuel McClintock (LaSalle Extension University, Chicago), 28 September 1916, MP. Like Fredericksen (p. 324), I have been unable to locate copies of Münsterberg's films. But the Münsterberg Papers include a number of the scenarios, under the title "Testing the Mind," Ms. Acc. 2443. George R. Meeker of Paramount refers to the "Paramount History of Mankind" in Meeker to HM, 5 April 1916, MP. Fredericksen (p. 22) quotes a report in *Motion Picture World* that Münsterberg used films to simulate actual conditions in tests of automobile driving. Münsterberg denied the story in the *New York Times,* 14 September 1916, sec. 7, p. 16.

54. Harry Alan Potamkin, "Movie Picture Criticism," *New Freeman* 2 (4 March 1931): 591. See Fredericksen, "Aesthetic of Isolation," p. 326.

55. HM, *Photoplay,* pp. 223, 228, 233, 220–21.

56. Ibid., pp. 183, 202–10, 220. Italics in original.

57. Ibid., 172, 69, 87, 88 (italicized), 95 (italicized).

58. Ibid., 74–76, 83.

59. Ibid., pp. 153–54. The phrase "promise of happiness" was originally Stendhal's. See Herbert Marcuse, "The Affirmative Character of Culture," *Negations: Essays in Critical Theory,* trans. Jeremy J. Shapiro (Boston: Beacon Press, 1968), p. 115.

60. HM, *Psychology and Social Sanity,* p. viii; HM, *Photoplay,* pp. 152, 230.

Chapter 10

1. For best-seller statistics, see "The Book Mart," *Bookman: An Illustrated Magazine of Literature and Life* 37 (June–August 1913): 4–6 and *passim.* To my knowledge there are no good accounts of the early development of industrial psychology and especially of its actual application in industry. For a general overview of the twentieth century, see Loren Baritz, *The Servants of Power: A History of the Use of Social Science in American Industry* (Middletown, Conn.: Wesleyan University Press, 1960). Leonard W. Ferguson, *The Heritage of Industrial Psychology,* 14 vols. (Hartford, Conn.: Finlay Press, 1963–64), offers a number of details, but is sketchy and uncritical. See also the brief accounts by Morris Viteles, *Industrial Psychology* (New York: W. W. Norton & Co., 1932), esp. chap. 5; and Arthur Mayer, "Die Betriebspsychologie in einer technisierten Welt," in *Betriebspsychologie,* ed. Bernhard Herwig and Arthur Mayer (Göttingen: Verlag für Psychologie, Dr. C. J. Hogrefe, 1970), esp. 14ff.

2. The most recent account of the emergence of the factory system and "systematic management" in the United States is Daniel M. Nelson, *Managers and Workers: Origins of the New Factory System in the United States, 1880–1920* (Madison, Wis.: University of Wisconsin Press, 1975). See also Henry Eilbirt, "The Development of Personnel Management in the United States," *Business*

History Review 33 (Autumn 1959): 345–64. An important new study that discusses the management of labor by the modern corporation is David A. Noble, *America by Design: Science, Technology, and the Rise of Corporate Capitalism* (New York: Alfred A. Knopf, 1977).

3. E. F. Peck, quoted in "Psychological Tests for Accident Prevention," *Electric Railway Journal* 39 (9 March 1912): 394; HM, *Psychology and Industrial Efficiency*, p. 99. For an example of the discussion among managers of accidents caused by employees, see the exchange on "Man Failure" in the *Electric Railway Journal* 39 (10 February 1912): 230–31, and (17 February 1912): 266, 282. On labor turnover, see U.S. Department of Labor, Bureau of Labor Statistics, *Proceedings of the Employment Managers' Conference, Philadelphia, Pa., April 2 and 3, 1917,* Bulletin of the United States Bureau of Labor Statistics, whole no. 227, Employment and Unemployment Series, no. 7 (Washington, D.C.: U.S. Government Printing Office, 1917); Eilbirt, "Personnel Management," *passim;* and Nelson, *Managers and Workers,* pp. 86–87, 149–50.

4. Baritz, *Servants of Power,* chap. 2; Noble, *America by Design,* chap. 10. For the Verein studies, see *Untersuchungen über Auslese und Anpassung (Berufswahl und Berufsschicksal) der Arbeiter in den verschiedenen Zweigen der Grossindustrie,* Schriften des Vereins für Socialpolitik, vols. 133–34 (Leipzig: Verlag von Duncker & Humblot, 1910); for the question of fatigue, see especially Josephine Goldmark, *Fatigue and Efficiency: A Study in Industry* (New York: Charities Publication Committee, 1912).

5. On the Taylor movement, see Samuel Haber, *Efficiency and Uplift: Scientific Management in the Progressive Era* (Chicago: University of Chicago Press, 1960); Hugh G. J. Aitken, *Taylorism at Watertown Arsenal* (Cambridge, Mass.: Harvard University Press, 1960); and Milton J. Nadworny, *Scientific Management and the Unions, 1900–1932* (Cambridge, Mass.: Harvard University Press, 1955). The Taylor quotations are from Nadworny, *Scientific Management,* p. 21, and Haber, *Efficiency and Uplift,* pp. 2–3.

6. Nadworny, *Scientific Management,* pp. 23, 59; Aitken *Taylorism at the Watertown Arsenal, passim.* Taylorism ran into labor difficulties in Europe, precipitating for example a violent strike at the Renault works at Billancourt, France, early in 1913. See Georges Friedmann, *Industrial Society: The Emergence of the Human Problems of Automation,* ed. and trans. Harold L. Sheppard (Glencoe, Ill.: Free Press, 1955), pt. 3, chap. 1.

7. Quoted in ibid., p. 58. See esp. chap. 1 of Friedmann's study and his more complete account in *La crise du progrès: esquisse d'histoire des idées, 1895–1935* (Paris: Gallimard [1936]), chap. 2. Friedmann discusses the emergence of industrial psychology as a reaction to Taylor. The word "technicist" is his. See also Baritz, *Servants of Power,* chap. 2, and Noble, *America by Design,* chap. 10.

8. HM, *Psychology and Industrial Efficiency,* pp. 165, 306. Harry Braverman, *Labor and Monopoly Capital: The Degradation of Work in the Twentieth Century* (New York: Monthly Review Press, 1975), describes this separation of planning from execution and the decline of skill as characteristic of work in the twentieth century.

9. Ibid., p. 143; HM, *Business Psychology,* p. 182; HM, *Psychology and Industrial Efficiency,* p. 257; O. V. Fry to HM, 28 October 1915, MP.

10. MM, *Hugo Münsterberg,* pp. 248–51; HM to William Wilson (Secretary of Commerce), 24 and 26 May 1913, and HM to *Geheimrat* Emil Fischer, 2 January 1911, MP.

11. HM, *Psychology and Industrial Efficiency,* p. 144.

12. Ibid., p. 309.

13. Ibid., pp. 195–96, 199.

14. Morris S. Viteles, *The Science of Work* (New York: W. W. Norton & Co., 1934), pp. 329–33.

15. Link, quoted in Eilbirt, "Personnel Management," p. 358; P. W. Gerhardt, "Scientific Selection of Employees," *Electric Railway Journal* 47 (20 May 1916): 222. For a similar argument, see Arthur Kornhauser, "The Psychology of Vocational Selection," *Psychological Bulletin* 19 (April 1922): 206. See also Noble, *America by Design,* esp. chap. 10.

16. Harry L. Hollingworth, *Vocational Psychology: Its Problems and Methods* (New York: D. Appleton & Co., 1915), p. 79.

17. MM, *Hugo Münsterberg,* pp. 209–11, HM, *Psychology and Industrial Efficiency,* chap. 11. A number of the responses from industrial spokesmen can be found in the Münsterberg Papers. For example, M. S. Green (Armour) to HM, 30 December 1911; Howard Elliott (Northern Pacific) to HM, 15 January 1912; G. E. Emmons (General Electric) to HM, 8 October 1913; W. E. Chamberlain (Armstrong Transfer Express Company, Boston) to HM, 14 February 1912; W. E. Nickerson (Gillette) to HM, 28 February 1912. This sort of "job analysis" became a common industrial practice within a few years. See Nelson, *Managers and Workers,* p.151.

18. Emil Leopold Boas to HM, 18 October 1911, MP; HM, *Psychology and Industrial Efficiency,* chap. 9. Münsterberg first published the details of this experiment in HM, "Experimentalpsychologie und Berufswahl," *Zeitschrift für pädogogische Psychologie und experimentelle Pädogogik* 13 (1912): 1–7.

19. "Psychological Tests for Accident Prevention," pp. 394–95; HM, *Psychology and Industrial Efficiency,* pp. 63–64. On the American Association for Labor Legislation, see Irwin Yellowitz, *Labor and the Progressive Movement in New York State, 1897–1916* (Ithaca, N.Y.: Cornell University Press, 1965), pp. 72–73, 108, and James Weinstein, *The Corporate Ideal in the Liberal State: 1900–1918* (Boston: Beacon Press, 1968), pp. 7, 48.

20. HM, *Psychology and Industrial Efficiency,* chap. 8. See also Viteles, *Industrial Psychology,* pp. 288–91, for a description and sketch of Münsterberg's machine.

21. Scott, review of *Psychology and Industrial Efficiency, Psychological Bulletin* 10 (15 July 1913): 283, Whipple, "The Use of Mental Tests in Vocational Guidance," *Annals of the American Academy of Political and Social Science* 65 (May 1916): 196. Whipple was the author of the standard text, *Manual of Mental and Physical Tests* (Baltimore: Warwich & York, 1910). See also Harry L. Hollingworth's generally unfavorable review in *Science* n.s. 38 (11 July 1913): 56–57.

22. Oscar T. Crosby, letter to the editor, *Electric Railway Journal* 39 (23 March 1912): 473. See also George Lawson, letter to the editor, *Electric Railway Journal* 47 (3 June 1916): 1046–47.

23. "Scientific Selection of Workmen," *Engineering Record* 57 (15 February 1913): 171; "The Beginnings of a New Science," *Survey* 30 (5 April 1913): 95. The comment on *Survey* is from Weinstein, *Corporate Ideal,* p. 56.

24. Gerhardt, "Scientific Selection," pp. 943–45; Scott, "The Scientific Selection of Salesmen," *Advertising and Selling* 25 (October 1915): 5–6; Morris Viteles, "Research in Selection of Motormen: Survey of the Literature," *Journal of Personnel Research* 4 (July 1925): 101ff.; Hollingworth, "Specialized Vocational Tests

and Methods," *School and Society* 1 (26 June 1915): 919. See also Leonard P. Ayres, "Psychological Tests in Vocational Guidance," *Journal of Educational Psychology* 4 (April 1913): 232–37, and Baritz, *Servants of Power,* 37–39. For later work by Münsterberg on vocational testing, see Harold E. Burtt, "Professor Münsterberg's Vocational Tests," *Journal of Applied Psychology* 1 (September 1917): 201–13.

25. HM, *Psychology and Industrial Efficiency,* pp. 208–9, 173.

26. HM, "Report to the National Electric Illumination Society," 11 April 1914, MP. Münsterberg was a member of the Advisory Committee of the NELA's Street Lighting Committee.

27. Preston S. Millar, "Outline of Further Investigations of Street Lighting Prepared and Issued for Criticism by Members of Joint Committee," 1 October 1914, MP; Charles P. Steinmetz to Preston S. Millar, 3 September 1914, included in Harold E. Burtt to HM, 8 September 1914, MP. On Burtt's experiments, see Burtt to HM, [June 1914?], 4 July 1914, 19 July 1914, and 17 August 1914, MP. Burtt's letters reflect a tension between him as a psychologist and electrical engineers like Steinmetz.

28. On industrial psychology and sociology of the 1920s, see Baritz, *Servants of Power,* and Robert Michael Smith, "The American Business System and the Theory and Practice of Social Science: The Case of the Harvard Business School, 1925–1945" (Ph.D. dissertation, University of Maine, 1976).

29. HM, *Grundzüge der Psychotechnik,* p. 407.

30. HM to Doubleday Page & Co., 27 September 1913, MP; HM to Lowell, 24 December 1913, LP, Series 1909–1914, Box 1289.

31. HM, "Circular for Questioning Men in Factories and Mills" [1913] and "Revised Circular" [1913], MP. Gompers's comment is handwritten on one of the returned questionnaires in the Münsterberg Papers (Ms. Acc. 2440). Gompers also wrote, "It is a matter of great gratification to me that men and women of all ranks of society are coming to a realization of the paramount importance of the labor problems." Gompers to HM, 1 October 1913, MP.

32. HM, "Circular" and "Revised Circular"; Gompers to HM, 1 October 1913, MP; Nelson, *Managers and Workers,* p. 150.

33. HM, *Grundzüge der Psychotechnik,* pp. 405–7.

34. See Herbert Gutman, *Work, Culture, and Society in Industrializing America: Essays in American Working-Class and Social History* (New York: Random House, 1976), pp. 29–32, and especially Betty Boyd Caroli, *Italian Repatriation from the United States, 1900–1914* (New York: Center for Migration Studies, 1973), chap. 1.

35. HM, *Grundzüge der Psychotechnik,* pp. 254–55.

36. HM, *Psychology and Social Sanity,* pp. 103, 108.

37. Ibid., p. 102.

38. Walter Dill Scott, *Psychology of Business,* Studies in Personnel and Management, no. 21 ([Austin, Tex.] Bureau of Business Research, University of Texas at Austin, 1969), p. 33. This volume originally appeared as a series of essays in *System* (later *Business Week*) in 1910–11. On Scott, see especially Jacob Z. Jacobson, *Scott of Northwestern: The Life Story of a Pioneer in Psychology and Education* (Chicago: Louis Mariano, Publisher, 1951), and Edmund C. Lynch, *Walter Dill Scott: Pioneer in Personnel Management,* Studies in Personnel and Management, no. 20 ([Austin, Tex.] Bureau of Business Research, University of Texas at Austin, 1968).

39. Leonard W. Ferguson, *The Heritage of Industrial Psychology*, vol. 3: *Walter Van Dyke Bingham: Dean of Industrial Psychologists* (Hartford, Conn.: Finley Press, 1963–64); Millicent Todd Bingham, "Beyond Psychology," in *Homo Sapiens Auduboniensis: A Tribute to Walter Van Dyke Bingham* (New York: National Audubon Society, 1953), p. 5ff.

40. "Economic Psychology Association, Printed Circular," MP.

41. Dorothy Ross, G. *Stanley Hall: The Psychologist as Prophet* (Chicago: University of Chicago Press, 1972), p. 420.

42. Robert M. Yerkes in *A History of Psychology in Autobiography*, ed. Carl Murchison and Edwin G. Boring, 6 vols. (Worcester, Mass.: Clark University Press, 1930–1961), 2:381–89; Elliott in ibid., 4:78. Daniel Kevles described Yerkes's role in the Army's psychological testing in "Testing the Army's Intelligence: Psychologists and the Military in World War I," *Journal of American History* 55 (December 1968): 565–81. See also Franz Samelson, "World War I Intelligence Testing and the Development of Psychology," *Journal of the History of the Behavioral Sciences* 13 (July 1977): 274–82. For a brief discussion of Münsterberg's influence in Germany, especially during the war years, see Frieda Wunderlich, *Hugo Münsterberg's Bedeutung für die Nationalökonomie* (Jena: Gustav Fechner, 1920), pp. 64–67.

43. Lewis M. Terman, "The Status of Applied Psychology in the United States," *Journal of Applied Psychology* 5 (March 1921): 3–4. See also Baritz, *Servants of Power*, pp. 44–48.

Chapter 11

1. HM to Karl Breul, 27 October 1910, MP. In a letter to the Prussian Ministry of Education on 6 February 1908, Münsterberg wrote: "The thought that German ideas must win stronger influence [*Macht*] over American intellectual life stands above all in the foreground. To see an American institute established in Berlin therefore would be an enticing thought for me." See "Professoren-Austausch mit Amerika, II," Handschriftenabteilung, Preussischer Kulturbesitz, Staatsbibliothek, Berlin. Films of this and other Münsterberg letters to the Prussian Ministry were lent to me by Professor Brigitte Schroeder-Gudehus of the University of Montreal. For an account of Münsterberg's career in German-American relations, see Phyllis Keller, "German-America and the First World War" (Ph.D. dissertation, University of Pennsylvania, 1969), chap. 6, a study which uses many of the same sources as this one but comes to somewhat different conclusions. See also Bruce Kuklick, *The Rise of American Philosophy: Cambridge, Massachusetts, 1860–1930* (New Haven: Yale University Press, 1977), chap. 23, for a discussion of the Harvard philosophers during World War I.

2. HM to Schmidt, 17 September 1910, MP. On this decline of prestige and the reaction of Germans to it, see Paul Forman, "Scientific Internationalism and the Weimar Physicists: The Ideology and Its Manipulation in Germany after World War I," *Isis* 64 (June 1973).

3. See esp. Arnold Sachse, *Friedrich Althoff und sein Werk* (Berlin: E. S. Mittler & Sohn, 1928), p. 311; Schmidt to HM, 15 January 1908, MP; HM to Eliot, 6 March 1908, MP.

4. HM to Schmidt, 17 September 1910, MP. See also HM to Breul, 27 October 1910, MP.

5. HM to Breul, 27 October 1910, HM to Schmidt, 17 September 1910, MP.

The Breul letter contains Münsterberg's most succinct account of the origins of the Amerika-Institut.

6. Lowell to Arthur N. Davis, 24 March 1919, LP Series 1917–19, Box 220. On the maneuvers to establish the Amerika-Institut, see Friedrich Schmidt-Ott, *Erlebtes und Erstrebtes, 1860–1950* (Wiesbaden: Franz Steiner Verlag, 1952), p. 112ff.; MM, *Hugo Münsterberg*, pp. 185–87.

7. Amerika-Institut Circular, 27 September 1910, MP, Ms. Acc. 2473.3.

8. HM, "Was das Amerika-Institut nicht ist," *Rundschau zweier Welten* 2 (January 1911): 45–47; HM to Johann von Bernstorff (German ambassador to the United States), 18 November 1910, MP; Georg Kartzke, "30 Jahre Amerika Institut: I. Oktober 1910–1940," *Geistige Arbeit* (Berlin) 7 (5 November 1940): 7–8. See also Sigmund Skard, *American Studies in Europe: Their History and Present Organization*, 2 vols. (Philadelphia: University of Pennsylvania Press, 1958), 1:135.

9. HM to Karl Breul, 27 October 1910, HM to Schmidt, 17 September 1910, MP; HM, *American Patriotism*, p. 11.

10. HM to Karl Jentsch, 12 February 1912, MP; HM, "Antrittsrede, Berlin, 1910," p. 2, MP, Ms. Acc. 2455; HM to Schmidt, 17 September 1910, MP.

11. See "Learned Professors at Odds in Berlin," *New York Times*, 4 March 1911, p. 1; "Such a Fuss at Court," *Washington Post*, 18 March 1911, p. 1.

12. "Münsterberg Reply to Smith's Charges," *New York Times*, 5 March 1911, p. 1; Lowell to HM, 9 March 1911, MP; *New York Times* editorial, 19 March 1911, p. 10; David Jayne Hill to Lowell, 27 April 1911, LP, Series 1909–14, 495. Münsterberg presented his side of the case in numerous letters. See HM to Lowell, 9 March 1911, MP.

13. In May, Münsterberg asked Wundt and Lamprecht if they could secure for him an appointment to replace the psychologist Ernst Meumann, who was vacating a chair at Leipzig. The position turned out to be for the training of teachers, not for experimental psychology. HM to Wundt, 13 May 1911, Wundt to HM, 28 May 1911, Karl Lamprecht to HM, 24 June 1911, MP. On Münsterberg's estrangement from the American community in Berlin, see HM to James Speyer, 12 August 1911, MP.

14. HM, *Ursprung der Sittlichkeit*, p. 112.

15. HM, *American Patriotism*, p. 5.

16. HM, "The Impeachment of German-Americans," *New York Times*, 19 September 1915, sec. 4, p. 2.

17. HM, *The Peace and America* (New York: D. Appleton & Co., 1915), p. 250.

18. HM, *The War and America* (New York: D. Appleton & Co., 1914), pp. 184–85; HM, *American Patriotism*, p. 17.

19. HM, "Germany: A Land of Peace and Industry," *Proceedings of the National Arbitration and Peace Congress, New York, April 14th to 17th, 1907* (New York: 1907), pp. 65–69; Max Dessoir, "Zur Erinnerung an Hugo Münsterberg," in *Gründzuge der Psychotechnik*, by HM, p. xv; *New York Herald*, 16 April 1907, p. 1.

20. HM, *Peace and America*, p. 248; George Sylvester Viereck, "Hugo Münsterberg: Hail and Fairwell!" *Fatherland* 5 (27 December 1916): 346.

21. On the reaction of German academics to the war, see Klaus Schwabe, *Wissenschaft und Kriegsmoral: Die deutschen Hochschullehrer und die politischen Grundfragen des Ersten Weltkrieges* (Göttingen: Munsterschmidt-Verlag, 1969). Drechsler's pamphlet was reprinted, with rebuttal, as Douglas Sladen, *The Real*

"Truth about Germany": Facts About the War (New York: G. P. Putnam's Sons, 1914). For a complete English translation of "To the Civilized World!" see Ralph H. Lutz, The Fall of the German Empire, 1914–1918, 2 vols. (Palo Alto: Stanford University Press, 1932), 1:74–78.

22. HM, Amerika und der Weltkrieg: Ein amerikanisches Kriegstagebuch (Leipzig: Verlag von Johann Ambrosius Barth, 1915), p. 11; HM, "Fair Play," Boston Herald, 5 August 1914, p. 12; HM to Gerald Stanley Lee, 5 April 1914, MP; Frederick Luebke, Bonds of Loyalty: German-Americans and World War I (DeKalb, Ill.: Northern Illinois University Press, 1974). Münsterberg reprinted "Fair Play" in War and America, pp. 23–30. Viereck briefly described his relationship with Münsterberg in a set of remarks sent to Gertz in connection with his biography. See Gertz Papers, Library of Congress, Box 129.

23. See, for example, E. Haniel to HM, 15 August 1914, Friedrich Schmidt to HM, 24 August 1914, Alfred Rau to HM, 5, 15, and 21 October 1914, MP; Arthur S. Link, Wilson: The Struggle for Neutrality, 1914–1915 (Princeton, N.J.: Princeton University Press, 1960), pp. 32–33. The most recent account of German propaganda activities in the United States is Reinhard R. Doerries, Washington-Berlin: Die Tätigkeit des Botschafters Johann Heinrich Graf von Bernstorff in Washington vor dem Eintritt der Vereinigten Staaten von Amerika in den Ersten Weltkrieg (Dusseldorf: Pädogogischer Verlag Schwann, 1975). See also Luebke, Bonds of Loyalty, passim; Link, Struggle for Neutrality, pp. 31–36; and U.S. Senate Subcommittee on the Judiciary, Brewing and Liquor Interests and German and Bolshevik Propaganda, Report and Hearings, 3 vols., 65th Cong., 1919.

24. HM, "Fair Play," p. 12; HM, War and America, pp. 190, 200, and passim. On the "ideas of 1914" among German academics, see Schwabe, Wissenschaft und Kriegsmoral, pp. 43–45.

25. Schmidt to HM, 7 April 1915, MP; Brigitte Schroeder-Gudehus, "Caractéristiques des relations scientifiques internationales, 1870–1914," Cahiers d'histoire mondiale 10 (1966-67): 168. On the wartime academic environment in America, see Carol S. Gruber, Mars and Minerva: World War I and the Uses of Higher Learning in America (Baton Rouge: Louisiana State University Press, 1975), chap. 2. On the situation at Harvard, see Samuel Eliot Morison, Three Centuries of Harvard: 1636–1936 (Cambridge, Mass.: Harvard University Press, 1965), pp. 450–51.

26. Archibald Coolidge to Walter Lichtenstein, 26 June 1915, cited in Gruber, Mars and Minerva, p. 52; HM, "How the Boston Transcript Does It," Fatherland 1 (7 October 1914): 8–9; Dean Hodges of the Episcopal Theological School, cited in the Boston Globe, 18 December 1916, p. 4.

27. Robert Lansing to Woodrow Wilson, 9 December 1914, in U.S. Department of State, Papers Relating to the Foreign Relations of the United States, The Lansing Papers, 1914–1920, 2 vols. (Washington, D.C.: U.S. Government Printing Office, 1939), 1:166 (at the time Lansing was counselor to the State Department); "The Kaiser's American Agents," Times (London), 26 September 1914, p. 3; Emil Witte, Revelations of a German Attaché: Ten Years of German-American Diplomacy, trans. Florence Clarkson Taylor and Francis Payne Mason (New York: George H. Doran Co., 1916); Morison, Three Centuries, p. 453.

28. Clarence Wiener to the Dean, Harvard University, 26, 30 September 1914, LP Series 1914–17, 5.

29. A. H. Propper to Lowell, 10 October 1914, Edmund von Mach to Lowell, 11 October 1914, Lowell to Mach, 13 October 1914, LP Series 1914–17, 5; Ralph

Barton Perry to HM, 13 October 1914, MP; "Ignore $10,000,000 Threat," *New York Times,* 11 October 1914, sec. 2, p. 6; "Wiener's Offer a Joke?" *New York Times,* 16 October 1914, p. 10. For an example of Lowell's standard letter, see Lowell to William H. Dennis, 13 October 1914, LP Series 1914–17, 5.

30. HM to the President and Fellows of Harvard University, 13 October 1914, LP Series 1914–17, 45; "Keep Prof. Münsterberg," *New York Times,* 15 October 1914, p. 5; George Sylvester Viereck to HM, 13 October 1914, MP.

31. HM to Lowell, 3 May 1916, LP Series 1914–17, 231; Lowell to Dean E. R. Thayer, 24 October 1914, LP Series 1914–17, 5; Morison, *Three Centuries,* pp. 453–56; MM, *Hugo Münsterberg,* p. 264.

32. HM to Adolph S. Ochs, 14 October 1914, MP.

33. HM to Charles Eliot, 18 November 1914, HM to Hugo and John Jarburg, 12 November 1914, Johann von Bernstorff to HM, 31 December 1914, MP.

34. Link, *Struggle for Neutrality,* p. 32n; Otto Hammann (Foreign Office) to HM, 16 December 1914, MP; HM to Woodrow Wilson, 7, 19 November 1914, Wilson Papers, Library of Congress. See also U.S. Department of State, *Lansing Papers,* 1:161–79.

35. On this attempt to politicize German-Americans in the interest of neutrality and an arms embargo, see Clifton James Child, *The German-American in Politics, 1914–1917* (Madison, Wis.: University of Wisconsin Press, 1939), chap. 3; Luebke, *Bonds of Loyalty,* pp. 120–24; Kuno Francke, *Deutsche Arbeit in Amerika: Erinnerungen* (Leipzig: Felix Meiner Verlag, 1930), p. 67ff. On Münsterberg's role, see, for example, HM to Charles John Hexamer, 19 December 1914, and HM to Harry Rubens, 28 December 1914, MP.

36. Francke, *Deutsche Arbeit,* p. 72; Doerries, *Washington-Berlin,* pp. 86, 90–91; Bernstorff as cited by Link, *Struggle for Neutrality,* p. 378; Johann Heinrich von Bernstorff, *My Three Years in America* (New York: Charles Scribner's Sons, 1920), pp. 54–57. On American reactions to the sinking of the *Lusitania,* see Luebke, *Bonds of Loyalty,* pp. 130–34, 145.

37. HM, *Amerika und der Weltkrieg,* p. 11; Josiah Royce to HM, 10, 12, 13 May 1915, MP.

38. HM to Royce, 11, 14 May 1915, MP. For Royce's views on the war, see especially his *The Hope of the Great Community* (New York: Macmillan Co., 1916). See also Gruber, *Mars and Minerva,* p. 62ff.

39. HM, *Peace and America,* pp. 2, 165, 184 and *passim;* HM, "Lebenslauf."

40. HM, "Impeachment of German-Americans," pp. 1–2; HM, "Hugo Muensterberg Defines Theo. Roosevelt as a Presidential Possibility," *Fatherland* 3 (22 December 1915): 346–48; HM to Alphonse G. Koeble, 16 March 1916, MP.

41. On Germany's covert operations in the United States, see Doerries, *Washington-Berlin,* chap. 5, and Link, *Struggle for Neutrality,* pp. 554–64.

42. Bernstorff to HM, 25 February 1916, MP. See also other letters from Bernstorff during this period in the MP.

43. HM to Robert Lansing, 31 January 1916, MP.

44. Bernstorff to HM, 30 December 1915, and 25 February 1916, MP; "Wilson or Hughes: Germans in Doubt," *New York Times,* 8 August 1916, sec. 10, p. 1. This article contains translated passages from Münsterberg's intercepted letter of 12 May 1916 to Bethmann-Hollweg.

45. HM, "Allies of the Future," *New York Times,* 30 July 1916, sec. 5, pp. 1–3; HM, *Tomorrow: Letters to a Friend in Germany* (New York: D. Appleton and Co., 1916).

46. HM, *Tomorrow,* pp. 189, 205, 260–62, 227, 214–15. On the "demobilization" of the moderate wing of German academics, see Schwabe, *Wissenschaft und Kriegsmoral,* pp. 95ff., 179–81.

47. HM, "Antrittsrede," p. 6, MP, Ms. Acc. 2455; Arthur Lovejoy, letter to the editor, *Nation* 99 (24 September 1914): 376; Troeltsch as cited by Forman, "Scientific Internationalism," pp. 159–60.

48. HM, *Peace and America,* chap. 2; HM, *Tomorrow,* pp. 36–38.

49. Ibid., pp. 230–31; HM, *Peace and America,* pp. 151–52.

50. Alden March to HM, 2 August 1916, Bernstorff to HM, 1 August 1916, Alexander Fuehr to HM, 18, 23 August 1916, G. S. Viereck to HM, 15 August 1916, MP. Münsterberg slightly enlarged his territorial demands for Germany in *Tomorrow.* Compare "Allies of the Future," p. 3, with *Tomorrow,* pp. 260–62.

51. Herbert C. Sanborn to HM, 16 March 1916, MP; Edwin B. Holt, *The Freudian Wish and Its Place in Ethics* (New York: Henry Holt and Co., 1915), pp. 38–39. Holt described Münsterberg as "a fairly well educated business man," who, according to Münsterberg, possessed several characteristics that pointed clearly to him. In particular, Münsterberg cited four similarities between the businessman and himself: he sharply disapproved of Freudianism; he often said "I confess frankly that" to introduce sentences; he had never had any dreams and he frequently said so; and he once said to Holt, "The word lie is not in my lexicon" (HM to Holt, 30 March 1916, MP). Rather than explicitly denying Münsterberg's charge, Holt wrote, "I do not 'want to point to' you 'as being "one of the most unconscionable liars who ever lived" ' " (Holt to HM, 3 April 1916, MP).

52. HM to Holt, 24, 30 March 1916, MP; HM to Lowell, 3 May 1916, LP Series 1914–17, 231; Holt, *The Freudian Wish,* p. 105. On Holt, see Herbert S. Langfeld, "Edwin Bissel Holt: 1873–1946," *Psychological Review* 53 (September 1946): 251–58; and Kuklick, *Rise of American Philosophy,* pp. 420–32.

53. Holt to Lowell, 30 March 1916, LP Series 1914–17, 1054; HM to Lowell, 3 May 1916, LP Series 1914–17, 231.

54. *New York Times,* 8 August 1916, p. 10; *New York Times,* 10 October 1916, p. 7; HM to Lowell, 18 October 1916, LP Series 1914–17, 231; HM to Woodrow Wilson, 24 October 1916, Wilson Papers; Hocking to HM in *New York Times,* 18 October 1916, p. 3.

55. Richard C. Cabot (Secretary to the American Rights League) to the President and Fellows of Harvard College, 20 October 1916, LP Series 1914–1917, 231b; "Suggest That Harvard Oust Münsterberg," *New York Times,* 22 October 1916, p. 3; Reginald Robbins to HM, 22 November 1916, MP.

56. *Chicago Post,* 25 October 1916. Clipping in the Münsterberg Papers.

57. HM to William Phillips (Third Assistant Secretary of State), 22 April 1916, MP; HM to Lowell, 5 September 1916, LP Series 1914-17, 462; *Boston Globe,* 17 December 1916, p. 17.

58. *Boston Globe,* 18 December 1916, p. 4; Robert Yerkes to Lowell, 22 December 1916, LP Series 1914–17, 462; Lowell to Yerkes, 23 December 1916, LP Series 1914–17, 462; Doerries, *Washington-Berlin,* p. 64n. Selma Münsterberg did receive a Carnegie Foundation pension, for which she was not technically eligible, because her husband had taught in the United States for twenty-four years and four months instead of the required twenty-five. See Carnegie Foundation for the Advancement of Teaching, *Annual Report of the Treasurer* (New York, 1917), 12:8.

59. As an example of these rumors, see Leigh H. Irvine to Lowell, 5 May 1918,

LP Series 1917–19, 220. There is little reason to give the rumors any credence, especially because Münsterberg's doctor had warned him of his failing health. See George Herbert Palmer, "Philosophy," in *The Development of Harvard University since the Inauguration of President Eliot, 1869–1929*, ed. Samuel Eliot Morison (Cambridge, Mass.: Harvard University Press, 1930), p. 20.

60. "Word from Muensterberg," *New York Times*, 28 December 1916, p. 2.

61. Abraham Aaron Roback, *History of American Psychology* (New York: Library Publishers, 1952), p. 208; "Münsterberg Was Painted Out," *Harvard Alumni Bulletin* 58 (18 February 1956): 384–85.

Chapter 12

1. Edwin G. Boring, *A History of Experimental Psychology* (New York: Appleton-Century-Crofts, 1942), p. 421; Frank R. Angell, review of *Hugo Münsterberg: His Life and Work*, by Margaret Münsterberg, in *Psychological Bulletin* 19 (August 1922): 454.

2. Watson quoted by Arthur Upham Pope, "The Real Münsterberg," *New Republic* 27 (17 August 1921): 327.

3. John B. Watson, "Psychology as the Behaviorist Views It," *Psychological Review* 20 (March 1913): 168.

4. Kenneth Keniston, *The Uncommitted: Alienated Youth in American Society* (New York: Delta Books, 1965), p. 17. For a similar argument in anthropology, see Clifford Geertz, *The Interpretation of Cultures* (New York: Basic Books, 1973), p. 43.

5. Charles Edward Merriam, *A History of American Political Theories* (New York: Macmillan Co., 1903), p. 310 and *passim*.

6. HM to Roosevelt, 20 November 1905, Roosevelt Papers.

7. See Aileen S. Kraditor, *The Ideas of the Woman Suffrage Movement, 1890–1920* (New York: Doubleday, 1965), esp. chap. 3, for a discussion of this argument among feminists.

8. HM, *Grundzüge der Psychotechnik*, p. 195; Franz Samelson, "World War I Intelligence Testing and the Development of Psychology," *Journal of the History of the Behavioral Sciences* 13 (July 1977): 274–82.

9. Sigmund Freud, *Introductory Lectures* (1916–17), in *The Standard Edition of the Complete Psychological Works of Sigmund Freud*, ed. James Strachey, 24 vols. (London: Hogarth Press, 1953–74), 16:285.

10. Ross, "The Mob Mind," *Popular Science Monthly* 51 (July 1897): 390.

11. See especially Leonard Krieger, *The German Idea of Freedom: History of a Political Tradition* (Boston: Beacon Press, 1957).

12. Eugene D. Genovese, *Roll, Jordan, Roll: The World the Slaves Made* (New York: Random House, 1974), p. 164. Genovese makes much of Hegel's argument that slavery "constituted an outrage, for, in effect, it has always rested on the falsehood that one man could become the extension of another's will" (p. 88). This is exactly the relationship that Münsterberg hoped to bring about through applied psychology, albeit nominally in the interests of society as a whole rather than a particular member of it.

13. In his essay "Self-Reliance," Emerson wrote, "I would write on the lintels of the door-post, *Whim.*" *Selected Writings of Ralph Waldo Emerson*, ed. William H. Gilman (New York: New American Library, 1965), p. 261.

14. See, for example, Morton White, *Social Thought in America: The Revolt against Formalism*, rev. ed. (Boston: Beacon Press, 1957).

applied psychology, albeit nominally in the interests of society as a whole rather than a particular member of it.

13. In his essay "Self-Reliance," Emerson wrote, "I would write on the lintels of the door-post, *Whim.*" *Selected Writings of Ralph Waldo Emerson,* ed. William H. Gilman (New York: New American Library, 1965), p. 261.

14. See, for example, Morton White, *Social Thought in America: The Revolt against Formalism,* rev. ed. (Boston: Beacon Press, 1957).

Index

Abitur examination, 15, 16, 193
Action Theory, 41–42, 80–83, 83–84, 85, 114, 128, 146
Adorno, Theodor, 142
Advertising, 140–42
Aesthetics, 142–47, 220
Aliotta, Antonio, 70
Allport, Floyd, 81
Allport, Gordon, 58
Althoff, Friedrich, 87, 98, 103–4, 165–66
American Association of Labor Legislation, 109, 154–55
American Psychological Association, 49, 56, 73, 172
American Rights League, 181
Amerika-Institut, 5, 165–68, 171, 174, 225
Angell, Frank, 58, 121
Angell, James, 203
Anti-Semitism, 21, 53, 203
Apperception, 35, 37
Applied psychology: development of, 106–8, 162–63; Münsterberg on,

3–4, 8–9, 35, 72–73, 108–10, 184–85, 187–88. *See also* Industrial psychology; Legal psychology; Münsterberg, Hugo, influence of; Psychotherapy
Army Alpha and Beta tests, 163
Arrhenius, Svante, 212
Associationism, 24, 38. *See also* Psychology, nineteenth-century

Bain, Alexander, 24
Bakewell, C. M., 49
Balance, William D. G., 203
Baldwin, James Mark, 46, 49, 54, 58–59
Barthold, Richard, 174
Bastian, H. C., 24, 38
Beard, George M., 114, 136–37
Behaviorism, 41, 159, 186
Beiträge zur Psychologie der Aussage (Stern), 108
Bell, Charles, 38
Berchthold, Johann, 113
Bergson, Henri, 36, 70, 179

Bernstorff, Johann von, 174–75, 176–77, 180
Bethmann-Holweg, Theodor von, 177, 181
Binet, Alfred, 107, 113, 126
Bingham, Walter V., 162
Bolton, Frederick, 17
Borah, William E., 116
Boring, Edwin G., 184
Boston Vocation Bureau, 109, 122, 123
Brandeis, Louis, 149
Breul, Karl, 167
Brooks, Stratton, 124
Brown, Thomas, 38
Brücke, Ernst, 29
Bryce, James, 96, 97
Büchner, Ludwig, 27
Buck, S. M., 210
Buckhout, Robert, 115–16
Buckle, Henry, 77
Burgess, John W., 168, 172, 185
Burtt, Harold E., 158, 215
Busch, Adolphus, 119
Butler, Nicholas Murray, 64, 93–94, 168, 171

Calkins, Mary Whiton, 57, 63, 83
Cambon, Jules, 88
Carnegie, Andrew, 103, 171
Carnegie Institute of Technology, 162
Cattell, James McKeen, 21, 46, 73; and applied psychology, 107, 114, 122, 124, 184; and Münsterberg, 57, 79, 97, 109
Christian Science, 126, 127
Christian Socialist Workers' Party, 19
Christison, J. Sanderson, 111
Claparède, Edouard, 39, 113
Coates, A. W., 95
Cohen, Hermann, 53
Columbia University, 103, 168. See also Butler, Nicholas Murray
Committee for Psychology (National Research Council), 162–63
Comte, Auguste, 77
Coolidge, Archibald, 172
Cooley, Charles Horton, 44
Croly, Herbert, 106
Cultural diplomacy, German

(Kulturpolitik), 87–90, 103–4, 165–67, 168–69, 172, 179, 211, 225

Danzig, 11–13, 192
Darrow, Clarence, 116
Darwin, Charles, 29–30, 31, 32, 34; Münsterberg on, 32–33
Darwin, Erasmus, 38
Davidson, Thomas, 51
Debs, Eugene V., 116
Delbruck, Hans, 177–78
Dernburg, Bernhard, 20, 174
Dessoir, Max, 97; on Münsterberg, 71, 134
Dewey, John, 39, 41, 59, 73, 82; educational theory of, 64–65; on Münsterberg, 85, 94
Dilthey, Wilhelm, 40, 70, 76, 84
Docenten, 22; at Harvard, 66–68
Drechsler, R. W., 171
DuBois-Reymond, Emil, 29, 35, 36–37, 44, 48–49, 202
Dunlap, Knight, 81; on Münsterberg, 6, 57

Eastern Rate Case, 149
Ebbinghaus, Hermann, 35, 198
Economic Psychology Association, 162
Eddy, Mary Baker, 127
Edwards, Jonathan, 186
Efficiency: as theme of Progressive era, 7–9, 106, 148–50, 187–88; Münsterberg on, 6, 9–10, 163, 167. See also Expertise
Eliot, Charles W., 115, 209, 210; and Münsterberg, 52, 54, 67, 89, 90–91, 102–5, 165, 216
Elliott, Richard, 163
Emerson, Ralph Waldo, 186–87, 231
Emerson Hall, 102–3
Emmanuel Movement, 127
Eucken, Rudolf, 36, 179
Exner, Sigmund, 200
Expertise, 8–9, 35, 110, 115, 120–21, 156, 185–86; Münsterberg on, 106, 110, 117–18, 123–24, 125. See also Efficiency

Fatherland, The, 171–72, 176–77
Fechner, Gustav, 35, 142

Fichte, Johann Gottlieb, 28, 35, 36; and Münsterberg, 34, 41–42, 71, 75, 145
Filene, Lincoln, 122
Film, 144–47, 221
Fouillée, Alfred, 36
Francke, Kuno, 67, 88, 89–90, 96, 103, 209; and World War I, 172–73, 174
Freiburg: Münsterberg at, 22–23, 25, 52, 53; school of psychophysics, 23
Freud, Sigmund, 9, 51, 126, 186, 215; and Münsterberg, 129–31, 133–34, 136, 219
Freudian Wish and Its Place in Ethics, The (Holt), 118
Fritsch, Gustav, 36
Fry, O. V., 151
Fuehr, Alexander, 180
Functionalism, 41, 80–81, 82

Galton, Francis, 107
Gary, Elbert, 154
German-Americans, 3, 89–90; and Münsterberg, 92–93, 171, 174, 176–77, 180–81; and prohibition, 119
Germanic Museum (Busch-Reisinger), 89–90, 119, 209
Germany: applied science in, 106–7; influence of, on American education, 46, 165, 201–2; relations of, with the U.S., 87–93, 174–75, 176–77; view of America in, 46–47, 48, 202. See also Cultural diplomacy; World War I
Gestalt psychology, 84–85
Goethe, Johann von, 30
Gompers, Samuel, 159, 224
Gorky, Maxim, 116
Gross, Hans, 113, 117
Grundzüge der physiologischen Psychologie (Wundt), 30–31
Gymnasium, 15, 17–18, 193

Haeckel, Ernst, 28, 30, 32
Haines, George, 95
Hale, Nathan, Jr., 131
Hall, G. Stanley, 21, 30, 48–49, 59,
136, 162; on child study and education, 60, 64
Hamburg-American shipping line, 154
Hamburger, Ernest, 20
Hanus, Paul H., 122
Harnack, Adolf, 87, 88
Harper, William Rainey, 93
Harris, William T., 64
Hartmann, Eduard von, 36
Harvard-Berlin exchange professorship, 88, 103–5
Harvard University: Docenten at, 66–68; Münsterberg's early years at, 49–50, 52, 54–55, 56, 57–58, 66–68, 90–91; Münsterberg's estrangement from, 4–5, 98–105, 165, 169, 173–74, 180–81, 182; psychology at, 45–46, 49, 81, 88; during World War I, 172–73, 175, 180–82
Haywood, Big Bill, trial of, 116–18, 215–16
Helmholtz, Hermann von, 27, 29, 35–36, 41, 44, 76, 89
Helpach, Willy, 113
Henry, Prince, 90–91, 169, 209
Hensel, Paul, 71, 97–98
Herbart, J. F., 37, 142
Hill, David J., 165–66, 168
His, Wilhelm, 21, 30
Hitzig, Eduard, 36
Hocking, William, 181, 182
Holleben, Edmund von, 89–90, 91–92, 93, 210
Hollingworth, H. L., 124, 140, 153–54, 157, 162
Holls, Frederick, 93–94
Holt, Edwin B., 81, 131; and Münsterberg, 58, 118–19, 134, 180–81, 216, 229
Holtz, Hermann von, 47, 48
Horkheimer, Max, 142
Huizinga, Johan, 141
Hume, David, 38

Idealism: German, 27, 34, 71–72, 76, 83, 142–43, 145, 171, 186; late-century revival of, 36, 70
Iggers, Georg, 83
Industrial psychology: development

of, 148–50, 222; and employee
selection, 122–23, 152–57; and job
satisfaction, 150, 157, 158–63; and
Münsterberg, 5–6, 150–61. *See also*
Scientific Management
Institut für angewandte Psychologie,
108
International Congress of Arts and
Science (1904), 93–97, 211
International Congress of
Physiological Psychology (1889),
45–46, 201
Ivens, Richard, trial of, 111–12, 214

Jackson, Frederick, 95
James, William, 183; on American
society, 60, 62; compared with
Münsterberg, 6–7, 40–41, 111,
187; on education, 65, 74; as
Idealist, 36, 70; and Münsterberg,
4, 45–46, 48, 49, 52, 98–103, 110;
Münsterberg on, 77; on
Münsterberg, 3, 15, 24, 57, 86;
personality of, 135–36;
psychological theory of, 38–41, 82;
on St. Louis Congress, 97
Janet, Pierre, 126
Jastrow, James, 46, 73, 110, 126, 186
Jews, in Germany, 13–14, 16, 19–21,
25, 193, 196
Jones, Ernest, 219
Journal of Abnormal Psychology, 126
Journal of Applied Psychology, 162
Jung, Carl, 117, 130

Kant, Immanuel: Idealism of, 28, 29,
35–37, 186–87; and Münsterberg,
42, 71, 142–43, 145
Kampf im Organismus, Der (Roux),
31–32
Katz, Jacob, 13
Keniston, Kenneth, 185
Klein, Julius, 117
Königsberg, University of, 97–98
Kraepelin, Emil, 107, 113, 149
Kraft-Ebing, Richard von, 137
Kries, Johannes von 47
Kühnemann, Eugen, 104
Külpe, Oswald, 23, 84–85, 199, 212
Kulturpolitik. See Cultural diplomacy

Lahy, J. M., 123
Langbehn, Julius, 16
Lansing, Robert, 173
LeBon, Gustav, 186
Legal psychology: development of,
112–14, 215; and eye-witness
testimony, 110, 112–16, 120–21;
and Münsterberg, 110–12, 114–20.
See also Lie-detection
Leibniz, Gottfried Wilhelm, 35, 37
Leuckart, Rudolf, 21, 31
Levenstein, Adolf, 159–60
Lie-detection, 116–18, 120–21, 215
Link, Henry, 153
Lippmann, Otto, 108
Loeb, Jacques, 202
Lotze, R. H., 200
Lovejoy, Arthur, 178
Lowell, A. Lawrence: and Amerika-
Institut, 166–69; and Münsterberg,
109, 119–20, 159, 180–82; and
Wiener incident, 173–74
Ludwig, Karl, 21, 29
Lusitania, 174–75

McCombs, William F., 174
McDougall, William, 84
McParlan, James, 116
Malthus, Thomas, 34
Mannheim, Karl, 9, 26, 179–80
Marston, William M., 120
Mauthner, Fritz, 20
Meinecke, Friedrich, 170, 178
Mendelsohn, Everett, 29
Mental testing, 122–24, 144, 152–58,
163, 186, 221
Methodenstreit, 74, 76
Merriam, Charles, 185
Meumann, Ernst, 53, 226
Miller, Dickinson, 58
Minor, Jakob, 211
Moore, Charles C., 115
Mosse, George, 143
Mosso, Angelo, 116, 120, 149
Moyer, Charles, 116
Müller, G. E., 23–24, 49
Müller, Johannes, 29, 35, 36–37, 38,
80
Münsterberg, Anna, 13–14, 22
Münsterberg, Emil, 13, 15, 19

Münsterberg, Hugo: birth of, 13;
childhood of, 13–15, 17–19;
conversion to Lutheranism of,
19–20, 194; death of, 119–20, 230;
German academic career of, 20–25;
influence of, 4, 6, 57, 162–63,
184–85; personality of, 15, 47,
53–54, 57–58, 71, 85–86, 118–19,
134–36; philosophy of, 6–7,
70–72, 73–77, 82–83;
psychological theory of, 22, 23–24,
37–42, 72–73, 77–83, 83–85,
108–9; as "spy," 93, 173, 177, 181,
210; in World War I, 5, 171–83.
Views of: on American society, 51,
59–69, 88, 136–38; on education,
17–18, 63–69; on evolution,
31–35, 42–44; on nationalism,
164–65, 169–71, 178; on sex, 43,
130, 131–33; on social symbols,
127, 134, 138–41; on society as an
organism, 43, 163, 164–65, 169–70;
on women and the family, 43,
60–64, 66–67, 110, 138. Works:
American Patriotism, 138, 169;
*American Traits from the Point of
View of a German*, 4, 60–65, 88;
The Americans, 5, 202; *Die
Amerikaner*, 88–89; *Beiträge zur
experimentellen Psychologie*, 23–24,
46; *Business Psychology*, 123;
Eternal Values, 85–86, 135; "Fair
Play," 171–72; *Grundzüge der
Psychologie*, 50, 56–57, 68, 74, 77,
80–81, 83–84, 86, 98; *Grundzüge
der Psychotechnik*, 109, 125, 159,
160, 184, 186; *On the Witness
Stand*, 115, 120, 124; *Peace and
America*, 172, 175–76, 178, 179;
Philosophie der Werte, 83, 85–86,
141; *The Photoplay*, 6, 144–47, 176;
Psychologie der Wirtschaftsleben,
148, 155; *Psychology and Industrial
Efficiency*, 139, 148, 151–53,
155–56; *Psychology and Life*, 60,
72–73, 86; *Psychology and Social
Sanity*, 138; *Psychology: General
and Applied*, 82, 83, 144;
Psychotherapy, 126, 127–29,
131–34, 135; "Testing the Mind,"
145, 221; *Tomorrow*, 178–79; *Ueber
Aufgaben und Methoden der
Psychologie*, 48, 52; *Der Ursprung
der Sittlichkeit*, 42–44, 61, 76, 169;
Verse, 56, 134–35, 194; *Vocation
and Learning*, 123; *War and
America*, 172; *Die Willenshandlung*,
22–24, 40, 41, 43, 81; *Zur Lehre
der natürlichen Anpassung*, 31–34.
See also Action Theory; Applied
psychology; Cultural diplomacy;
Efficiency; Expertise; Harvard
University; Industrial psychology;
Legal psychology; Psychology;
Psychotherapy
Munsterberg, Hugo, 192, 194
Münsterberg, Margaret, 14, 190–91
Münsterberg, Moritz, 12–14, 16,
17–18, 19, 21
Münsterberg, Oscar, 13, 15, 19, 183,
192
Münsterberg, Otto, 12, 13, 15
Münsterberg, Rosalie, 13
Münsterberg, Selma Oppler, 22,
182–83
Murray, Henry, 57
Myers, C. S., 150

National Arbitration and Peace
Congress (1907), 103, 170–71
National Electric Light Association,
109, 157–58
National Research Council, 162–63
Naturphilosophie, 27–31, 35, 36, 84
Nelson, Daniel, 160
Neurasthenia, 136–38
Newcomb, Simon, 94–95
Nichols, Herbert, 58
Nietszche, Friedrich, 16, 71, 146–47

Olson, Harry, 214
Orchard, Harry, 116–17
Organic view of society, 32–35, 43,
58–59, 122, 125, 185–86. *See also*
Münsterberg, Hugo, views of
Origin of Species, The (Darwin),
29–30

Pabst, Gustav, 119
Palladino, Eusapia, 4, 110

Palmer, George Herbert, 49, 102, 183; on Münsterberg, 57, 58, 135–36
Parsons, Frank, 121–23, 124, 153, 185
Paulsen, Friedrich, 15–16, 36
Perry, Ralph Barton, 135, 175
Pettibone, Richard, 116
Planck, Max, 171
Poincaré, Henri, 95
Positivism, 23, 40–41, 77, 195
Prince, Morton, 126, 127
Progressive education, 60, 64–66
Prohibition, 119–20, 139
Psychological testing. See Mental testing
Psychology: nineteenth-century, 21–22, 35–40; profession of, 45–46, 47–48; purposive, 83–85. See also Action Theory; Applied psychology; Behaviorism; Gestalt psychology; Harvard University, psychology at; Industrial psychology; Legal psychology; Münsterberg, Hugo, psychological theory of; Psychotherapy
Psychophysics (physiological psychology), 35–38
Psychotherapy, 126–28; Freudian, 129–31, 133–34; Münsterberg's practice of, 110, 128–30, 131–34, 136, 218. See also Freud, Sigmund
Putnam, James Jackson, 126–28, 134

Rádl, Emanuel, 32
Ranke, Leopold von, 35
Reductionism, 21, 27, 29–30; in psychology, 35–36
Reisinger, Hugo, 119
Rickert, Heinrich, 25, 57, 71–72, 74, 75, 83, 101
Ridder, Hermann, 174–75
Rieff, Philip, 127
Riehl, Alois, 25, 171
Riesman, David, 138
Ringer, Fritz, 15, 26, 193
Roback, Aaron Abraham, 192, 203
Robbins, Reginald, 181–82
Robertson, Croom, 24
Rockefeller, John D., 154
Roosevelt, Theodore, 59–60, 62–63, 69, 91–94, 170, 210; on Haywood

trial, 116, 215–16; in World War I, 174, 176
Ross, Edward A., 58–59, 68–69, 186
Roux, Wilhelm, 30, 31, 32
Royce, Josiah, 49, 58–59, 70, 183; and Münsterberg, 97, 144, 174–75
Rubens, Harry, 174
Rutherford, Ernest, 94

St. Louis Exposition. See International Congress of Arts and Science
Santayana, George, 49
Sauer, August, 211
Schelling, Friedrich, 28
Schiff, Jacob, 166, 167, 174
Schiller, F. C. S., 102
Schmidt-Ott, Friedrich, 89, 104, 166, 167–68, 172
Schopenhauer, Arthur, 23, 36
Schrenck-Notzing, Albert, 113, 214
Schwann, Theodor, 29
Scientific Management, 149–53, 157, 158, 222. See also Industrial psychology; Taylor, Frederick W.
Scott, Walter Dill, 107, 124, 140, 155–56, 157, 161–62, 184, 186
Scripture, Edward, 46, 72–73
Seashore, Carl, 107–8
Sex: and psychotherapy, 131–33; and "repeal of reticence," 130–31
Sexual education, 131
Shaw, Mrs. Quincy Adams, 122
Simmel, Georg, 8
Skinner, B. F., 120
Small, Albion, 94–95
Smith, C. Alphonso, 168–69
Smithsonian Institution, 165–66
Spanish-American War, 91–92
Specht, Wilhelm, 130
Spencer, Herbert, 42, 43, 200
Speyer, James, 166, 174
Spiritualism, 4, 41, 102, 110, 183
Starch, Daniel, 140
Steinmetz, Charles, 158
Stern, L. William, 57, 84–85, 186; and applied psychology, 107–8, 113; on Münsterberg, 4, 71, 74
Sternburg, Speck von, 92–93
Steunenberg, Frank, 116
Stoecker, Adolf, 19

Stout, G. F., 24
Structuralism. *See* Psychology, nineteenth-century
Stumpf, Carl, 53, 202
Sud-Baden (Southwestern) School, 71–72, 85

Taylor, Alfred E., 79–80
Taylor, Frederick W., 44, 149–53, 222
Taylorism. *See* Scientific Management; Taylor, Frederick W.
Terberg, Hugo (pseudonym for Hugo Münsterberg), 56
Thorndike, Edward, 73, 82, 124, 162, 217
Titchener, Edward B., 36, 198, 203; on Münsterberg, 6, 23, 24
Tonnies, Friedrich, 8, 43
"To the Civilized World!" 171
Troeltsch, Ernst, 178
Troland, Leonard, 181

Uber Psychologie der individuellen Differenzen (Stern), 108

Venezuela crisis, 91–92
Verein für Socialpolitik, 149
Viereck, George Sylvester, 171–72, 173, 174–75, 180, 218
Virchow, Rudolf, 21, 29
Viteles, Morris, 153, 217
Vocational guidance, 121–25
Vogt, Carl, 27
Voluntarism, 31–32, 36–37. *See also* Will

Watson, John, 9, 159, 184–85
Weber, Max, 8, 18, 27, 43, 76, 84, 95; and Münsterberg, 57, 58, 74; on World War I, 177–78
Wertheimer, Max, 117
Whipple, G. M., 114, 156

White, Morton, 63
Wiebe, Robert, 7
Wiener, Clarence, 173–74
Wigand, Albert, 30
Wigmore, John H., 120
Wilhelm II, 87–88, 90–92, 151, 162, 166, 168
Will: Münsterberg on, 40; theories of, 36–37, 39–40, 41, 82, 200; turn-of-the-century crisis of, 59–60, 62, 126–27, 136–37
Wilson, Woodrow, 94, 151, 162, 173, 174, 176, 185
Windelband, Wilhelm, 40, 71, 77, 83, 95, 171
Winthrop, John, 186
Witmer, Lightner, 46, 107; on Münsterberg, 110
Witte, Emil, 93, 173, 210
Worcester, Elwood, 127
World War I: German academics in, 171–72, 177–78; German diplomacy and propaganda in, 173–75, 176–77, 180–81. *See also* Harvard University, during World War I; Münsterberg, in World War I
Wundt, Wilhelm, 38, 49, 113, 140, 203; on evolution, 30–31; and Münsterberg, 49, 52, 53–54, 55, 57, 77, 226; psychological theory of, 35, 36–38; psychological theory of, compared to Münsterberg's, 21–22, 23–24, 28, 40; and World War I, 171

Yerkes, Robert M., 163; and Münsterberg, 57, 81, 183, 186

Ziehen, Theodor, 200, 220
Zurich, University of, 52–54, 203